Confucian Cultures of Authority

SUNY series in Asian Studies Development
Roger T. Ames and Peter D. Hershock, editors

Confucian Cultures of Authority

EDITED BY

*Peter D. Hershock
and Roger T. Ames*

STATE UNIVERSITY OF NEW YORK PRESS

Published by
State University of New York Press, Albany

For information, address State University of New York Press, 194 Washington Avenue, Suite 305, Albany, NY 12210-2384

Production by Diane Ganeles
Marketing by Anne M. Valentine

Library of Congress Cataloging-in-Publication Data

Confucian cultures of authority : edited by Peter D. Hershock and Roger
T. Ames.
    p. cm.—(SUNY series in Asian studies development)
    Includes bibliographical references and index.
    ISBN-13: 978-0-7914-6797-8 (hardcover : alk. paper)
    ISBN-10: 0-7914-6797-X (hardcover : alk. paper)
    ISBN-13: 978-0-7914-6798-5 (pbk. : alk. paper)
    ISBN-10: 0-7914-6798-8 (pbk. : alk. paper)
    1. Philosophy, Confucian. 2. Confucianism. I. Hershock, Peter D. II. Ames,
Roger T., 1947– . III. Series.
    B127.C65C625 2006
    181′.112—dc22

                                                            2005023942

10 9 8 7 6 5 4 3 2 1

Contents

Introduction:
Confucian Cultures of Authority

Peter D. Hershock and Roger T. Ames

It has often been said that change is the only constant. So often, in fact, has the claim been made recently that it has taken on the softly tarnished patina of a cliché. Yet, there is perhaps nothing so strikingly characteristic of the present postmodern, postindustrial, and (according to some) even posthistorical era than its refusal to assume any fixed form or identity. The pace and scale of change taking place in virtually all sectors of all societies is arguably, if not obviously, without precedent. Equally unprecedented is the unpredictability of the directions in which change is taking place. For good reason, the language of paradigm shifts—once reserved for rare, epochal events—has also become a commonplace.

Under such circumstances of ironically sustained inconstancy, the foundational values and strategies by means of which any given society negotiates the complementary needs for both continuity and change are inevitably brought under critical scrutiny. When, as is presently the case, the conditions giving rise to deep, rapid, and multidimensional change are overwhelmingly global in nature, it is likewise inevitable not only that a society's foundational values and strategies are called into question, but its critical tool chest as well. The nature of authority itself—the capacity and right to author and to authorize—is opened to sweeping, categorical contest.

This has become a staple of commentators on the political, economic, social, and cultural effects of a globalizing process that is evidently far from smooth and trouble-free. Contemporary patterns of globalization place considerable stress on already existing local, national, and regional communities even as it has challenged them to enter into new kinds of relationship. To take but a single example, the disparate benefits reaped by nations of the "North" and those of the "South" have made it clear that in spite of the rhetoric of "free" trade, globalization has not been egalitarian in effect. The result has been a complex pattern of cultural and national polarizations that have led some to speak—with varying degrees of perspicuity—of an oncoming "clash of civilizations" (Huntington: 1998), of tensions between globalism and tribalism (Barber: 1996), and of epochal shifts in authoritative capital (Friedman: 1999). What is clear is that by placing conflicting systems of values into increasingly dense proximity, the process of globalization has precipitated widespread crises of identity, the intense foregrounding of ethnic and religious differences, and has significantly raised the volume of communal dissonance.

With the rapid spread of telecommunications technologies, this transition has become increasingly self-reflective. To a perhaps unique degree, authority can no longer be taken for granted, and along with this "fact" of the present era have come powerful incentives for assessing prevalent cultural axioms and for improvising or evolving new forms of community. This has, in turn, placed new and very considerable demands on educators—particularly those responsible for crafting and delivering the undergraduate core curriculum that establishes a shared generational ground for responsibly taking up active and critically aware roles in working through the local and global challenges of deep and unpredictable social, economic, political, and cultural change.

The present volume emerged out of an effort to address the needs of educators faced with these demands and with the corollary challenge of furthering commitments to global literacy through infusing Asian content into the undergraduate curriculum. With funding from the National Endowment for the Humanities, the Asian Studies Development Program—a joint project of the East-West Center and the University of Hawai`i—held a two-year series of workshops and a culminating on-line conference on *Cultures of Authority in Asian Practice: A Seminar Series for Undergraduate Educators.* The aim of this project was: to examine critically the values that have historically guided the negotiation of identity, both practical and ideal, in different Asian contexts; to consider how these values play into the conception and exercise of authority; to assess their contemporary relevance in a rapidly globalizing world; and to develop resources for using the theme of cultures of authority in infusing Asian content throughout the undergraduate humanities curriculum.

Beginning with the premise that cultures are continuously improvised patterns of value and conduct, this two-year project explored, in pedagogically relevant detail, the ways in which Asian cultures of authority establish the conditions of communal continuity. In particular, the four workshops engaged in comparative examination of how different cultures of authority in East Asia, South Asia, and Southeast Asia both canonize and challenge apparent constants in the ongoing play of values and conduct that compose a given culture. A primary aim of the series of workshops was to highlight the diversity of Asian cultures of authority as well as the ways in which studying the dynamics of authority in each of Asia's major cultural spheres can shed incisive, critical light on both their intrinsic complexity and their unique approaches to accommodating often contending indigenous impulses and exogenous influences.

Not infrequently, authority is associated with authoritarianism and hence with uncritical, often coerced, compliance with "elite" dogmas. But the exercise of authority can also be seen in the sensitively appropriate translation of an existing constellation of values and customs into novel and changing contexts—a personalization of tradition uniquely suited to prevailing circumstances. Authority in this sense is allied with authoring and hence with initiative, openness, and creativity. Indeed, it is precisely the ambiguities surrounding authority that make it so appropriate as a thematic focus for studying the ways different Asian societies have negotiated the contrary demands of change and constancy. Because the role of authority is equally pronounced in Western societies, this theme opens fertile ground for comparative studies of culture within the frame of existing undergraduate courses.

The four workshops took complementary approaches to the organizing theme of authority, with each workshop focusing on different sets of academic disciplines in the humanities and social sciences and contributing to an overall understanding of the place of authority in Asian cultural contexts.

The first two workshops examined Asian cultures of authority in terms of the construction and representation of authority, focusing on the relationship between authority and order, between the authoritative and the heroic, and between authorship and the pragmatics of contributing to communal flourishing and endurance. What does it mean to be an authoritative person? How does gender affect the acquisition or claim of authority? What is the relationship between personal forms of authority and those evident in the spheres of nature, society, and the spiritual or divine? How is authority transmitted—be it religious, artistic, social, or political? What makes a particular artistic work authoritative? By what means are artists and their works able to challenge authority, both artistic and otherwise?

The third and fourth workshops investigated authority through comparative discussion of the institutional frameworks associated with leadership and governance, and through the ways in which cultures of authority implicate the subaltern, invite their own revision, and both create room for and procedures for responding to dissent. What are the institutions by means of which a culture conserves key traditions? How open are these institutions to innovation? What is the relationship between political authority and the cultures of authority associated with cultural production or religious observation? To what degree is authority distributed, and with what presuppositions regarding the value of equity? What are the mechanisms for challenging authority or critically assessing the effects of its exercise in historically unprecedented times? What opportunities and resources are there for expressing and evaluating dissent?

The articles on *Confucian Cultures of Authority* included in this volume have been selected thematically from those prepared by participants in these workshops and constitute the culminating event of the *Cultures of Authority* project. In an essay entitled "Two Loci of Authority: Autonomous Individuals and Related Persons," Henry Rosemont Jr. begins from a series of startling snapshots about the configuration of wealth and power in the world in which we live. The fact that we have a systemic problem is all too clear. His argument is practical: there is a real tension between the freedom that we celebrate as the centerpiece of American culture and our aspirations to live in a world in which the values of equality and justice prevail. While the civil and political rights of autonomous individuals developed over the past several centuries have increased the quantum of human freedom in the world markedly—certainly a good thing—these same rights have lead to an increasing concentration of wealth and power, both within the structure of American society and in the world broadly, that conflicts fundamentally with our sense of justice—a situation that will have an increasingly corrosive effect on the democracy that we want. Rosemont then turns to a portrait of the classical Confucian model of the authoritative person cultivated within the context of ritualized roles and relationships as a heuristic for rethinking the relative weight we want to invest in the values of liberty and justice, and for determining an appropriate balance between them. Can we learn something from the construction of personal and communal authority in classical China—a construction that seeks a balance between freedom and responsibility—that might allow modern America to achieve its most cherished and defining ideals?

In identifying what is distinct about political authority in Confucian China, much has been made of the contrast between ritually constituted social order and rule by law. Tao Jiang in "Intimate Authority: The Rule of Ritual in Classical Confucian Political Discourse" marshals the distinction made by the comparative philosopher Thomas Kasulis between "intimacy" and "integrity" to attempt to resolve the question: is family-centered Confucianism a particularist philosophy, or is it a more ambitious universalism? Abandoning the particularist/universalist dualism as having little relevance for the Confucian sensibility, Jiang argues that "the rule of ritual" can be a productive way of thinking through the political discourse of ancient China. Jiang disputes the familiar distinction between "rule by man" and "rule by law" as failing to appreciate the vectoral force of the ritualized context in establishing and perpetuating normative authority. Jiang then uses "intimacy" as defined by Kasulis to show how ritually constituted authority for the always familial community is at once personal and objective, internal and external, rational and affective, somatic and psychical, and so on. Beginning in the classical period with the Legalists, law has certainly had a role in effecting order in Chinese history, but it has been a much "Confucianized" application of law in which the conditions of intimacy have prevailed. This entrenched tradition of "rule by ritual" leaves us with the open question: what will be the real substance of rule by law in the irreversible democratization of modern China?

How are we to make sense of "culture of authority" as a theme in a contemporary Confucian vocabulary? Wenshan Jia in his essay, "The *Wei* (Positioning)-*Ming* (Naming)-*Lianmian* (Face)-*Guanxi* (Relationship)-*Renqing* (Humanized Feelings) Complex in Contemporary Chinese Culture" provides terminology that allows us to reflect again on the resolutely hierarchical Confucian social dynamic described by Rosemont and Jiang. *Lianmian*—literally "face"—is a social capital accumulated through moral self-cultivation that enables persons to establish themselves in community and to reposition themselves as circumstances require. As a social display of who one is, "face" is a concrete and pervasive factor in all dimensions of social living. Importantly, *wei*—status, position, rank—is always hierarchical and is open to the dynamics of personal transformation. It is something accomplished and sustained through effective social living. *Ming*—not just naming, but naming properly—allows us to discriminate and acknowledge discursively the shifting grammar of the community as it is expressed in meaningful relations. Having defined these Confucian terms of art, Jia then uses several case studies to demonstrate the contemporary relevance of these terms by showing how they are still alive and well in the social, political, and educational dynamics of modern China.

In these discussions of the ritually constructed authority that defines Confucianism, the institution of the family has been alluded to as the governing cultural metaphor. In "Creeping Absolutism: Parental Authority as Seen in Early Medieval Tales of Filial Offspring," Keith Knapp turns to the early literary corpus to construct a more focused picture of how family authority functioned under concrete circumstances.

To establish a clear and indeed necessary distinction between the Chinese experience and the power of the father in the Roman *paterfamilias*, Knapp is able to demonstrate that Confucian filial piety (*xiao*) was understood to have more to do with the duties that children owe their parents than it does with the exercise of parental authority. Citing the classical philosophical and historical texts, Knapp shows that the model of filiality recommended in the formative period of this culture was far from simple, entailing a combination of both obedience and appropriate remonstrance. The picture he is able to glean from the early medieval literature, however, places a clear emphasis upon doing as one is told without assuming any latitude for a child's own critical assessment. In explanation of this changing phenomenon, Knapp suggests that in this early medieval period, parents had come to be portrayed as having the unconditional authority of rulers within their own homes, a situation that reflects the weakened power of the central government and the rise of the extended family. This authoritarian picture of parental power, however, far from reflecting real conditions, instead suggests insecurity on the part of the parents, mothers as well as fathers. In order to corroborate his argument that these literary sources are compensatory, Knapp turns to an evaluation of *shengfen* during this same period—the prevailing practice of sons splitting off from the father to establish a separate financial identity. In establishing a separate household, the husband-wife relationship came to supercede that of parent and child. In showing that the household heads were far weaker than previously thought, Knapp is able to establish and explain a distinction between the representation of parents in the literature and the actual state of affairs.

Of course, integral to the institution of family is gendered authority. Robin Wang in "Virtue (*de*), Talent (*cai*), and Beauty (*se*): Authoring a Full-Fledged Womanhood in *Lienüzhuan*" explores the biographies of notable women to identify the criteria according to which the authority of women was constructed and evaluated. In using this literary source, Wang must struggle with the same equivocation between representation and actual circumstances—between normative standards and real lives—that Keith Knapp has engaged in his research. Although there is a clear separation of roles between men and women advocated in the *Lienüzhuan*, and although the circumstances in which virtue is demonstrated are different because of this, what in fact constitutes excellence is the same for both. That is, a woman is celebrated to the extent that her personal example is deserving of deference by the family and community in which she is located. The fact that the commentary on each story is frequently able to associate the anecdote with a particular passage in the *Analects* reflects the androgynous character of Confucian virtue. Of particular importance is her pivotal role as teacher of and model for her children—a role in which she constitutes the primary formative authority for the next generation. In their role of wife and counselor, women portrayed as exemplary persons (*junzi*) are able to transform the social restrictions imposed upon them into a context in which their own personal dignity and self-worth are displayed. Confucian selfhood, male or female, is defined in a network of relations, and moral autonomy is to be achieved through virtuosity in those relations. Even female beauty is defined as the outside of an inside—an acknowledgment of moral worth. Although *Lienüzhuan* is a didactic idealization of the woman's experience, by representing excellence as a possibility for both women and men, an argument can be made that the Confucian tradition has the resources within it to resolve its own problem of gender discrimination.

Roberta Adams makes use of a different genre of literature—the folk novel—to explore "Aspects of Authority in Wu Cheng'en's *Journey to the West.*" *Journey to the West* is a legendary recreation of the adventures of the Tang dynasty Buddhist monk Xuanzang who in the seventh century travels to South Asia to bring Buddhist scriptures back to Emperor Taizong. While authority in the story resides in political and religious personages, mortal and immortal, and of course in the Buddhist scriptures, there is a key antinomian figure in this 100-chapter sixteenth century novel who through his subversive antics establishes himself as a major icon in the evolution of Chinese culture—the figure of Monkey. There is a sustained tension between the boundless talents and audacious arrogance of Monkey and the many attempts that the Heavenly authorities make to rein him in. Whatever violence is inflicted on Monkey, he repeatedly rises to the occasion and hurls Heaven into chaos. In the end, it is only with the intervention of Buddha that Monkey is finally contained and sent down to accompany Xuanzang on his many adventures. Although the story is Buddhist, it also prompts reflection on the Confucian virtues of loyalty and selecting worthy officials, and echoes the old story of how so often literati merit has gone unappreciated by the Confucian state. There are also allusions to Daoist alchemical practices and the secrets of immortality, and the Five Phases *qi* cosmology that is a shared assumption of all of these traditions. Xuanzang is the human everyman whose innocence and purity—yet another kind of authority—make him both victim and hero as he wins the absolute loyalty of Monkey and his other disciples, and proceeds on his hazardous journey. Perhaps the main message of the entire novel is that it is the irrepressible authority of the cultivated human spirit that is to be prized over any other kind of power. The sheer complexity of this fabulous tale as a cross-section of Chinese cultural sensibilities has made it a contested landscape plowed by commentators over the centuries, and continues to absorb the lifelong interest of some of our best interpreters of Chinese ways of living and thinking.

In reflecting on the construction of authority in late imperial China, Steven B. Miles endorses the trend of contemporary social history to argue that general discussions of central political authority must be balanced by the hydraulics of power found at more local levels of family and society. In his essay, "Establishing Authority through Scholarship: Ruan Yuan and the Xuehaitang Academy," Miles explores authority as it is constituted by scholarship, culture, and education at a specific time and place. An account of Guangzhou's Xuehaitang Academy founded by the prominent political and cultural figure, Ruan Yuan, in the 1820s is itself a story of contested authority. Ruan Yuan was a powerful patron of the Han evidential learning movement that sought to challenge both the tenets of orthodox Song dynasty "neo-Confucianism" and the political legitimacy of its adherents. The Cheng-Zhu interpretation of Confucianism that had emerged in late Song became the standard commentary for the civil service examinations that provided aspirants access to political power, and it was the function of most academies to educate students in this curriculum. It was Ruan Yuan's personal prestige as both research scholar and regional governor-general that enabled him to become a force for educational reform by expanding the authority of Han learning from the north into the southern quarters of Qing China. But it was the institutionalization of evidential research in the curriculum at the Xuehaitang that perpetuated this redirection of education among the Cantonese elite long after Ruan Yuan as a person departed the scene. Miles examines one leading "immigrant" Cantonese scholar, Chen Li— perhaps the most prominent product of Xuehaitang—as a case study of how the prestige of this academy, its famous founder, and its authoritative scholarly methods demonstrated in new anthologies was used to certify the cultural authority of a small gentry elite.

While notions of orthodoxy and the inertia of authority are familiar themes in recounting the long story of imperial China, the beginning of the twentieth century was a period in which the old principles and the traditional institutions of authority had become thoroughly discredited, and political reformers and intellectuals—divided and conflicted among themselves—had to embark upon a transformation of the social and political order. The choice they faced was between Kang Youwei and Liang Qichao's revisionist "enlightened despotism," in which a modernized monarch would use the weight of tradition to effect sorely needed change, and the motley advocates of democratic reform—anarchists, radical nationalists, and republicans—who envisioned the wholesale modernization of Chinese political institutions. But nothing comes or goes easily in China. In his "Intellectual and Political Controversies over Authority in China: 1898–1922," Lawrence R. Sullivan rehearses the contesting forces that joined the struggle in the early days of Republican China and recounts the many false starts on the march toward demo- cratic reform that only fed the disgust of the New Culture critics of tra- ditional Chinese. By establishing the crucial distinction between power and authority, Sullivan is able to underscore the key role that culture plays in galvanizing legitimate authority—a communally shared sense of what is right. The May Fourth intellectuals believed that real political change required nothing less than a thoroughgoing cultural emancipa- tion that allowed China once and for all to throw off the chains of entrenched ethical, religious, philosophical, and linguistic values that bound the population to promonarchical thinking. The painful comedy of errors that continued among the political elite was only symptomatic of a chronic malaise that afflicted the general population, expressed almost universally as a numbing apathy and an irrepressible indifference. You cannot have a democracy without the people, and in the eyes of the reformists, the defect preventing the emergence of a new China lies ultimately in the Chinese character itself. Indeed, it was the inability of the often cynical and always frustrated reformers to move the masses and overcome popular complicity in the familial and political tyranny of Confucian culture that in the fullness of time led China to embrace Marxism-Leninism as an alternative despotism.

Lawrence Sullivan has certainly provided the context. And Virginia Suddath then asks "Ought We Throw the Confucian Baby out with the Authoritarian Bathwater?" adding yet another twist to the complex history of early twentieth-century China. In this critical inquiry into Lu Xun's extreme "anti-Confucianism," Suddath locates the discussion within the context of the continuing encounter between Chinese and Western cultures, and speaks to the very pressing question: what kind of democracy will emerge in contemporary China? After all, the contro- versy over the value of Confucianism in the construction of a new China—does it serve as an authoritative or an authoritarian normative force?—still divides our best interpreters of Chinese culture in our own historical moment. What is unique to Lu Xun and the stinging critique he directed at China's degenerate past is that unlike other reformers, he had on offer neither an idealized Western future for his countrymen, nor a nostalgic return to the Han past. Having been educated as a traditional intellectual, even in his rebellion against the content of the canons, he could not entirely escape their influence. In demanding change, he advocated a transformation of the existing social order rather than disjunction with it, and a retail rather than a wholesale solution to China's recalcitrant problems. The question that Suddath asks is: how do we reconcile Lu Xun's strident anti-Confucianism and what Li Zehou would call his own "psychocultural construct"? In response Suddath shows that Lu Xun is indeed something of a paradox in that, in his iconoclastic assault on Confucian feudalism, at the same time he perpetuates the high status of remonstrance (*jian*) and its place in the Confucian project of self-cultivation. In reflecting on Lu Xun's legacy and his relevance for contemporary China, Suddath is keen to distinguish the Confucian sense of protest from dialectical dissent, personal realization from liberal individualism, and the ritually constituted, flourishing community from the ideal state. Indeed, there must always be room for a Lu Xun-like indeterminacy within the Confucian construction of authority.

It is hoped that this collection of essays will benefit teachers of the undergraduate curriculum in their commitment to help foster global literacy among all college and university graduates. While separate courses focused on the histories and cultures of Asia, Central and South America, Africa, and the Pacific are an important and even necessary element in any comprehensive university or college curriculum, they are not a sufficient response to the broad needs of all American undergraduates. Teaching Asia, for example, can no longer be the sole responsibility of the area specialist. Indeed, the segregation of Asian cultures, religions, literatures, and histories from those of the European and American traditions has tended to perpetuate the erroneous impression that "they" have not been members of "our" community for centuries.

In today's colleges and universities, teachers previously responsible for conducting lower division courses with a traditional Euro-American focus are being asked to add comparative emphases including other world cultures, Asian exemplars among them. The challenge these teachers face is formidable: to provide American students with an understanding of how the more familiar European and American values compare with and—in many cases—have been informed by those of other peoples, often in the context of intellectual, artistic, and commercial dialogue. This involves not only introducing alternative ways of thinking and living that merit study on the basis of their own intrinsic worth, it also involves highlighting the uniqueness and complexity of the contributions made by Europe and the Americas to world history and their role (for good and ill) in the emergence of global cultures. An integrated approach to the humanities is not only conducive to, but grounded on, an explicitly critical engagement with values proper to both our own and other cultural lineages.

These essays examining authority in cultural context shed considerable light on the continuities and contentions underlying the vibrancy of Chinese culture. In spite of their common footing in the Sinitic world, they also exemplify the substantial merits of a thematic (rather than geographic or area studies) approach to infusing Asian content throughout the undergraduate experience. It is hoped that such an approach promises broad applicability across the undergraduate curriculum, increased opportunities for critical and pedagogically relevant cross-cultural comparisons, and a ready forum for encouraging values-centered conversation in the undergraduate classroom.

Two Loci of Authority: Autonomous Individuals and Related Persons[1]

Henry Rosemont Jr.

I want to consider the concept of authority in cross-cultural perspective, with specific reference on the one hand to the contemporary United States, and on the other, to China, and even more specifically, classical Confucianism. Nuances aside, there are two ways authority may be exercised: by coercion, or threats thereof, based on strength and power; or by persuasion, based on knowledge and reason. In the former case, if the authorities have not come to their positions by democratic means we call them *author*itarian, and in the latter case, the reasoned persuaders are considered *author*itative. Hereafter I will say only very little about authoritarianism, concentrating on authoritative persons, who assist others in becoming the true *authors* of their lives.

Authoritative persons usually are highly knowledgeable; we tend to do what our doctors tell us because they know more about health and disease than we do. Others are simply "wise in the ways of the world" (think of grandmothers). Authoritative persons appeal to some combination of reason (logic) and emotion (rhetoric—which is not devoid of reason).

Given that persuasion involves getting people to act in ways they may not be inclined to act—it takes little persuasion to get a hungry person to eat—authoritative persons must offer arguments based on some basic assumptions shared by the other(s) they are endeavoring to influence. Their worldviews must overlap significantly, and at rock-bottom level, as I shall attempt to show, all parties should more or less share a similar conception of what it is to be a human being. Differing conceptions will thus lead to differing patterns of persuasion and have somewhat different consequences for the way a society is structured in its institutions, and in its values. Given one model of personhood (the modern West) justice will be valued, but freedom even more so; given

1

another model (the classical Confucian) the ordering will be reversed. Harking back to my title, authoritative persons will invoke the concept of the autonomous individual—free, rational, and self-interested—in the course of developing their arguments in the modern West, while the early Confucians based their arguments and concerns on the social and interpersonal nature of related persons.

No one would insist that we are altogether autonomous individuals or altogether social, interrelated beings. By definition, self-consciousness implies an awareness of who and what I am as a unique person against all others. It is equally obvious that my sense of myself has been overwhelmingly influenced by my parents, relatives, teachers, friends, and many others. Thus the issue is not whether we are all one or the other of these conceptions, but which of them we take to be most fundamental, when others attempt to persuade us of the value of a particular course of action, or to weigh our values in a specific way.

In what follows I will discuss these differing conceptions of what it is to be a human being in the context of the values of freedom and justice, and most specifically as these are implicated in the discourse on human rights as invoked by ostensibly authoritative persons. First I will briefly and critically sketch some major themes in contemporary Western moral, political, and legal philosophy, and some facts about the world today, with the aim of suggesting that the values of equality and justice—deeply rooted in Western culture—cannot be fully realized so long as we continue to more highly esteem other values, especially those pertaining to individual freedom and liberty.

In the second part, I will sketch an alternative vision for ordering our values, the vision of the classical Confucians, with the aim of suggesting how and why we must begin to rethink what it is to be a human being, and what the good society might be, if the twenty-first century is to be a more peaceful and humane one than the twentieth. We are certainly not off to a good start.

To avoid misunderstanding the nature of the arguments that follow, I must emphasize at the outset that in questioning the primacy of the value of individual freedom—which I will do—I am not going to suggest it be *dis*valued. In the same way, in championing classical Confucianism—which I shall do—I will not be urging you to take on a whole new set of values, for both as a matter of fact and point of logic, such is not possible. Everyone mature enough to contemplate moral, political, or religious issues already has a set of values, weighted at least roughly in certain ways; hence the most any philosopher, authoritative or otherwise, can hope to do is provide arguments for changing the weighting or ordering of values already held.

In contemporary Western moral philosophy, political theory, and jurisprudence, the concept of freedom is central. The challenge of the question "Why did you do that?" has no moral force unless it is presupposed that the interrogated was free to have done otherwise. Most political theorizing—even if undertaken behind a veil of ignorance—still begins with the Hobbesian concept that human beings are fundamentally free and then attempts to justify subservience to a state (government) that restricts that freedom. And in jurisprudence, the demands of justice can seldom be addressed, either in civil or criminal law, without due consideration of the freedom—couched in the language of rights—of the parties involved. And of course punishment usually takes the form of sharply curtailing the freedom of the convicted.

The concept of freedom is no less central in practice than in theory, as is clearly evidenced by all three branches of the U.S. government, where freedom has achieved almost sacred status, in name if not in fact. At law, felony convictions based on confessions are overturned if it can be shown that the convicted were not told they were free to remain silent. A legislator promoting a welfare bill defends it on the basis of enhancing the freedom of opportunity of the poor. These bills will be opposed by those who see redistributive wealth measures as an infringement of the freedom of the affluent to dispose of their wealth as they see fit, and/or an infringement of the freedom of majorities to act in accordance with their beliefs. And a great deal of U.S. foreign policy is regularly justified as furthering freedom (and its cousin, democracy) in different parts of the world, even when the instruments of the policies are bombing raids on other countries, from Vietnam, Laos, and Cambodia to Libya, Kosovo, the rest of Serbia, Afghanistan, and Iraq twice, a decade apart.

We can see the philosophical importance of the concept of freedom in another way: it is an integral part of a larger Western concept-cluster, the terms for which—"liberty," "rights," "democracy," "justice," "choice," "autonomy," "individual," and so forth—cannot be clearly defined without also using "freedom." Absent this lexicon, it would be virtually impossible for English-speaking people to discuss morality, politics, or the law today.[2] Now given that both those who endorse and those who oppose any particular judicial decision, piece of legislation, or aspect of foreign policy will do so at least in part by invoking freedom, it must be the case that freedom is seen not only as conceptually fundamental, but also as an unalloyed good. It is something we have, simply in virtue of our being human; we are born free. And differing moral, political, and legal theories are defended and attacked significantly on the basis of the extent to which they do, or do not maximize human freedom.

Freedom is not, however, singular. There are many freedoms, and differing rank orderings of them is what largely distinguishes different moral, political, and legal theories from each other. I want to focus on a single theme that implicates all three areas, and at the same time is of immediate concern and a major source of conflict in the United States and in the world today: human rights, which are usually grounded in the concept of freedom as a defining characteristic of human beings.

If I am essentially free—and it is irrelevant here whether this is to be taken descriptively or prescriptively—then it would seem to follow that no one, and especially no government, should curtail my freedom to say whatever I want to say, associate with whomever I wish, accept any set of religious beliefs I hold true, and dispose of any land or material goods I have legally acquired as I see fit. In the United States, these are the most basic of rights (freedoms), without which I supposedly cannot prosper, and therefore I must be secure in their enjoyment, entering only the caveat that I do not infringe these same rights of others.

For Americans, these rights—these freedoms—are protected by the Bill of Rights. They are civil and political in nature and are now commonly referred to as "first generation" rights. Much of the plausibility of seeing these civil and political rights as the most basic of freedoms is the concomitant view of seeing human beings as basically rational individuals. If we are indeed such, we must also be capable of self-governance, i.e., we must be autonomous. But rational, autonomous individuals must also be free, else they could not realize the potential of that which supposedly makes them uniquely human. With the industrial development of the United States over the past century and a half, these rights have been extended beyond the human realm to include corporations; these, too are seen to be free, self-governing, supposedly rational and certainly self-interested profit-maximizing entities.[3]

The U.N. Universal Declaration of Human Rights,[4] however, goes far beyond civil and political rights. It declares that human beings also have fundamental economic, social, and cultural rights ("second generation" rights). First generation rights are often described as negative, which can be misleading. But they are surely passive, in that they are invoked to secure freedom *from* coercion. Second generation rights are active: they are intended to obviate social and natural impediments *to* the full realization of our human potential: the right to an education, a job, health care, and so on; without these rights, the argument runs, the concept of freedom becomes hollow. Noam Chomsky has put this point succinctly: "Freedom without opportunity is a devil's gift."[5]

"Freedom from" and "freedom to" are clearly distinct, and "freedom from" can loom large in our political thinking if our major concern is

focused solely on the threat of authoritarian governments or the supposed "tyranny of the majority." But if we combine moral and political
considerations, and ask what it means for each of us, not governments,
to respect the rights of others, things can look rather different. That first
generation rights are basically passive can be seen from the fact that 99
percent of the time I can fully respect your civil and political rights
simply by ignoring you; you surely have the right to speak, but no right
to make me listen. Second generation rights, on the other hand, are active
in the sense that there are things I must do (pay more taxes, at the least)
if you are to secure them. Put another way, schools, jobs, hospitals, and
so on, do not fall from the sky; they are human creations. And herein lies
a fundamental conflict in differing conceptions of freedom as expressed
in the discourse of human rights: to whatever extent I am obliged to assist
in the creation of those goods that accrue to you by virtue of having
second generation rights, to just that extent I cannot be an altogether
autonomous individual, enjoying first generation rights, free to rationally
decide upon and pursue my own projects rather than having to assist you
with yours.

That I, too, can have the second generation rights to these goods is
of no consequence if I believe, like libertarian theorists, that I can secure
them on my own, or in free contractual association with a few others,
and thereby keep secure my civil and political rights. It is equally irrelevant that I can freely choose to assist you in securing those goods necessary for the positive exercise of your freedom on my own initiative, for
this would be an act of charity, not an acknowledgment of your rights to
them.

Arguments for second generation rights have a special force in
developing nations but apply as well to the highly "developed" United
States. Of what value is the right of free speech if, unschooled,[6] it is
difficult for me to say anything intelligent, or I am too sick to say anything at all? How much freedom of speech does a single mother with
two small children working for minimum wage in the South Bronx have
compared to, say, Ted Turner, Rupert Murdoch, or the CEO of Mobil-
Exxon? What good is the right to freely dispose of what I own if I don't
own anything? What good is the right to freely choose a job if there
aren't any?

These questions lead to another: What might it take for me to see
that you do indeed have positive rights, and that it is not generous feelings but a moral/political responsibility that I must have to assist you in
securing them? What is required, I believe, is the rejection of the view
of human beings as *most fundamentally* free, autonomous, self-interested
individuals; rather must we come to see, feel, and understand each other

more basically as comembers of human communities where freedom is not a given, but achieved in the company of others.

Again, no one would insist that we are either solely autonomous individuals or altogether social beings, but it should be clear that in contemporary Western moral, political, and legal thinking, free, autonomous individuals have pride of place, and are the basis for virtually all theorizing in these three areas. And it should be equally clear that in these theories, and in legal fact, first generation rights consistently "trump" any claimed second generation rights; hence individual liberty is purchased at the expense of social justice.

In a world of even a roughly equitable distribution of wealth and property, protecting the freedom and liberty of these autonomous individuals and corporations might well be morally, politically, and legally of the utmost importance, infringements thereon to be guarded against at all times. Unfortunately, the real world is rather different.

Consider the following from a *Wall Street Journal* article of 1996:

> Forty years ago the world's 20 richest countries had a per capita GDP 18 times greater than that in the world's 20 poorest countries. The most recent statistics indicate the rich countries' GDP is now 37 times higher. Over 1.2 billion people around the world live on less than $1.00 a day.[7]

The *UN Human Development Report* for 1997 provides greater detail of the inequalities:

> The richest fifth of the world's peoples consume 86% of all goods and services while the poorest fifth consume just 1.3%. Indeed, the richest fifth consumes 45% of all meat and fish, 58% of all energy used, and 84% of all paper, has 74% of all telephones and owns 87% of all vehicles.[8]

And at the pinnacle, the *Report* goes on, "the world's 225 richest individuals, of whom 60 are Americans with total assets of $311 billion, have a combined wealth of over $1 trillion—equal to the annual income of the poorest 47% of the entire world's population."[9] And at the peak of the pinnacle: "the 3 richest people in the world have assets that exceed the combined GDP of the 48 least developed countries."[10] As awful as these figures are to contemplate, they are made much more awful by considering just how relatively little it would take to begin seriously redressing the imbalance between those who have, and those who have not. The UN Report goes on to say: "For $40 billion a year, basic health, basic nutrition, basic education, reproductive health and family planning services, and water sanitation facilities could be extended to the entire world's population."[11] These figures are now a few years old, but overall the situation has at best remained the same, and in many areas have worsened in the interim. *The UN Human Development Report 2000* says that income inequality is growing, and then goes on: "Meanwhile, the super-rich get richer. The combined wealth of the top 200 billionaires hit $1,135 billion in 1999, up from $1,042 billion in 1998. Compare that with the combined incomes of $146 billion for the 582 million people in all the least developed countries."[12]

The *Report* for 2003 gives little reason to believe things will get better for the poor:

> At constant inequality levels, a country needs to grow by 3% or more a year to double incomes in a generation—say from $1 to $2 a day. Yet of 155 countries with data, only 30 had annual per capita income growth rates above 3% in the 1990s. Among the rest, 54 countries saw average incomes fall, and in 71 countries annual income growth was less than 3%.

> The consequences of this dismal growth performance? At the turn of the millennium more than 1.2 billion people were struggling to survive on less than $1 a day—and more than twice as many, 2.8 billion, on less than $2 a day. Living on $1 a day does not mean being able to afford what $1 would buy when converted into a local currency, but the equivalent of what $1 would buy in the United States—a newspaper, a local bus ride, a bag of rice.[13]

Thus, even if the1997 UN estimate of $40 billion annually for the provision of basic human needs and services for everyone is revised upward by 50 percent, to $60 billion, that is less than 50 percent of the increase in wealth of the richest 200 billionaires in 1999, and extrapolating from the earlier figures, the $60 billion represents less than one-quarter of 1 percent of the projected income for the entire world next year.

With statistics like these, it is easy to see why so many U.N. members endorse second-generation rights: 137 countries have ratified the International Covenant on Economic, Social, and Cultural Rights, but the United States is not among them (it is the only developed country not on the list). The government's official attitude toward second-generation rights was well summed up by former U.N. Ambassador Jeanne Kirkpatrick, who referred to them as "a letter to Santa Claus."[14]

Closer to home, it is becoming increasingly difficult to ignore the fact that 13 million young children in the U.S. live in families whose income is below the poverty line, and 45 million Americans have no health insurance, both of which figures went up in 2003.[15] Meanwhile, the *Multinational Monitor* reports that the top 400 income earners here earned more than *the entire population* of the twenty poorest countries in Africa.[16]

What I am suggesting here is that our preoccupation with maintaining and enhancing the formal freedom and liberty attendant on first generation rights is at least partially to blame for our failure to achieve greater equality and justice in a capitalist society, and worldwide. Consider the following statement from the well-known theoretical economist Mancur Olson:

> A thriving market economy requires, among other things, institutions that provide secure individual rights. The incentives to save, to invest, to produce and to engage in mutually advantageous trade depend particularly upon individual rights to marketable assets—on property rights. Similarly,
>
> . . . If there is no right to create legally secure corporations, the private economy cannot properly exploit . . . productive opportunities . . .[17]

Now it may appear at first that when referring to private property, we are speaking of economic, and hence second generation rights, but in actuality we are not. Excepting the two inaugurating and then repealing Prohibition, all twenty-seven Amendments to the U.S. Constitution are either procedural, or deal with civil and political rights, and being able to keep, own, and be secure with one's property is stated explicitly in the Second, Third, Fourth, Fifth, and Fourteenth Amendments. In 1972 Justice Potter Stewart said: "A fundamental interdependence exists between the personal right to liberty and personal right to property . . . That *rights in property are basic civil rights* have long been recognized."[18]

To see why this is so, we must understand that the concept of property rights does not refer either to physical possession, nor is it a relation holding between owners and things; rather is it a set of relations between owners and other persons with respect to things, from which it follows that those with a great deal of money to buy things will have far more "rights" with reference to real property, material goods and services, than those persons living in abject poverty.

To illustrate how Olson's reasoning plays out in practice, and to underscore the significance of giving first-generation property and economic rights primary over second generation economic rights, let me give an example that I have used before in a slightly different context, one which involves the transnational British Petroleum Company. According to a report and analysis in *The Nation*, British Petroleum closed a plant in Lima, Ohio, not because it was losing money, but because it wasn't considered *profitable enough* for the corporation. Being the town's major employer, BP's decision was, of course, devastating for the entire community. A spokesman for the company acknowledged the suffering and dislocation, but defended the decision to close the plant, and to refuse to sell it either to the town or the local union, by saying "Our first responsibility is to our stockholders."[19]

Never mind that at the time this was said, one of the largest stockholders in BP was the government of Kuwait, which thereafter sold a number of its shares at a large profit. This is important, but not my present point, which is conceptual: If no one can abridge my freedom to do whatever I wish with what is mine, then British Petroleum was only claiming its legitimate first generation rights in closing the plant and letting it sit idle instead of selling it to the town and/or the union. And the courts agreed. But if we think the Lima workers had a right to security in their jobs so long as they competently performed them, and the company was making a profit, then BP's action becomes morally suspect, and would, in a just society, very probably be illegal.

By challenging first generation human rights based on freedom and liberty in this way, it may seem that I am at least implicitly championing one form of totalitarianism or another, Stalinist or Fascist. But these are not the only philosophical alternatives and are seen as such only because of the spell of the concept of the free, rational, self-interested autonomous individual, which leads in turn to dichotomies between selfishness and altruism in the moral sphere, and between individualism and collectivism in the political sphere. These dichotomies have been much too sharply drawn, in my opinion, making it difficult for us to entertain very new, or very old ways of envisioning what it is to be a human being.

To sum up the argument thus far: the civil and political rights of autonomous individuals have done much to increase human freedom since the Enlightenment, and to secure justice in many areas as well. But with an increasing concentration of wealth and power both intra- and internationally, we should understand how these rights contribute to that concentration, with justice continuing to elude us, poverty and inequality increasing, democracy eroding, and the achievement of freedom but a distant dream for a majority of the world's peoples.

Turning now to ancient China, the doctrines gathered under the heading of "classical Confucianism" were set down in four texts written and edited roughly between 450–150 BCE: The *Analects of Confucius*, the *Mencius*, the *Xun Zi*, and the *Records of Ritual*. These works are by no means in full agreement on all points, and there are several tensions within each work itself; nevertheless, in conjunction with a few other texts that came to be classics—the Books of *Changes*, *Poetry*, and *History*—these texts do present an overall coherent view of the good life for human beings. This good life is an altogether social one, and central to understanding it is to see that Confucian sociality has aesthetic, moral, and spiritual no less than political and economic dimensions, all of which are to be integrated.

None of the early texts address the question of the meaning *of* life, but they do put forward a vision and a discipline in which everyone can find meaning *in* life. This meaning will become increasingly apparent to us as we pursue the ultimate goal of being human, namely, developing ourselves most fully as human beings to become *jun zi*, "exemplary persons," or, at the pinnacle of development, *sheng*, or sages. And for Confucians we can only do this through our interactions with other human beings. Treading this human path (*ren dao*) must be ultimately understood basically as a religious quest, even though the canon speaks not of God, nor of creation, salvation, an immortal soul, or a transcendental realm of being; and no prophecies will be found in its pages either. It is nevertheless a truly religious path; Confucius definitely does not instruct us about the Way (*dao*) strictly for the pragmatic political consequences of following his guidance. For Confucius we are irreducibly social, as he makes clear in the *Analects*:[20] "I cannot run with the birds and beasts. Am I not one among the people of this world? If not them, with whom should I associate?" (18:6)

Thus the Confucian self is not a free, autonomous individual, but is to be seen relationally: I am a son, husband, father, grandfather, teacher, student, friend, colleague, neighbor, and more. I live, rather than "play" these roles, and when all of them have been specified, and their interrelationships made manifest, then I have been fairly thoroughly individuated, but with very little left over with which to piece together an autonomous individual self, free to conclude mutually advantageous contracts with other rational individuals.

While this view may seem initially strange, it is actually straightforward: in order to *be* a friend, neighbor, or lover, for example, I must *have* a friend, neighbor, or lover. Other persons are not merely accidental or incidental to my goal of fully developing as a human being, they are essential to it; indeed they confer unique personhood on me, for to the extent that I define myself as a teacher, students are necessary to my life, not incidental to it. Note in this regard also, that, again, while Confucianism should be seen as fundamentally religious, there are no solitary monks, nuns, anchorites, or hermits to be found in the tradition. Our first and most basic role, one that significantly defines us in part throughout our lives, is as children; familial deference is one of the highest excellences in Confucianism. We owe unswerving loyalty to our parents, and our obligations to them do not cease at their death. On unswerving loyalty:

> The Governor of She in conversation with Confucius said, "In our village there is someone called 'True Person.' When his father took a sheep on the sly, he reported him to the authorities."
>
> Confucius replied, "Those who are true in my village conduct themselves differently. A father covers for his son, and a son covers for his father. And being true lies in this." (13:18)

On constancy: "The Master said: 'A person who for three years refrains from reforming the ways of his late father can be called a filial son.'" (4:20) And the demands of filial piety are lifelong: "While [the parents] are alive, serve them according to the observances of ritual propriety; when they are dead, bury them and sacrifice to them according to the observances of ritual propriety." (2.5)

From our beginning roles as children—and as siblings, playmates, and pupils—we mature to become parents ourselves, and become as well spouses or lovers, neighbors, subjects, colleagues, friends, and more. All of these are reciprocal relationships, best generalized as holding between benefactors and beneficiaries. The roles are thus clearly hierarchical, but each of us moves regularly from benefactor to beneficiary and back again, depending on the other(s) with whom we are interacting, when, and under what conditions. When young, I was largely the beneficiary of my parents; when they were aged and infirm, I became their benefactor, and the converse holds for my children. I am benefactor to my friend when she needs my help, beneficiary when I need hers. I am a student of my teachers, teacher of my students, colleague of my colleagues. Taken together, the manifold roles we live define us as persons. And the ways in which we live these relational roles are the means whereby we achieve dignity, satisfaction, and meaning in life.

The differences between Western autonomous individuals and Confucian relational persons are significant. In the first place, while autonomous individuals have general moral obligations that they must meet in accordance with some set of universal rational principles, they have no *specific* moral obligations save those they have freely chosen to contractually accept: toward spouses or lovers, their children, friends. But we have not chosen our parents, nor our siblings and other relatives, yet Confucius insists that we have many and deep obligations to them, and they to us. That is to say, unlike individual selves, relational selves must accept responsibilities and ends they have not freely chosen; there is a good for human beings independent of individual conceptions of it.

From this emphasis on familial deference it should be clear that at the heart of Confucian society is indeed the family, the locus of where, how, and why we develop into full human beings. A central government is also important to the good society, because there are necessary ingredients of human flourishing—especially economic—that the family (and local community) cannot secure on their own: repairing dikes, ditches and roads, distributing grain from bumper harvest to famine areas, establishing academies, etc. The early Confucians thus saw the state not as in any way in opposition to the family, but rather saw both as complementary; stated in contemporary terms, if the state insists that I meet my fatherly responsibilities, it should insure that I have the wherewithal— i.e., an education, job, etc.—to do so. Similarly, the state must assume responsibility for the well-being of those who have no family networks for support. Xunzi argued: "If [rulers] choose the worthy and the good, promote the sincere and the respectful, stimulate familial deference and respect for elders, shelter orphans and widows, help the son and poor and disabled, the people will be content with their government."[21]

As an aside, we may note that if the goal of human life is to develop one's humanity to the utmost, then we have a clear criterion for measuring the worth and quality of our interactions with others in the groups (family, clan, village, school, state) to which each of us belongs; we are not merely to accept them as unalterable givens. Rather must we consistently ask to what extent do these groups, and interactions, conduce to everyone's efforts to realize (make real) their potential? That is to say, while deference and loyalty had to be learned and practiced, remonstrance was obligatory when things were not going well. As the Master said: "To see what it is appropriate to do, and not do it, is cowardice." (2:24)

The ideal Confucian society is thus basically communally oriented, with customs, tradition, and rituals serving as the binding force of and between our many relationships. The rituals described in the early classics and basic Confucian texts were largely based on archaic supernatural beliefs that were being questioned during the rationalist period in which Confucius lived, and a part of the genius of the Master and his followers lies in their giving those ritual practices an aesthetic, moral, political, and spiritual foundation that was independent of their original inspiration. To understand this point, we must construe the term *li*, translated as "ritual propriety" not simply as referring to weddings, bar and bat mitz-vahs, funerals, and so on, but equally as referring to the simple customs and courtesies given and received in greetings, sharing food, leave-takings, and much more: to be fully social, Confucians must at all times be polite and mannerly in their interactions with others.

This, then, is Confucian humanism in action: interacting with others as benefactors and beneficiaries in an intergenerational context. Confucius himself was absolutely clear on this point, for when a disciple asked him what he would most like to do, he said: "I would like to bring peace and contentment to the aged, to share relationships of trust and confidence with friends, and to love and protect the young." (5:26)

Both within the family, and in the larger society beyond it, custom, tradition, manners and rituals—civility in the highest sense—are the glue of our intergenerational, interpersonal relationships. Even civility at a low level—performed perfunctorily, "going through the motions"—is obligatory and politically essential to resolving conflict by nonviolent means. But for the early Confucians, rituals, customs, and traditions served other political functions as well. They did not believe laws or regulations were the proper way to govern society:

> The Master said: "Lead the people with administrative injunc-tions and keep them orderly with penal law, and they will avoid punishments but will be without a sense of shame. Lead them with excellence and keep them orderly through observing ritual propriety and they will develop a sense of shame, and moreover, will order themselves." (2:3)

Even more strongly put:

> The Master said: "If rulers are able to effect order in the state through the combination of observing ritual propriety and deferring to others, what more is needed? But if they are unable to accomplish this, what have they to do with ritual propriety?"(4:73)

Thus the Confucians did not believe that society should be governed by monarchical fiat either; the good ruler was to reign more than rule: "The Master said: 'Governing with excellence can be compared to being the North Star: The North Star dwells in its place, and the multitude of stars pay it tribute.'" (2:1)

If customs, traditions—ritual propriety—can perform the same functions in the political realm as laws and regulations, or the orders of a despot, they can also serve in place of universal principles in the moral sphere. Confucian morality is particularistic, in that it insists that at all times we do what is appropriate, depending on who we are interacting with, and when. This particularism is normally seen in Western moral philosophy as decidedly inferior to universalism (Kant thought Confucius knew nothing of morality.[22]) But we may nevertheless make generalizations from the canon that are no less important today than two thousand years ago: when interacting with the elderly, be reverent, caring, obedient; when dealing with peers, treat them as you would be treated; with the young, be nurturing, careful, loving, exemplary. Of course we did not learn these generalizations as moral principles when we were young. But it is on the basis of many and varied loving interactions with my grandmother that I learned long ago to interact appropriately with other grandmothers. Now compared to most issues in contemporary Western moral philosophy—abortion, suicide, genetic engineering, etc.—the importance of making birthday cards for our grandmothers seems incredibly trivial, not even deserving probably of consideration as a moral issue.

But as the early Confucian canon reveals with surety, these homely little activities are the basic "stuff" of our human interactions, and Confucius is telling us that if we learn to get the little things right on a day-in and day-out basis, the "big" things will take care of themselves. And in addition to grandmothers and other elders, the "little things" involve our deep interactions with peers, and those younger than ourselves, and in this way begin to bring home to each of us our common humanity. Hence early Confucianism is not liable to the accusation of say, countenancing racism even if it has been customary in one's family to do so; such upbringing does not conduce to our fullest development as human beings, and hence must be condemned. I can only fully realize my potential when I have learned from my interactions with my own grandmother that grandmothers share qualities, live roles, and interact with others such that, in one sense, when you've seen one grandmother, you've learned to see them all, despite differences in skin color, ethnicity, or other characteristics.

Put another way, if our task is to meet our obligations to elders, peers, and the young in ways that are both efficacious and satisfying, then the specific customs, manners, and rituals we employ in our interactions must contribute to these ends; if not, they must be changed: "The Master said: 'The use of a hemp cap is prescribed in the observance of ritual propriety. Nowadays, that a silk cap is used instead is a matter of frugality. I would follow the newer accepted practice in this.'" (9:3)

This argument will undoubtedly still seem forced to those who would be justifiably skeptical that learning to be polite (civil) when young—absorbing customs and traditions, participating in rituals—could overcome racism, sexism, patriarchy, or any other form of oppressive behavior that has been all too customary and traditional in far too many families and communities. It is for this reason that I have insisted that the efficacy of ritual propriety for the early Confucians is not simply to be seen for its social, political, or moral effects, but rather must be understood spiritually as well. The rituals, even if only followed formally, are essential for social harmony and justice, as noted earlier. But unless they are made one's own, internalized and become productive and satisfying, we can never realize our potential to be fully human.

Consider another statement on filial piety: "As for the young contributing their energies when there is work to be done, and deferring to their elders when there is wine and food to be had—how can merely doing this be considered being filial?" (2:8) And relatedly, on rituals: "The Master said: 'In referring time and again to following ritual propriety, how could I just be talking about gifts of jade and silk?'" (17:11) As we mature, then, we cannot simply "go through the motions" of following custom, tradition, and ritual, nor should we fulfill our obligations mainly because we have been made to feel obliged to fulfill them, else we cannot continue to develop our humanity. Rather must we make them our own and modify them as needed. Remember that for Confucius, many of our obligations are not, cannot be, freely chosen. But he would insist, I believe, that we can only become truly free when we *want* to fulfill our obligations, when we want to help others (be benefactors), and enjoy being helped by others (as beneficiaries).

Being thus altogether bound to and with others, it must follow that the more I contribute to their flourishing, the more I, too, flourish; conversely, the more my behaviors diminish others—by being racist, sexist, homophobic, etc.—the more I am diminished thereby. In saying this, I must insist that I am *not* proffering here a Confucian view of selfless or altruistic behavior, for this would imply that I have a (free, autonomous, individual) self to surrender. But this of course would beg the question against the Confucians, whose views clearly show the supposed dichotomy between selfishness and altruism as a Western conceit, as well as the equally Manichean split on which it is based: the individual *vs.* the collective. Overcoming these deeply rooted dichotomies in Western thought is not at all easy, but when it can be done, very different possibilities for envisioning the human condition present themselves.

For the Confucians, then, civility thus becomes personal, not merely social, and by following custom, tradition, and ritual we mature psychologically and religiously. This is what the Master meant when he said: "What could I see in a person who in holding a position of influence is not tolerant, who in observing ritual propriety is not respectful, and who in overseeing the mourning rites does not grieve?" (3:26)

Some, perhaps, will not grieve at funerals. Going through the rituals merely to "keep up appearances" is socially superior to flaunting them, but such persons are lacking some essential human quality. Confucius believed such people were few in number, however: Master Zeng said: "I have heard the Master say 'Even those who have yet to give of themselves utterly are sure to do so in the mourning of their parents.'" (19:17)

Now this way of seeing ourselves, as most basically comembers of a family, of groups, of communities, of the human race, can easily lead to a conception of social justice far more robust and substantial than that which currently dominates our moral, political, and legal thinking. If what binds us together is felt more strongly than what separates or individuates us, we can come to appreciate that every person has dignity and insist on a more equitable distribution of material goods sufficient for each person to maintain their dignity, flourish, and contribute to the flourishing of others.

But I am not thinking solely of the less fortunate among us here or abroad, those who are currently sick, unschooled, and/or unemployed. Rather am I also thinking now of the very young, the very old, the severely disabled mentally or physically, i.e., those who are in a state of dependency, those who can seemingly only be beneficiaries. What the members of these groups share—and there are millions of such persons— is that they cannot fulfill their side of an individualistic social and political contract. Toward such persons, especially the very old and the severely disabled, we can only be benefactors, and if those disabled are our own close kin, our benefactions will take up a staggering amount of our time, sufficient to make it almost impossible to enjoy the supposed individual freedom we have to pursue our own projects.

In such contract-oriented situations autonomous individuals are getting the worst of a bad bargain even though no bargaining could be done. Kant will be of no help here, for if we can formulate a maxim to care for the wholly dependent close to us, we can equally formulate a maxim to institutionalize them, given Kant's insistence that we have duties to ourselves, and might also will to be institutionalized when we can no longer care for ourselves.

But even if we feel a Kantian duty to care for these wholly dependent persons, either at home or in conjunction with a nearby care facility, purely on the basis of rationality—Kant's only foundation for morality—our lives will not be as satisfying as they might be if we see ourselves as relational persons rather than autonomous individuals, because relational persons interact with others emotionally no less than cognitively. As benefactors to the wholly dependent we interact with the heart as well as the head, and in working with *this* particular child, or *this* particular parent or grandparent, we can come to see, and continuously see, the dignity in their lives, we can come to celebrate them as recipients of our care and love, and can enjoy immensely the love they bestow on us in return; though wholly dependent on us, they can yet be benefactors. We are all taught to say "thank you"—a small ritual—when we receive a gift or a kindness from someone. From the Confucian perspective, however, to say "thank you" is also to give a gift, a kindness, signaling to the other that they have made a difference, great or slight, in your life.

Of course one may have this sense of being basically a comember of families and communities without ever reading a Confucian text. Many Americans give a great deal of themselves to their dependent elders, and many even adopt severely disabled children. But such efforts play no important role in contemporary political theory and in practice continue to be seen largely as women's work, with nowhere near adequate resources provided by the larger society to assist them, which true justice would demand. What the Confucians would insist on, however, is that this is not women's work, but basic human activity, male or female, gay or straight, black, white, yellow, red, or brown.

The Confucian person must thus be seen as relationally whole, as leading an integrated life. In addition to the aesthetic, social, moral, and political features attendant on following this Way—being benefactors and beneficiaries to and of our elders and ancestors on the one hand, and to our fellows and succeeding generations on the other—the Confucian vision displays an uncommon yet religiously authentic sense of transcendence, a human capacity to rise above the concrete spatio-temporality of our existence, enabling us to form a union with all those human beings who have gone before, and all those who will come after.[23]

In summary, others are essential for leading a meaningful Confucian life. Herbert Fingarette put this point well when he said, "For Confucius, unless there are at least two human beings, there are no human beings."[24] By constantly doing what is appropriate we can come to see ourselves as fundamentally, not accidentally, intergenerationally bound to our ancestors, contemporaries, and descendents. All of our interactive relations, with the dead as well as the living, are to be mediated by the customs, traditions, and rituals we all come to share as our inextricably linked personal histories unfold and by fulfilling the obligations defined by these relationships, we are following the Confucian Way.

If the Confucian vision still seems blurred, it is due to the Western lenses through which we attempt to see it, as free autonomous individuals, individuals who are strongly inclined to agree with Aldous Huxley that: "We live together, we act on, and react to, one another; but always and in all circumstances we are by ourselves. The martyrs go hand in hand into the arena; they are crucified alone."[25]

Everyone with eyes to see is aware of the manifold problems attendant on Huxley's description of the self, but we do not yet take those problems as seriously as we should, evidenced clearly by the fact that barren notions of individual freedom and autonomy remain foundational for virtually all contemporary, social, moral, and political theorizing, in our courts, and in our foreign policies. Ever since the Enlightenment at least, individualism has been deeply rooted in Western culture and philosophy, especially in the United States, and in my opinion is significantly responsible for much of the malaise increasingly infecting it.

Worse, insisting that we are basically autonomous individuals can become a self-fulfilling prophecy, especially in a consumptive, property and thing-oriented capitalist society like our own: the more we believe we are isolated, rational, self-interested profit-maximizing atoms, the more we incline to become such.

To return to the beginning, some authoritative persons and groups continue to enhance human well-being by appealing to the conception of autonomous individuals in their arguments: Amnesty International, the American Civil Liberties Union, and Human Rights Watch come immediately to mind. But as wealth and power become more concentrated in fewer individual and/or corporate hands, we may expect more and more authority figures to become more authoritarian, and one way to halt this tendency is to place individuals more dependently in their social contexts as related persons.

A final comment. It may strike some of you as paradoxical that while I have been championing a non-Western philosophical tradition, I have not invoked any arguments for relativism in the attempt. Thus the thrust of my arguments appear universalistic, despite the cogent critiques of some postmodernist, postcolonial, and feminist thinkers that universalism in the history of Western philosophy has too often been totalizing, confining, and oppressive. But these critiques, I believe, while largely correct, are directed at the wrong target. There is nothing wrong with seeking a worldwide consensus on a proper ordering of basic human values; indeed, that search must go forward if we are to see an end to the ethnic, racial, religious, and sexual violence that have so thoroughly splattered the pages of human history with blood and gore since the Enlightenment. Rather does the wrongness lie in the belief that we—especially in the United States—are already fully in possession of those values in the proper order, and therefore feel justified, backed by superior economic might and a military juggernaut, in foisting that particular order on everyone else.

Notes

1. Parts of the first part of this paper are taken—and updated—from my "On Freedom and Inequality" in *The Aesthetic Turn: Reading Eliot Deutsch on Comparative Philosophy*, edited by Roger Ames. Open Court Publishing Company, 2000. Adding the Confucian materials, the paper was given as a keynote address at the annual meeting of ASIANetwork in March 2002 and given roughly in its present form at the KCCC Workshop in March 2003. I am grateful to all these audiences for their comments, questions, and most important, their general support for the views I have advanced herein.

2. None of these terms have close lexical equivalents in classical Chinese, a theme I have discussed in "Against Relativism" in G. Larson and E. Deutsch, eds., *Interpreting Across Boundaries*. Princeton, NJ: Princeton University Press, 1987.

3. Peter Kellman has described well how corporations became individual persons with respects to rights (but not responsibilities) in *Building Unions*. Seattle, WA: Apex Press, 2001.

4. The Declaration is published in several different works, one of which is *The UN Declaration of Human Rights 1948–1988: Human Rights, The United Nations, and Amnesty International*, published by the AIUSA Legal Support Network. Though published in 1988, the work is by no means dated.

5. "Market Democracy in a Neoliberal Order," in *Z Magazine*, September 1997.

6. See "Appalachian Focus Must Change" by Barry Wilson in the *Resist Newsletter* of April 1999: In some parts of Appalachia, illiteracy runs as high as 50 percent.

7. April 14, 1996.

8. As reported in *The New York Times*, September 27, 1998, p. 16.

9. Ibid.

10. Ibid.

11. Ibid.

12. *Human Development Report—2000*. New York, NY: Oxford University Press, 2000, p. 82.

13. *Human Development Report—2003*. New York, NY: Oxford University Press, 2003, pp. 40–41.

14. Quoted in Noam Chomsky, *Rogue States*. Boston, MA: South End Press, 2000, p. 112.

15. *Providence Journal*, August 29, 2004, p. E 6.

16. Cited in "The Top 25 Censored Stories" in *The Progressive Populist,* October 15, 2004, p. 12.

17. "Development Depends on Institutions," in *College Park International,* April 1996, p. 2.

18. Quoted in James W. Ely Jr., *The Guardian of Every Other Right.* New York, NY: Oxford University Press, 1992, p. 141. (Italics added.)

19. See "A Town Betrayed" by Marc Cooper in the *Nation,* June 14, 1997, pp. 13–17.

20. All quotes from the *Analects* are taken from the translation by Roger T. Ames and myself, published by Random House/Ballantine Books, 1998.

21. See my "State and Society in the Xunzi" in T. C. Kline and P. J. Ivanhoe, *Nature, Virtue and Moral Agency in the Xunzi.* Boston, MA: Hackett Publishing Company, 2000.

22. See Julia Ching, "Chinese Ethics and Kant" in *Philosophy East and West,* vol. 28, no. 2, April 1978, p. 169.

23. This point is developed more fully in my *Rationality and Religious Experience.* La Salle, Ill: Open Court Publishing Company, 2001, pp. 82–90.

24. "The Music of Humanity in the Conversations of Confucius," in the *Journal of Chinese Philosophy*, 10, 1983.

25. *The Doors of Perception.* London: Penguin, 1963, p. 12.

Intimate Authority: The Rule of Ritual in Classical Confucian Political Discourse

Tao Jiang

This chapter is a discussion of the nature of political authority in the normative political discourse of classical Confucianism. It is set against the background of the perceived particularism that characterizes a significant portion of the classical Confucian teaching. Classical Confucianism, as an ethical, political, and religious teaching, has often been regarded as advocating family-centered moral particularism. This is in sharp contrast with the universalism of Legalism advocating a universal legal code (Bodde & Morris, p. 29). However, both universalistic and particularistic elements are clearly present in the Confucian teaching. Those who claim that Confucianism is exclusively advocating particularism will have a hard time explaining why it became the orthodox teaching of a universal empire for much of the two thousand years of Chinese imperial history. The fact that Confucianism came to dominate the official political, ethical, and religious discourse in imperial China points to its universal appeal. It is hardly conceivable that an exclusively particularistic teaching could have become the source of political, moral, and religious legitimacy for a universal empire. On the other hand, however, one who claims that Confucianism advocates universalism exclusively will run into the apparent difficulty of explaining the family-centered nature of its moralism. The fact that orthodox Confucian texts often lean towards the interest of the family when there is a potential conflict between family and state is suggestive of its particularism. Hence, we find ourselves in a dilemma on how to categorize classical Confucianism in terms of universalism vs. particularism, since such categories appear to be misfits with respect to the nature of classical Confucianism.

David Hall and Roger Ames have proposed a focus/field model to solve the dilemma of universalism vs. particularism: "The focus/field model results from understanding an item's relation to the world to be constituted by acts of contextualization" (1995, p. 275).[1] That is,

> At any given moment, items in a correlative scheme are characterizable in terms of the focal point from and to which lines of divergence and convergence attributable to them move, and the field from which and to which those lines proceed . . . Fields are unbounded, pulsating in some vague manner from and to their various transient foci. This notion of field readily contrasts with the one-many and part-whole models (ibid., p. 273).

Applying this focus/field model to classical Confucianism would help us to see it in terms of both a family-centered moral particularism (focus) and "the kind of inclusive pluralism that is achieved with the flourishing community" (field).[2] The focus/field model retains particularism as the focus while dissolving universalism into inclusive pluralism as the field.

In this essay I would like to propose another way to approach the issue. I will make the case that it is better not to interpret classical Confucian teaching along the lines of universalism vs. particularism at all, which presupposes a clear boundary between the two; rather, universalism and particularism are not even clearly separated to begin with in classical Confucianism. The difficulty in applying the two categories to describe the nature of the classical Confucian teaching points to its peculiar orientation. To be more specific, classical Confucianism is an intimacy-oriented discourse and to interpret it along the line of universalism vs. particularism is an integrity-oriented analysis that is premised upon a separation between the two. I am using the terms "intimacy" and "integrity" as they are defined by Thomas Kasulis in his comparative study of cultures, *Intimacy or Integrity: Philosophy and Cultural Difference.* Accordingly, intimacy refers to a cultural model whose dominant orientation is characterized by personal—instead of public—objectivity, no sharp distinction between self and other, an affective dimension of knowledge, the connection between the somatic and the psychological, and a nonself-conscious ground for knowledge. By contrast, integrity refers to a cultural orientation with just the opposite characteristics.

I will use the classical Confucian political discourse as an illustration of the overall intimacy orientation of classical Confucianism. I will argue that the classical Confucian paradigm of political authority is what I call "the rule of ritual," idealized in the rule by sage rulers and scholar/officials who exercise a personal form of authority, the source of which is their moral exemplarity in observing ritual propriety, and that it is essentially a model of intimate authority. Such a form of political authority is analogous to the traditional familial and communal authority exercised by respected elders, as opposed to the impersonal, coercive form of authority in the execution of law. The whole premise of this intimate authority is the analogical relationship between family and state, with family as the central metaphor. The efficacy of such a form of authority is established on the educated observance of ritual propriety, *li*, in every aspect of one's life, as opposed to being coerced into obeying the (penal) law, *fa*. *Li* and *fa* belong to two distinct domains of political discourse in ancient China, with Confucians advocating *li* and Legalists *fa*. We will first examine the rule of ritual in the classical Confucian political discourse; then we will see how it is an intimacy-oriented discourse, with its advantages and disadvantages; at the end, we will look into how the intimacy-oriented rule of *li* has shaped the legal practice in traditional China and explore implications it has on China's current transition towards some form of the rule of law.

Li and the Rule of Ritual

Li, usually translated as ritual, ceremony, propriety, ritual propriety, etiquette, and politeness, etc., is a core Confucian notion, and the centrality of the teaching of *li* is one of the distinguishing characteristics of Confucianism. As summarized by Benjamin Schwartz:

> The word *li* on the most concrete level refers to all those "objective" prescriptions of behavior, whether involving rite, ceremony, manners, or general deportment, acting roles within the family, within human society, and with the numinous realm beyond. . . . What makes *li* the cement of the entire normative sociopolitical order is that it largely involves the behavior of persons related to each other in terms of role, status, rank, and position within a structured society. (p. 67)

What is striking is the fact that *li* is an all-embracing realm prescribing every aspect of social, including familial, and political relationships and regulating every detail of interpersonal behavior. More importantly, it is also a gateway through which human beings are connected with the divine. Being such a highly charged concept, *li* covers an extraordinarily wide spectrum of relations and behaviors, from familial to social and political, from the human realm to the divine. No clear demarcation is made between private and public, secular and sacred, or particular and universal. This is one of the fundamental premises of the Confucian thought.[3] In this section, I will argue that *li* legitimizes the kingship and that it offers the ideal form of governance in classical Confucian political discourse.

Li's role in legitimizing the kingship has to do with its origin, which can be traced to the practice of ancestral worship. Ancestor worship was a prevalent form of religious practice in ancient China that is based upon the belief that the ancestral spirits dwell in the world of the divine or numinous, and that the well-being of posterity relies on the blessing of those ancestral spirits. Sociologically, what is significant for ancestor worship as a religious orientation lies in the fact that it "highlights the kinship group as a paradigm of social order—that is, as a network of intimately related roles" (Schwartz, p. 23). In other words, the practice of ancestor worship, in which a clan participates as a group, provides a way of managing the intraclan relationship and regulating the behavior of clan members within the networks of that relationship. As such, as Schwartz notes, "[i]n exploring the wide implications of ancestor worship, . . . we already discern the germ of the later category of *li* which bridges a gamut of prescriptions, ranging from religious ritual to proper social behavior and even etiquette, to use our terms" (p. 22). Ancestral worship represents the embryonic form of *li* in its early development, and as *li* is perfected later on, it is gradually expanded to incorporate other domains, becoming what Schwartz calls "the cement of the entire normative sociopolitical order" (p. 67).[4]

Ancestor worship was the quintessential religious practice in ancient China, and even the king practiced it, as an exemplar of filial piety to his subjects. Be so as it may, the legitimization of a king's rule over others could not be entirely dependent upon the ancestral cult of the royal family, since all people have their ancestors and kin. The king needs a spiritual authority with universal power that can legitimate his rule over the kingdom. Heaven, worshipped by the Zhou house, fulfilled such a role. It is clearly a supreme being with universal power: "Heaven, or the dome of the sky, was worshipped as the supreme being by the Zhou"; "Heaven was not tied to any nation as kin but was omnipresent" (Hsu & Linduff, pp. 106, 108). The legitimization of a king's rule lay, in addition to his military might, in his symbolic ability[5] to communicate with Heaven. Such a communication with Heaven, however, was not a direct one, but through the mediation of ancestral spirits (Schwartz, p. 25).

The ancestral spirits of the royal lineage played a mediating role between Heaven and the king, while the king was the intermediary

between the divine realm and the human world. Through the ritual performance of ancestral worship, a unique avenue was thus established
between the king, the universal ruler of the human world, and Heaven,
the supreme governor of the cosmos, via the ancestral spirits of the
royal lineage. This is how ancestor worship and the worship of Heaven
were linked together, through *li*. We can clearly see why ancestor worship
was so central to the Chinese, from the royal family down to the commoners, even though the ancestral spirits of the common people are
not believed to be as powerful as those of the royal lineage. To the
kings, the observance of *li*, of which ancestor worship constituted one
essential part, was the source of political authority, and the appropriate
fulfillment of *li* was the springboard of political legitimization.[6] Therefore,
the king, in worshiping the royal ancestor, also worshiped Heaven, as
the Son of Heaven (*tianzi*) in receiving the blessing of Heaven (*tianming*)
to rule over the kingdom (Dubs, p. 114). Failure in its observance could
even lead to the downfall of a dynasty.[7] The familial nature of the relationship between the king and Heaven is striking. Ancestor worship
served as the prototype of the worship of Heaven. It is through *li*
that kinship and kingship, family, and state, the two social and political
pillars of traditional China, were linked together.[8] It is, therefore, no
exaggeration to claim that *li* was the cultural cement of traditional
China.

In addition to its legitimizing power, *li* was also a very potent means
of governance, and this is demonstrated in the early Zhou, when the
government was run by ritual.[9] For Confucius, early Zhou represents the
ideal age of unity, peace, and justice, and ritual is *the* perfect means of
governing.[10] What is truly remarkable, however, is Confucius's conviction
that "all government can be reduced to ceremony [*li*]" (Graham, p. 13).
This is what I call "the rule of ritual," representing the Confucian ideal
of governance. Such an ideal is explicitly advanced in the *Analects*. For
example,

> Rulers should employ their ministers by observing ritual propri-
> ety, and ministers should serve their lord by doing their utmost.
> (3.19)

> If rulers are able to effect order in the state through the combi-
> nation of observing ritual propriety (*li*) and deferring to others,
> what more is needed? But if they are unable to accomplish this,
> what have they to do with observing ritual propriety? (4.13)

> If those in high station cherish the observance of ritual propriety,
> the common people will be easy to deal with. (14.41)

Traditionally, the Confucian ideal of governance is regarded as rule of the sage-king, or the rule of men (Peerenboom, p. 131):

> Confucius rejects such limiting notions as rule ethics, pure procedural justice, and a normatively predetermined way. That there are no hard and fast rules means that one must respond to the particular circumstances with an open mind, with a willingness to be flexible and to join in a cooperative search for a harmonious solution. (Ibid., p. 130)

While not disputing the validity of such an almost universally accepted characterization, I would argue that the rule of ritual is a more accurate description of the Confucian paradigm. That is, rule in the Confucian political paradigm is not, strictly speaking, personal rule, since the early Zhou king, the ideal Confucian model of kingship, "did not have an unfettered discretion to act as he pleased, but was very considerably circumscribed by precedent and expected to follow the 'right way to rule' as established by earlier dynasties or his own ancestors" (MacCormack, xiv). The political process in the Confucian paradigm is a rule-based operation, not a haphazard one. Such a rule is the rule of *li*, ritual propriety, constituted by various cultural, religious, ethical, political, and kinship norms.

According to Anthony Cua, *li* has three major functions: delimiting function, supportive function, and ennobling function (pp. 256–58). The delimiting function of *li* refers to the fact that "the main objective of *li* or its primary function is to prevent social disorder, which for Xunzi is an inevitable result of humans' conflicting pursuit of things to satisfy their desires" (Cua, p. 256). *Li's* supportive function provides "conditions or opportunities for satisfaction of desires within the prescribed limits of action" (ibid., p. 257). The ennobling function refers to its conduciveness to the cultivation of beautiful virtues (ibid., p. 258). Interestingly, in direct contradiction with R. P. Peerenboom's characterization of Confucius's aversion to the rule ethics, procedural justice and a normative predetermined way, Cua's characterization of the delimiting and supportive functions of *li* is analogous to "negative moral injunctions or criminal law" and the "procedural law, which contains rules that enable us to carry out our wishes and desires, for example, the law of wills and contracts" respectively (ibid., p. 257). Therefore, the rule of men does not describe the whole picture of the normative Confucian political paradigm on kingship. On the other hand, to characterize the Confucian political paradigm as the rule of ritual has the merit of drawing our attention to the rule-based normative function of *li*, whose flexibility should not be exaggerated as the rule of men implies.

In the following, we will examine how the rule of ritual can be instituted as a viable form of governance envisioned by the classical Confucians. The central concept of *li* has received the most systematic and comprehensive treatment in Xunzi's writings. As one of the most important figures in classical Confucianism,[11] Xunzi has exerted a lasting impact on the subsequent development of the Confucian thought. Hence, our examination of the Confucian paradigm of the rule of ritual will be based on Xunzi's writings.[12] According to Xunzi, observance of ritual principles is a life-and-death matter for a ruler and his state:

> Rites are the highest expression of order and discrimination, the root of strength in the state, the Way by which the majestic sway of authority is created, and the focus of merit and fame. Kings and dukes who proceed in according with their requirements obtain the whole world, whereas those who do not bring ruin to their altars of soil and grain. Hence strong armor and keen soldiers will not assure victory; high walls and deep moats will not assure defensive strength; stern commands and manifold punishments are not enough to assure majestic authority. If they proceed in accordance with the Way of ritual principles, then they will succeed; if they do not, then they will fail. (Knoblock, 15.4)

Here Xunzi is unequivocally clear about the importance of observing ritual principles, which alone can ultimately assure the well-being of a kingdom. By contrast, strong military and severe punishment are no guarantee of success in governing the world. Such a profound commitment to the Confucian ritual principles renders Xunzi an arch defendant of the Confucian project of humane government through observing ritual proprieties, even though some other elements of his writings might sometimes lead one to regard him as non-Confucian, for example the explicit appeal to the penal law, etc.

As Xunzi conceives it, at the heart of *li* is the notion of hierarchy:

> Where the classes of society are equally ranked, there is no proper arrangement of society; where authority is evenly distributed, there is no unity; and where everyone is of like status, none would be willing to serve the other.

Just as there are Heaven and Earth, so too there exists the distinction between superior and inferior, but it is only with the establishment of intelligent kingship that the inhabitants of a kingdom have regulations.

Two men of equal eminence cannot attend each other; two men of the same low status cannot command each other—such is the norm of Heaven. When power and positions are equally distributed and likes and dislikes are identical, and material goods are inadequate to satisfy all, there is certain to be contention. Such contention is bound to produce civil disorder, and this disorder will result in poverty. The Ancient Kings abhorred such disorder. Thus, they instituted regulations, ritual practices, and moral principles in order to create proper social class divisions. They ordered that there be sufficient gradations of wealth and eminence of station to bring everyone under supervision. This is the fundamental principle by which to nurture the empire. (Knoblock, 9.3)

To Xunzi, as well as to other Confucians, hierarchy is the way of nature, as exemplified by the different natural positioning between Heaven and Earth, high and low respectively. Hence human society should also model itself after this natural hierarchy.[13] Social hierarchy is the effective way to put the society in order so that social chaos can be prevented. Equality, on the other hand, is against nature, and it gives rise to confusion leading to chaos. Therefore, the best way of governance is to follow the natural way of hierarchy that the ritual principle embodies. Xunzi declares that a true king is a ruler who can act in accordance with ritual propriety and moral principles (Knoblock, 9.10).

Li is a powerful way to regulate various dimensions of human relationship, which is the basis of social order and political stability. "The relationships between lord and minister, father and son, older and younger brothers, husband and wife, begin as they end and end as they begin, share with Heaven and Earth the same organizing principle, and endure in the same form through all eternity" (Knoblock, 9.15). Only when *li* is observed, hierarchy is instituted, and social roles are performed accordingly can the society function as a whole. This is what Xunzi means by the "unitary principle":

In mourning and sacrificial rites, in court and diplomatic ceremonies, and in military organization there is a unitary principle. In elevating or degrading, in decreeing death or life, in bestowing or taking away, there is a unitary principle. In the lord acting as lord, the minister as minister, the father as father, son as son, the older brother as older brother, the younger brother as younger brother, there is a unitary principle. In the farmer functioning as a farmer, the knight as a knight, the artisan as an artisan, and the merchant as a merchant, there is a unitary principle. (Knoblock, 9.15)

If the way of a society is properly structured, then each of the myriad things acquires its appropriate place, the Six Domestic Animals can properly increase, and every living thing will have its allotted fate. (9.16a)

It is clear that the ideal Confucian state, according to Xunzi, is one in which the natural hierarchy is respected and enforced through ritual propriety. For those who are not worthy enough to respect such a hierarchical system, punishment is in order (9.2).

However, Xunzi does not advocate hereditary social hierarchy. Rather, he proposes some form of meritocracy, based upon a person's moral quality and ability to observe ritual propriety; he also thinks that people should be regulated by rewards and punishment (Knoblock, 9.1). As Knoblock points out, "In both these views, Xunzi follows Mozi rather than the moral traditional Ru teaching, but unlike Mozi he uses ritual as the means to accomplish these ends" (vol. 2, p. 85).

To sum up, we have discussed in this section the central Confucian notion of *li*, ritual propriety, both as the source of political legitimization of the king's right to rule over his kingdom and as a viable way of governance. That *li* can play such a critical role in the political discourse in classical Confucianism is premised upon the analogical relationship between the family and the state. This family model of the state has dominated the orthodox Confucian political discourse (Knoblock, vol.1, p. 87). The potency of such a model on the political discourse in classical Confucianism can be seen in two aspects. The first aspect concerns the legitimacy of a kingdom or empire. To be more specific, on this model, the legitimization of kingship is achieved through an establishment of a familial relationship between the universal Heaven and the king as the Son of Heaven. Such a model of political legitimacy clearly taps into the popular sentiment of the centrality of family/kinship in ancient China. The second aspect has to do with the governance itself. As a political model, the rule of ritual is predicated upon an extension of the natural hierarchy observed within a family to the whole kingdom or empire. It is through the observance of *li* that such a form of authority is exercised.

This family model of the state authority with family interests often outweighing state interests points to the rather peculiar orientation of classical Confucian teaching. Normally, the state/empire is a universal entity and the family a particular unit within it. To establish a correlative relationship between the two is to reject the universalistic model of the state. However, a mere particularistic model of the political authority would not have worked, and the appeal to *tian*, usually translated as Heaven, in the classical Confucian political discourse is a clear indication of the presence of universal elements. I will argue that the categories of universalism and particularism fail to capture the basic orientation of classical Confucian political discourse. In order to understand the Confucian political discourse, we need a better model so that its peculiar orientation can come to light. This is precisely what we will do in the next section.

The Rule of Ritual: Intimate Authority

In this section we will examine the peculiar orientation of the Confucian paradigm of political authority, the rule of ritual. I will argue, in using Thomas Kasulis's vocabulary, that the rule of ritual is an intimacy-oriented political model, as opposed to the integrity-oriented one. Kasulis, in his *Intimacy or Integrity: Philosophy and Cultural Difference*, postulates two cultural models with different prevailing orientation, intimacy-oriented and integrity-oriented. Intimacy is characterized by the following:

1. Intimacy is objective, but personal rather than public.
2. In an intimate relation, self and other belong together in a way that does not sharply distinguish the two.
3. Intimate knowledge has an affective dimension.
4. Intimacy is somatic as well as psychological.
5. Intimacy's ground is not generally self-conscious, reflective, or self-illuminating. (p. 24)

Integrity, on the other hand, emphasizes the opposites:

1. Objectivity as public verifiability.
2. External over internal relations.
3. Knowledge as ideally empty of affect.
4. The intellectual and psychological as distinct from the somatic.
5. Knowledge as reflective and self-conscious of its own grounds. (p. 25)

We will first explain in some detail the major characteristics of the intimacy-orientation—since the integrity-orientation is not the focus here, I will not go into details with it. Following this, we will show that the Confucian paradigm of political authority, the rule of ritual, is clearly a model of intimate authority. We will conclude this section with a brief investigation of the advantages and disadvantages of the intimate model of political authority.

The first characteristic of intimacy is that it embraces a personal, instead of public, form of objectivity. Usually, personal and objective are regarded as incompatible with each other. To search for the objectivity of knowledge is to remove as much personal, hence subjective, elements as possible. Scientific knowledge is a paradigm case of objectivity that is characterized as nonpersonal. However, such an attitude towards objectivity is merely reflective of our integrity-dominated modern mentality. In fact, there are two species of objectivity: the objectivity of publicly verifiable knowledge and that of intimate knowledge (Kasulis, p. 35). What distinguishes the latter from the former is the expert nature of the latter:

> If we believe that any reasonable person *who spent thirty years in gymnastics* would come to the same evaluation as the gymnastic judges, then we believe their judgment is objective, though not publicly so. The universality assumption of positivism differs only in omitting the italicized phrase, making the objectivity "public" rather than "expert." The common core of the objectivity claim in both public and nonpublic knowledge, however, is in their common phrase "any reasonable person." (ibid., p. 36)

Clearly, the amount of training that expert knowledge requires marks it off from being merely public. Any reasonable person, after the required training, can expect to achieve a similar level of expertise. Hence, intimate knowledge is by no means subjective. In fact, knowledge requires expertise. That is, knowledge has an intimate core to it that only a trained expert can have access to.

Furthermore, "[i]ntimacy is not merely personal, but personal in a special way. When in the locus of intimacy, one feels he or she *belongs* there" (ibid., p. 36). This points to the second characteristic of intimacy, namely there is no sharp distinction between the self and the other within the locus of intimacy. Here Kasulis makes a crucial distinction between external and internal relations:

> In an external relation, the relatents (the things in relation to each other) exist independently. . . . In an internal relation, by

> contrast, it is part of the essential nature of the relatents that
> they are connected as they are; they are interdependent, not
> independent, entities.... To dissolve an internal relationship
> would not merely disconnect them; it would actually transform
> an aspect of the relatents themselves. (pp. 36–7)

Intimate relations are experienced as internal, rather than external, to
the parties involved. In other words, that to which we are intimately
related is not just our connection; it is part of me. Such a relationship is
often the result of many years of cultivation, to the extent that it becomes
constitutive of me. Family relationship is a clear example in this regard.

Thirdly, intimate knowledge has an affective dimension. While it is
an admirable achievement of modern scientific rationality to maintain a
strict separation between feeling and knowing, it is also important to
recognize the limitation of such a rationality, as Kasulis points out:

> Many of life's most anguishing decisions are not resolvable
> on logical and empirical grounds alone.... Many decisions
> require not only logic and factual information, but also an
> imagination and conjecture nourished by experience. Expe-
> rience, especially expert experience, can undergird rational
> hunches, suspicions, and intuitions. Such phenomena often
> involve feelings. (p. 40)

Despite its phenomenal success and efficacy, the potency of scientific
rationality is confined to a well-guarded and self-defined boundary
outside of which it does not possess a magic power. Apparent examples
include moral and aesthetic sensitivities whose development requires
empathic imagination based upon one's personal experience rather than
discursive reasoning. What is significant with respect to knowledge based
upon the empathic imagination is that it "is generally transmitted or
taught in a nondiscursive way. That is: the content and rules of an intimate form of knowing are of secondary importance to the practical
training under a master or expert." (p. 40) Put simply, knowing in such a
form is preceded by training and practice under a teacher. As a result,
the mind is molded in a certain way that it becomes attuned to some
aspects of the world that are not so readily available to an untrained
mind.

Closely related to the affective dimension of intimacy is its embodied nature, the fourth characteristic of the intimacy orientation. Here
praxis involving human body becomes the key to the intimate relation-

ship. Praxis refers to "a pattern of practical behavior enacting a precon-
ceived model" (ibid., p. 43):

> Praxis is fundamental to intimacy in two respects: First, in cases
> wherein intimacy involves a person, the intimate relation itself
> is established only through praxis. . . . intimacy must be physi-
> cally enacted. The second point about praxis is that intimacy
> deepens as the praxis is repeated or habitualized. That is: after
> getting the right idea about—indeed the right *feel* for—log split-
> ting I established a proper posture and imitated the correct
> movements. (p. 43)

In this regard, intimacy is an accomplishment, through praxis that involves
reconditioning of one's body. Reconditioning of the body is achieved
through habitualization of the praxis until it becomes one's second
nature. The somatic dimension of intimate knowledge distinguishes it
from a mere abstract form of knowledge that belongs to the privileged
domain of the "rational" mind, often dualistically conceived as being
against the "irrational" body. To highlight the somatic aspect of knowledge is to acknowledge the profound and often ignored intelligence that
the human body possesses. Implicit in such a view is the assumption that
a human being is always an embodied being, and her physical condition
is intricately related to her mental life. Mind and body are taken to be a
unity, or at least there is a continuum between the physical and the
mental, as opposed to the modern Cartesian understanding of the body
as an intricate machine.

The somatic nature of intimacy means that its ground is not generally self-conscious, reflective, or self-illuminating. This is the fifth characteristic of intimacy. It points to the somewhat "esoteric" or "dark" nature
of intimacy. "By saying intimacy is 'dark' I mean that the foundation or
ground of intimate knowledge is not obvious even to those involved in
the intimate locus" (p. 47), just as we are not usually aware of the way
our body moves in an everyday routine situation. There is a certain sense
of magic in the way intimate knowledge works. Esoteric refers:

> specifically to the context in which a nonpublic, but objective,
> insight is available only to members of a certain group who have
> undergone special training . . . In our sense, then, the esoteric is
> not necessarily secretive or exclusive. It is open to everyone who
> has entered the intimate circle. How does one do that? By
> undergoing the appropriate praxis. (p. 48)

Once again, praxis and training, instead of abstract analysis and rationality, make such a shared "esoteric" knowledge possible.

Our brief summary of key characteristics of intimacy should make it immediately clear that classical Confucianism is an intimacy-oriented discourse. In no other place within the Confucian system is such an intimacy-orientation more clearly demonstrated than the teaching of *li*. Consequently, the political authority in the classical Confucian discourse, grounded on the rule of ritual, is best described as a model of intimate authority. In the following, we will analyze the central Confucian notion of *li* in light of this intimacy orientation and examine its impact upon the politics of imperial China. I will use mainly Robert Eno's highly original work on Confucian *li*.

As we have seen earlier, *li* is a central Confucian notion, especially in the writings of Xunzi. The centrality of *li* in Confucianism is further emphasized by Robert Eno when he argues that *li* is the defining characteristic of Confucianism, or what he calls Ruism. That is, it is better to understand Confucianism:

> more as a community of men than as a body of doctrine. Programs of ritual activity will appear as the distinguishing core of that community. Consequently, the explicit doctrines that were articulated as a product of these activities will be most coherently expressed by their relation to the activities themselves: either as reports of perspectives generated through core practices, or as defensive rationalizations possessing the instrumental value of promoting and preserving the ritual core. (Eno, p. 7)

This insightful observation captures Confucianism at its heart. That is, when understood as a body of doctrine, classical Confucianism might appear unsystematic and unstructured, or even messy. It is usually full of claims and sayings that do not lend themselves to logical or self-evident axiomatic analysis, as is expected in a philosophical project. However, what Eno proposes here is that to interpret Confucianism as a body of doctrine is to miss a major part of its teaching. According to Eno, classical Confucianism was first and foremost a community of men gathering together around a master studying classics and various ritual skills. Much of the collected Confucian writings are related to such activities those men were engaged in and experiences arisen therein.

What is distinctive about such a community of learners is their shunning away from abstract reasoning. Instead, their focus was on studying and practicing ritual skills. This emphasis on learning ritual skills points to an underlying assumption essential to Confucianism, namely "an individual's repertoire of skills determines the interpretative options available to him for understanding the world" (Eno, p. 9). In other words, the interpretative options are not themselves the product of nature, but are rather conditioned by one's repertoire of skills which in turn comes from training. "The heart of Ruism lay outside its texts in a detailed training course of ritual, music, and gymnastics" (ibid.). For the Confucians, those who have mastered the ritual skills after the vigorous training and praxis would find at their disposal power of wisdom that is inaccessible to ordinary people. In other words, such power is the result of the ritual praxis that provides the basic framework for the subsequent rational thinking and political action.

A disciple who was trained to be a Confucian committed himself to "the practice of *li* and to the notion that mastery of *li* was the path to Sagehood" (Eno, p. 33). Confucian political activism is therefore preceded by the program of *li*-centered self-cultivation. Such a commitment to *li* would be shared by the educated elite literati class, whose members filled the imperial bureaucracy as scholar/officials after the Confucian triumph in the early Han Dynasty. In other words, the commitment to *li* became a shared group mentality of the Chinese ruling elite. Only those who have successfully cultivated themselves by completely ritualizing their personal conducts and becoming a moral exemplar would be regarded as qualified to engage in political action.

> For the master of ritual, government is simple. But a man unskilled in the art of ritual will only blunder if he attempts to exploit the political power of *li*: "Can *li* and deference be used to rule a state? Why, there is nothing to it. He who cannot use *li* and deference to rule a state, how can he manage *li* at all?" (A: 4.13). For the Ruist, then, the study of ritual and a grasp of the values that govern the application of *li* must precede ritual government. The Ruist disciple must begin by cultivating his virtue within the Ruist group: political action must be deferred. (Eno, p. 44)

The magic power of a ritual government can be tapped into only by a person who is a master of ritual and has become a moral exemplar. To be able to run the government by ritual, or to use Eno's word, "to transform society into a field of ritual action" (p. 41), is a clear indication of a virtuous sage-king, since only a virtuous sage who is a master of ritual propriety can effectively use ritual politically. For those who are unqualified due to the inadequacy in their self-cultivation of *li* and virtue, the political power of the ritual cannot be exploited. Hence the conclusion is that one should cultivate oneself first before taking up political action. Or simply, in order for *li* to generate order in society, it would require a sage-king and his officials who are superb ritual actors and moral exemplars.

To recap what we have covered so far in this section, when Confucianism is understood as a community of men who were engaged in the study of classics and ritual praxis in cultivating themselves, shared insights about the world as the result of such a cultivation, became experts in ritualized actions in both daily life and the political arena, and were able to exploit the magic power of ritual action in government, it clearly demonstrates an intellectual discourse with an intimacy orientation. The ideal Confucian political norm, the rule of ritual, is built upon a model of intimate political authority, exercised by the sage-king and a group of learned scholar/officials whose shared experience of moral and ritual cultivation gives them the authority to govern. The Confucian education molded the Chinese ruling elite in such a way that there was a shared commitment to the observance and praxis of *li*. This ruling literati class became an intimate group with intricate relationships among themselves, governing the empire on behalf of the emperor.

If our analysis of the normative Confucian political authority, grounded on the rule of *li*, is of some validity, let us briefly examine the advantages and disadvantages of this intimacy model of political authority. The clear advantage of the model of intimate authority is that it fosters a harmonious relationship among participants of the political order of *li*, with a background of common experience in the self-cultivation through the study of classics and ritual praxis.[14] The clear disadvantage, on the other hand, is that "insofar as intimacy privileges a form of knowledge that is unsaid, intuitive, and cannot be shared with nonexperts, it is difficult, maybe impossible, for an outsider to analyze and challenge this knowledge" (Kasulis, p. 145). Furthermore, to criticize and challenge it from the inside is rendered difficult, as the challenger faces the scenario of being ostracized as a traitor of the ruling elite (ibid., pp. 145–46). Such a tendency in the intimacy-oriented political practice prompts Kasulis to characterize such an orientation as "inherently totalitarian" (p. 147).[15]

This charge of totalitarianism poses a serious challenge to the Confucian model of intimate authority. While we might not agree that the Confucian model of political authority is inherently totalitarian, its authoritarianism is less controversial. In this connection, we do find that Xunzi's discussion of *li* leans towards authoritarianism, more so than Confucius's. In A. C. Graham's observation,

Confucius himself had conceived the ideal of a society in which all relations between persons function not by force but by ceremony, so that punishments will lapse. It is possible to think of this as one of the varieties of Chinese 'anarchism', with some stretching of the word; one would have to conceive a hierarchical anarchism, in which the ceremonial acts which are perfectly voluntary for all participants include the issuing and obeying of a properly ritualised command of ruler to minister. (p. 302)

If it is still possible to construe Confucius as a hierarchical anarchist, the image of Xunzi is decidedly a hierarchical authoritarian, even though both uphold the rule of *li* as the supreme way of governance. To be fair to Xunzi, he lived at a time when China was plunged into unprecedented social chaos and suffering. Consequently, a stronger measure was called for in order to deal with the grave situation. Despite his struggle, sometimes visibly intense as manifested in his writings, Xunzi was still committed to the rule of ritual as the ideal form of governance, and this puts him within the orthodox Confucian school. If Xunzi's political thought has demonstrated a clear authoritarian tendency, such a tendency would become a full-blown totalitarianism in the hands of Legalists, some of whom, not surprisingly, were his own disciples, including Han Fei Zi and Li Si, the former being the grand synthesizer of Legalist philosophy and the latter the first prime minister of the first unified Chinese empire, Qin, who was instrumental in implementing policies and measures in consolidating the unification and establishing a centralized government bureaucracy followed by the subsequent Chinese empires. The role the Confucian notion of *li* has played in the political practice of imperial China was not a clear-cut positive or negative case. Let us direct our attention to the influence the Confucian rule of *li* has exerted in the *actual* political practice of imperial China.

The Rule by *Fa* and Its Confucianization

In contrast to the Confucian ideal of governance by *li*, the rule of ritual, the Legalists formulate a powerful instrument of statecraft, the core of which is the rule by *fa*, penal law.[16] Legalism calls for a much more powerful and centralized form of government, to absolutize the power of the ruler so that he can fend off the intense pressure from both within and without the kingdom. We will briefly examine the Legalist teaching on *fa* through the writings of its great synthesizer, Han Fei Zi, whom Graham regards as "the most immediately relevant to his times of all Chinese thinkers" (p. 269).

At the core of Legalism was the conviction that "good government depends, not as Confucians and Mohists supposed on the moral worth of persons, but on the functioning of sound institutions" (Graham, p. 268). According to Legalists, if the institution was established strictly based on rules and standards with vigorous enforcement, it could work automatically by itself. The effectiveness of the Legalist theory is grounded upon their observation of human nature as articulated by Han Fei Zi:

> In ruling the world, one must act in accordance with human nature. In human nature there are the feelings of liking and disliking, and hence rewards and punishments are effective. When rewards and punishments are effective, interdicts and commands can be established, and the way of government is complete. (qtd. in Fung, p. 162)

Since the Legalists saw people as selfish and responsive only to the hope of reward and fear of punishment, penal law and rewards were necessarily the most effective means for the ruler to bring the people to his feet.

Han Fei Zi synthesized three of his predecessors' theories, namely *fa* (law) of Shang Yang, *shu* (statecraft) of Shen Buhai and *shi* (authority) of Shen Dao (Chan trans., pp. 255–56), to create an amazingly coherent theory of power politics:

> Statecraft involves appointing officials according to their abilities and demanding that actualities correspond to names. It holds the power of life and death and inquires into the ability of all ministers. These are powers held by the ruler. By law is meant statutes and orders formulated by the government, with punishments which will surely impress the hearts of the people. Rewards are there for those who obey the law and punishments are to be imposed on those who violate orders. These are things the ministers must follow. On the higher level, if the ruler has no statecraft, he will be ruined. On the lower level, if ministers are without laws, they will become rebellious. Neither of these can be dispensed with. They both are means of emperors and kings. (ibid., p. 255)

Apparently, *fa* (law) here mainly refers to the penal laws instituted by the ruler to deal with the masses, while *shu* (statecraft) is the means to manipulate ministers and the whole bureaucratic system. The purpose of *fa* is to keep people "from doing any evil." The intent of *shu* is to ensure that the ministers picked by the ruler are qualified both in their abilities and loyalty, and that the whole bureaucratic system is functioning properly. There are always too few in the state who can please the ruler, and if the ruler relies on these few, he would be ineffective in dealing with the whole populace (De Bary et al., p. 141). *Fa* is proclaimed to the public, while *shu* remains secret to the ministers—clearly the Legalists believe that officials are harder to control, therefore some flexibility is necessary on the part of the king to keep them in line.

Han Fei Zi incorporated *shi* (authority), introduced by Shen Dao but neglected by Shang Yang and Shen Buhai, into his Legalist framework as the authority of rulership. In light of his scheme, the source of authority, or the power-base, lies in the function of kingship instead of the person of the king.[17] In other words, for Han Fei Zi, political power depended upon the power-base itself being ordered through the vigorous enforcement of laws instead of the particular person of the king, or his charisma or morality. Han Fei Zi realized that it would be a disastrous mistake to rely on the sage-kings to bring peace and prosperity to the state, since sages are always in the extreme minority, and therefore such reliance would condemn the world to almost endless chaos with few exceptions of peace whenever some true sages happen to be at the throne. His concern was more worldly: he felt that through his theoretical framework the world could avoid the extreme scenario of despotic rulers like Jie and Zhòu (Graham, p. 281). His solution was to build a solid power-base, structured in such a way as to function automatically and by itself, no matter who was in charge. Were this the case, the moral integrity of the ruler would become irrelevant. Han Fei Zi's theory, and for that matter the Legalist theory in general, was essential in replacing the rule by a sage-king who follows the ritual propriety—idealized in the Zhou feudal system—with an impersonal rule by the bureaucratic machine.

Both the Confucians and the Legalists were seeking ways to accomplish peace and stability over the known world, but what distinguished the one from the other was twofold: the nature of that peace and stability and how to achieve it. The Confucians, by preaching a return to rule of ritual, *li*, betrayed their commitment to a noncentralized form of governance wherein the political operations are under the guidance of cultural and religious order, embodied in the practice of *li*; the practice of *li* put some restraint upon the execution of political power through the mechanism of traditional religious and moral values and kinship rule.[18] On the other hand, Legalists advocated an absolutization of power by placing it in the hands of the ruler, under whom an impersonal bureaucratic system operates of itself by following the laws of punishment and reward, but the laws do not apply to the ruler himself.

The Confucian triumph over Legalism in the Han Dynasty, at least from the perspective of the normative political discourse, signals the failure of *fa* and the political model it represents in dealing with Chinese society, which was organized into clan families based upon blood ties rather than legal norms. Nevertheless, the Legalists have left an indelible mark on the Chinese political operation, the most important of which are the increasing bureaucratization of the state and centralization of power in the hand of the ruler. However, Confucianism, through its control of the educational system that produced scholars who later entered the imperial bureaucracy as officials, was able to exert a powerful influence over the political and social life of the Chinese people. The most substantive influence is reflected in what T'ung-tsu Ch'ü calls "Confucianization of law" (p. 267). Let us take a closer look at this unique phenomenon of legal practice in traditional China.

Li and *fa* represent two fundamentally different governing models in the Chinese political discourse. At the heart of *li* is the social hierarchy, whereas equality under the ruler is at the core of *fa*.

> The Confucian School denied that uniformity and equality were inherent in any society. They emphasized that differences were in the very nature of things and that only through the harmonious operation of these differences could a fair social order be achieved. Any attempts to equalize what was unequal, to give all men an identical way of life, would be irrational and would only result in the destruction of the rational division of labor and inevitably in the overthrow of the social order itself. (Ch'ü, p. 226)

Li fulfills exactly such a differentiating function in traditional China. *Li* dictates various distinctions according to nobility or baseness, old or young, poor or rich, insignificant or important (Knoblock, 19.1c).

This is in sharp contrast with the Legalist vision of society. Despite its totalitarianism, the notion of equality in advocating one unifying legal system without differentiation in treating both the noble and the commoner deserves some recognition, although it was put forth in the sense that *under the ruler*, everybody should be equally treated, albeit equally harshly, before the law, meaning that the ruler remained in a privileged position outside the legal system:

> The law no more makes exceptions for men of high station than the plumb line bends to accommodate a crooked place in the

wood. What the law has decreed the wise man cannot dispute nor the brave man venture to contest. When faults are to be punished, the highest minister cannot escape; when good is to be rewarded, the lowest peasant must not be passed over . . . Were the ruler of men to discard law and follow his private whim, then all distinction between high and low would cease to exist. (Han Fei Tzu, pp. 28–9)

With the Confucian victory in the Chinese political discourse, efforts were made to reconcile the conflict between *li* and *fa*, resulting in the Confucianization of law. Confucianism stamped itself upon the legal code in several important ways: "the legal bolstering of the human relationships [was] held to be necessary for the well-being of society" (MacCormack, p. 7), "factors of benevolence and individual merit or position [were allowed] to influence the incidence of punishment" (ibid., p. 5), and punishment "was carefully proportioned to the gravity of the offense" (ibid.). Put differently, the consequence of the Confucianization of law was at least twofold: it moderated the harshness of punishment and took circumstances of the crime into consideration; it also rejected the principle of equality before the law, taking into consideration the different social and political status of the offender.

However, the relationship between *li* and *fa* remained an uneasy one within the traditional Chinese political system. This uneasy balance between the two can be characterized as the practice of "the rule of ritual and the rule by law" in imperial China, accommodating both the Confucian rule of ritual and the Legalist rule by law.[19] The ritual order, as an imitation of the natural order in regulating all facets of the society and the empire including even the imperial household, was deemed as higher than the legal order, regularly applied to the lower strata of the political system or the mass. As Derk Bodde and Clarence Morris point out,

The concern of the Legalists was political control of the mass man, for which reason they have been termed totalitarian. Yet in their insistence that all men high and low should conform to a single law, they were egalitarian. The concern of the Confucians was moral development of the individual man, for which reason they have been termed democratic. Yet in their insistence that for a graded society there has to be a graded law, they were undemocratic. (pp. 50–1)

The Confucian model of intimate authority that may regard "as not merely excusable but obligatory what for Legalists (and for us) is nepotism, corruption, the aggrandisement of one's family at the expense of the weaker" (Graham, p. 302) has often been blamed for the ills of contemporary China. Such a mixed legacy of the Confucian impact on the legal practice in traditional China poses a serious challenge to the possibility of the rule of law[20] in China's future, assuming that China is still largely Confucian (Hall & Ames 1999, p. 9). In light of our discussion of different cultural orientations, the rule of law instituted in the West is clearly an integrity-oriented political practice. For Confucian China to accept the ideal of the rule of law, it will require nothing short of a radical cultural transformation from the intimacy-dominated political culture to the integrity-dominated one, even as intimacy retains its influence on the Chinese society. As for the possibility of such an outcome, it is beyond the scope of this chapter.

To sum up, in this chapter, we have tried to solve the problematic of universalism vs. particularism in classical Confucianism by focusing on its peculiar orientation, which, strictly speaking, defies being characterized by the two categories. We have used the issue of the Confucian ideal political model as an example to illustrate the peculiar orientation of the Confucian discourse. We have argued that the ideal Confucian political model is that of the rule of ritual, instead of the rule of man. In using Thomas Kasulis's vocabulary, we have come to view the rule of ritual as a model of intimate authority, the basis of which is the analogical relationship between family and state. Based upon the discussion of its intimacy orientation, we have looked into the actual impact the Confucian rule of ritual had on the legal practice in imperial China. In that regard, we have come to realize the mixed legacy of the Confucian model of intimate authority, namely the moderation of harsh punishment but the promotion of unequal treatment before the law. Given the intimacy orientation of the Confucian political model of the rule of ritual and the integrity orientation of the rule of law enshrined in the West, a radical transformation is required in order for China to make the transition to some form of the rule of law. Another option is to establish the rule of law based on the intimacy model, but that would radically redefine the nature of the rule of law with its liberal rights-based premise. As for what shape that might eventually take, it will take another separate effort.

Notes

1. A more detailed discussion of the focus/field model can be found in Hall & Ames 1995, pp. 268–78.

2. This particular wording is from Roger Ames's comments during the online conference on "Cultures of Authority in Asian Practice" hosted by the East-West Center in September 2003.

3. "The ancients who wished to manifest their clear character to the world would first bring order to their states. Those who wished to bring order to their states would first regulate their families. Those who wished to regulate their families would first cultivate their personal lives. Those who wished to cultivate their personal lives would first rectify their minds. Those who wished to rectify their minds would first make their wills sincere. Those who wished to make their will sincere would first extend their knowledge. The extension of knowledge consists in the investigation of things. When things are investigated, knowledge is extended; when knowledge is extended, the will becomes sincere; when the will is sincere, the mind is rectified; when the mind is rectified, the personal life is cultivated; when the personal life is cultivated, the family will be regulated; when the family is regulated, the state will be in order; and when the state is in order, there will be peace throughout the world." *The Great Learning*, translated by Wing-tsit Chan, in *A Source Book in Chinese Philosophy* (Princeton: Princeton University Press, 1963), pp. 86–87. However divergent the Neo-Confucian interpretations might have been, the general theme is no different from the Confucian ideal of "inner sageliness and outer kingliness," further elaborated as engaging in the cultivation of the self, bringing harmony in the family, achieving order in the country and accomplishing peace over the world (*xiu qi zhi ping*). In *The Doctrine of the Mean*, there is a clear indication that human beings embody the sacred dimension in our nature: "What Heaven (Tian, Nature) imparts to man is called human nature. To follow our nature is called the Way (Tao). Cultivating the Way is called education. The Way cannot be separated from us for a moment. What can be separated from us is not the Way" (Chan, p. 98). The distinction between the transcendent and human, the sacred and the secular is not at all clearly demarcated.

4. As Anthony Cua summarizes, *li* evolves through three stages in its increasing extension, "The earliest usage . . . pertains to religious rites. . . . In the second stage, *li* becomes a comprehensive notion embracing all social habits and customs acknowledged and accepted as a set of action-guiding rules. In this sense, the scope of *li* is coextensive with that of traditional comprising established conventions, that is, customs and usages deemed as a coherent set of precedents . . . The third stage in the evolution of *li* is connected with the notion of right (*yi*) and reason (*li*). In this sense, any rule that is right and reasonable can be accepted as an exemplary rule of conduct" (p. 254).

5. Such a symbolic ability should not be looked down upon as merely a symbol, but rather as how the charisma of a ruler is revealed; charisma proved crucial in rulership, as Schwartz observes. (Schwartz, p. 43.)

6. "Ritual performance offers a means of legitimation of royal authority, demonstrating to the king's subjects his position as mediator between Heaven, Earth and human beings" (Ching, p. 23).

7. One of the most important apologies Zhou used to justify their action to drive the Shang house out of power is "failure to sacrifice properly to the gods" (Creel 1960, p. 147).

8. Robert Eno, in his *The Confucian Creation of Heaven*, argues that "the rise of *li* as a cardinal value can be seen as a function of the fall of T'ien" (p. 19). It is an interesting but radical interpretation between the relationship of *li* and Heaven. My argument, however, follows a more traditional interpretation.

9. As Cho-yun Hsu and Katheryn M. Linduff point out, "The conquest of Shang was symbolically proclaimed by the Chou not as a hostile act against the Shang, but rather as a pledge to continue the Shang level of domination over the world of the Chinese. Moreover, their commitment was countenanced by Heaven. The gesture made by the Chou king added coherence to rule and responded to particular circumstance of the moment. The Chou had accomplished the nearly impossible task of allying and uniting the semi-independent and independent powers of north China. The small armed force that they controlled directly was not strong enough to hold the vast territory by force. Part of their solution was to maintain the ties established by the Shang and to legitimate them through moral decree. Compromise and cooperation were necessary to succeed, and the first Chou gesture for so doing was to adopt the sacred ceremonies customarily conducted by the Shang in their old, sanctioned center. The Chou could then be seen as generous and licit. They expressed such authority because they were obligated to do so by Mandate and by political and psychological reality" (pp. 100–1).

10. "The ritual order remained the pivot of the patriarchal feudalism which supported kingship and kinship during the eight centuries of the Chou dynasty, and even long after" (Ching, p. 33).

11. "In many matters, especially as showing the fundamental authoritarian-ism of Confucianism, he reveals an attitude more truly Chinese than can be had from a cursory reading of either Confucius or Mencius" (Dubs, xviii).

12. In Dubs's opinion, Xunzi is even more of a representative of what he regards as the authoritarianism of Confucianism than Confucius or Mencius (xviii).

13. As Jean Escarra states, "One of the most ancient guiding principles of the Chinese spirit is the belief in the existence of an order of nature and in the efficacy of an accord between it and the social order" (quoted in Creel 1980, p. 42).

14. Since Kasulis's discussion here (pp. 144–45) does not specifically address the political domain, I will paraphrase his analysis by applying it to the political discourse, relevant to our purpose here.

15. There are two other disadvantages that Kasulis has listed (pp. 147–48), but since this one poses the most serious challenge to the Confucian model of intimate authority, we will focus our discussion on it.

16. In some important sense, the translation of the Chinese term *fa* into law is an unfortunate one, since *fa* in the traditional Chinese political discourse and law in the Western political parlance bear little resemblance. Law overlaps with both *li* and *fa* in various ways.

17. Legalists were fully aware of the fatality of relying on a sage-king who might come once every hundred years, as Han Fei sharply points out, "It is not that there is any ability in the power-base itself to get itself invariably employed by the worthy rather than the unworthy. The world is ordered when it is the worthy who are employing it, disordered when it is the unworthy. It belongs to man's essential nature that the worthy are fewer than the unworthy, and the benefits of authority and power being available to unworthy men who disorder the age, it follows that those who use the power-base to disorder rather than order the world are the majority. The power-base is what facilitates and benefits the orderly and the disorderly alike. . . . Supposing that Jie and Zhòu had been commoners, before they had taken the first step they would have been executed with all their kin. The power-base is the nurturer of the tigerish and wolfish heart and the accomplisher of tyrannical deeds. This is the world's greatest misfortune" (qtd. in Graham, p. 280). We have to admit that Legalists, at least in theory, realized the dilemma in the Confucian scheme, namely the rareness of sage-kings and the vast majority of common or even corrupted ones who might use the system to their advantage. They actually did recognize the sagehood of Yao and Shun, as reflected in another passage (ibid., p. 281), but their concern was, as Han Fei articulates, the rulers who did not "reach as high as Yao and Shun or sink as low as Jie and Zhòu" (ibid.).

18. "Eastern Zhou texts indicate that the head of the *tsung* maintained considerable authority over his member *tsu*: he could execute offenders or exile members; he must be consulted by the king in any action taken against his members; and he served as leader in military campaigns" (Chang, pp. 74–75).

19. I am making a distinction between "rule of law" and the "rule by law": the former enshrines the ideal that no one is above the law, whereas the latter deems the law only instrumentally as an effective way to govern the mass, which does not apply to the ruler. By the same token, the Confucian ideal is the rule *of* ritual with the ritual governing all facets of society including the ruler, not rule by ritual.

20. "The essential elements currently associated with the rule of law are constitutional guarantees for civil liberties (due process, equal protection), guarantees of the orderly transition of power through fair elections, and the separation of governmental powers" (Hall & Ames 1999, p. 215).

References

Ames, Roger T. and Henry Rosemont Jr., trans. 1998. *The Analects of Confucius: A Philosophical Translation.* New York: Ballantine Books.

Bodde, Derk. 1990. "The Idea of Social Classes in Han and Pre-Han China," in *Thought and Law in Qin and Han China*, 26–41, eds. By W. L. Idema and E. Zürcher. Leiden, the Neitherlands: E. J. Brill.

Bodde, Derk, and Clarence Morris. 1967. *Law in Imperial China: Exemplified by 190 Ch'ing Dynasty Cases, with Historical, Social, and Judicial Commentaries.* Cambridge, MA: Harvard University Press.

Cai, Shangsi. 1991. *Zhongguo Lijiao Sixiang Shi (History of the Thought of Ritual Teachings in China).* Hong Kong: Zhonghua Shuju.

Chan, Wing-tsit. 1963. *A Source Book in Chinese Philosophy.* Princeton: Princeton University Press.

Chang, Kwang-chih. 1976. *Early Chinese Civilization: Anthropological Perspectives.* Cambridge, MA: Harvard University Press.

Ching, Julia. 1997. *Mysticism and Kingship in China: the Heart of Chinese Wisdom.* Cambridge, UK: Cambridge University Press.

Ch'ü, T'ung-tsu. 1965. *Law and Society in Traditional China.* The Hague, The Netherlands: Mouton & Co.

Creel, Herrlee Glesssner. 1980. "Legal Institutions and the Procedures During the Chou Dynasty," in *Essays on China's Legal Tradition*, pp. 26–55, ed. by Jerome Alan Cohen, R. Randle Edwards, and Fu-mei Chang Chen. Princeton, NJ: Princeton University Press.

———. 1970. *The Origins of Statecraft in China.* Vol. 1. "The Western Chou Empire." Chicago: University of Chicago Press.

———. 1960. *Confucius and the Chinese Way.* New York: Harper & Row.

Cua, Anthony. 2003. "The Ethical and the Religious Dimension of *Li*," in *Confucian Spirituality*, vol. 1, pp. 253–86. Ed. by Weiming Tu and Mary Evelyn Tucker. New York: Crossroad.

De Bary, William Theodore, Wing-tsit Chan, Burton Watson (comp.) 1960. *Sources of Chinese Tradition.* New York, NY: Columbia University Press.

Dubs, Homer H. 1927. *Hsüntzu: The Moulder of Ancient Confucianism.* London: Arthur Probsthain.

Eno, Robert. 1990. *The Confucian Creation of Heaven: Philosophy and the Defense of Ritual Mastery.* Albany: State University of New York Press.

Fung, Yu-lan. 1966. *A Short History of Chinese Philosophy.* New York: Free Press.

Graham, A. C. 1989. *Disputers of the Tao: Philosophical Argument in Ancient China.* La Salle, Ill: Open Court.

Hall, David L., and Roger T. Ames. 1999. *The Democracy of the Dead: Dewey, Confucius, and the Hope for Democracy in China.* Chicago: Open Court.

————. 1995. *Anticipating China: Thinking Through the Narratives of Chinese and Western Culture*. Albany: State University of New York Press.

Hsu, Cho-yun, and Katheryn M. Linduff. 1988. *Western Chou Civilization*. New Haven, CT: Yale University Press.

Kasulis, Thomas P. 2002. *Intimacy or Integrity: Philosophy and Cultural Difference*. Honolulu: University of Hawaii Press.

Knoblock, John. 1988. *Xunzi: A Translation and Study of the Complete Works*. 3 Vols. Stanford, CA: Stanford University Press.

MacCormack, Geoffrey. 1996. *The Spirit of Traditional Chinese Law*. Athens, GA: The University of Georgia Press.

Peerenboom, R. P. 1993. *Law and Morality in Ancient China: The Silk Manuscripts of Huang-Lao*. Albany: State University of New York Press.

Schwartz, Benjamin. 1985. *The World of Thought in Ancient China*. Cambridge, MA: Harvard University Press.

Taylor, Rodney L. 1990. *The Religious Dimensions of Confucianism*. Albany: State University of New York Press.

Watson, Burton, trans. 1964. *Han Fei Tzu: Basic Writings*. New York: Columbia University Press.

The *Wei* (Positioning)-*Ming* (Naming)-*Lianmian* (Face)-*Guanxi* (Relationship)-*Renqing* (Humanized Feelings) Complex in Contemporary Chinese Culture

Wenshan Jia

Introduction

In search of a functional equivalent in indigenous Chinese culture for Roger Ames's term "culture of authority" in his call for papers, I have identified five native Chinese terms closest to the concept of "authority." They are *wei, ming,* and *lianmian, guanxi* and *renqing.* I define *wei* as a position or

> a positioning in the primary ontocosmology which should under-lie any other constructed or developed system, for it is most fundamental and has everything to do with the very existence of a thing and its worth. In this sense *wei* can be said to define the worth and "raison d'être" of anything, particularly those of the human person. (Cheng 1996, 149).

I define naming as a rhetorical instrument to bring about the exercise of *wei* and to translate *wei* into *lianmian.* I define *lianmian* as a practical social-moral construct of the Confucian personhood that stands for the very worth defined by *wei.* I define *guanxi* as the web of relationships that functions as the set of interlocking laces which connects people of different *wei*s together. *Renqing* is defined as a body of symbolic and/or material resources exchanged in this web of social relations to establish or strengthen relations in a mutually emotionally satisfactory manner in order to accumulate one's *lianmian.* It is used to complement *naming,* since naming is merely rhetorical and does not provide practical action. The more worth is attached to a thing, particularly a person, the more power, influence, access to truth and the right to rule, which includes the rights to think, speak, reward and punish, and access to wealth and privilege the person can have. In other words, *lianmian* is generated by *wei* via *ming*. While *wei* is the hub, *lianmian* functions as a team of spikes with *ming* as the spin, *renqing* as the lubricating oil, and *guanxi* as the joints. *Guanxi* is not only part of the absolute reality to the Chinese, which the love of *lianmian* makes possible, but also it can be pulled to elevate one's *wei*. Each *wei* is always relative and in relationship to all other *wei*s. As a result, a culture is structured hierarchically with different members of a society voluntarily or involuntarily occupying different positions, and the culture is maintained as a culture of authority. In this paper, I argue that *wei, ming, lianmian, guanxi,* and *renqing* conjointly construct and maintain contemporary Chinese culture as a culture of relational authority despite the economic reform and social change that have taken place in the past decades.

In the following, I will first conduct the critical review of the relevant scholarly literature on *wei, ming, lianmian, guanxi,* and *renqing*. Then, I will elaborate the *wei-ming-lianmian-guanxi-renqing* interpretive framework on the basis of the review. Furthermore, I will present several real-life cases from contemporary Chinese society and use them in illustrating the soundness of the *wei-ming-lianmian-guanxi-renqing* theory.

Review of Scholarly Literature

Many prominent studies on Chinese face practices (Ho 1976; Smith 1894; Hwang 1987; Chen 1990; Ting-Toomey 2003; Kipnis 1995), while acknowledging the relational dimension, seem to have ignored or downplayed the hierarchical nature of *lianmian* dynamics in Chinese culture thanks to a modern Western lens of equality. The theories used, such as the social exchange theory (Hwang, 1987), the Coordinated Management of Meaning (Chen 1990) and negotiation (Ting-Toomey 2003), all share an underlying assumption in modern Western culture that human beings are equal and individualistic. Such theories also do not take morality into consideration. These theories are primarily descriptive with the suggestion that humans are inherently free, rational, and have choices for the individual good. These ideas run counter to the Chinese Confucian normative view of humans as beings with inherent moral responsibility to cultivate themselves into gentle persons (*junzi*) or sages (*shengren*) who are morally superior only because they are selfless and emotionally invested in the community. The ideas are also opposite to the deeply held assumption of the Chinese that humans are unavoidably placed in different positions of moral and social hierarchies; that humans are onto-logically in mutual relations, yet as unequal as human fingers are not of equal length, as a Chinese folk saying goes.

The *Wei-Ming-Lianmian-Guanxi-Renqing* Complex

Wei is one of the first and the most fundamental dimensions in the complex. *Wei* is synonymous with *diwei, jibie* (grade or level differentia-tion), and in extension, *dengji* (class). *Wei* is such a pervasive construct in Chinese culture that Chung-ying Cheng, a scholar of Chinese philoso-phy, has systematically articulated a Chinese philosophical view of *lian-mian* (1986) and a Chinese philosophical view of *wei* (1996) respectively. Although the author does not cross-reference the two articles, his article on *wei* seems to have extended and deepened his view on the *wei-ming-lianmian* (positioning-naming-moral/social face) continuum (342).

Reading the two articles closely in relation to each other, one is likely to conclude that *wei*, as the process of standing up of a human being (*li*) or establishing himself in the society by accomplishing a virtue (1996, 151), is the most fundamental process of accruing *lianmian* resources. *Wei* is omnipresent, since every "situation in which a thing finds itself is both a position and a stage which constitutes and confines and defines the thing" (Cheng 1996, 157). *Wei*, a central theme in the *Zhouyi*, reflects the Chinese view of the world as a world made up of positions and life as a constant process of finding one's position and repositioning oneself in the world. This view of *wei* also makes the love of *wei* into a fundamental value of Chinese culture. *Wei* or status-consciousness has understandably become a prominent part of the Chinese cultural psyche. Contrary to the modern Western view of humans as free and equal individuals, the concept of *wei* suggests that the worth, dignity, power, influence, and access to resources of each and every human being should vary according to varying *wei*s or positions. Because of this value, Chinese culture has acquired a fundamental belief that humans are of *wei*, by *wei*, and for *wei*. The concept of *wei* has two impli-cations. First, the concept of *wei* implies that humans always live in a hierarchy of social and moral positions and thus are "naturally" unequal. The other implication is that *wei* is a dynamic process of transformation as well as a static entity. A person can "overcome the limitations of one's given position," (Cheng 1996, 157) transform oneself into a position higher than the current one by achieving more virtues, or deform oneself down into a lower position than the current one by losing the current virtues.

Underlying the concept of *wei* is *guanxi*, which is the context, means, and the motive for *wei*. *Guanxi* literally means connections across barriers. *Guan* means barriers and *xi* means connections. First of all, the concept of *guanxi* makes the awareness of the audience and community possible. *Wei* differentiates people from each other, which functions as a barrier, but the very meaning of *wei* resides in the connections embedded in the complex hierarchy of different *wei*s. People strive for *wei* in order for the communal respect or for power over and above the community.

Ming is between *wei* and *lianmian*, connecting the two. *Ming* is the Chinese word for language/rhetoric/communication. One can hardly tell one *wei* from another *wei* without each different *wei* being labeled differently. Proper naming is expected to bring about the very birth of proper *wei* and the accurate representation of *wei*. It also goes hand in hand with *wei* or positioning. Without naming, *wei* could not display its existence. Naming can be said to be the form for *wei* that is the content or substance. Most important of all, proper naming should be discriminating and differentiating. The hierarchy of *wei* depends on an appropriate hierarchy of names. This means that each *wei* should have a distinct name. The varying amounts of humanity attached to varying *wei*s should be denoted clearly and accurately by each different naming and proper communication. *Ming* differentiates different kinds of *guanxi*, while *guanxi*, by its very nature, defies fixed labeling created by *ming*. While *ming* creates stability, *guanxi* opens up new frontiers of society, for *guanxi* can be pulled and established in all possibly creative ways to achieve a targeted *wei*. The interaction between *ming* and *guanxi* creates this dialectic force that makes the striving for *wei*s all the more dynamic.

Lianmian and *renqing* function as the most practical dimensions of the complex. This means that *lianmian* and *renqing* are the closest to the lifeworld. *Lianmian* refers to the social display (both active and passive), loaning (both active and passive) of one's *wei* and its derivatives (such as resources, influence, power, and privileges etc.) in social interaction on the basis of the mutually shared experience and knowledge of the Confucian ethics and norms for proper human relations in a social world of hierarchy. It was and still is one of the central indigenous sociological constructs of Chinese culture. As early as 1894, Arthur Smith insightfully pointed out: "Once rightly apprehended, 'face' will be found in itself a key to the combination lock of many of the most important characteristics of the Chinese" (17). To Chung-ying Cheng, face plays as important a function in Chinese societies as law does in modern Western societies (1986, 340). To Xuewei Zai, face plays an even more comprehensive role in Chinese societies. He concludes after a field study that face "has been always exercising a tremendous influence on and even playing a decisive role in the politics, economy, education, physical training, military arts and all aspects of Chinese everyday life" (1995, p. 1997). Many studies (Chang and Holt, 1994; Cheng, 1986; Scollon & Scollon, 1994; Ting Toomey, 1988) emphasize the relational nature of *lianmian* in critique of Goffman's concept of face (1967) as instrumental and Brown & Levinson's facework (1987) as rationalist. However, the literature masks or ignores the hierarchical nature of the relational dimension of *lianmian*. In *lianmian* practice, hierarchy and relationality are almost inseparable. A person of a higher *wei* is supposed to provide a person of a lower *wei* sufficient safety and security. To reciprocate, the latter is expected to remain loyal to, give and save as much face as possible to the former by being loyal and obedient. The relationship between the two can be described as mutually relational. However, this relationality occurs in the context of inequality and hierarchy. The latter may never be able to move to a higher *wei* so long as s/he stays in the relational loop. In reality, this relationality could be just a rhetorical device to mask, legitimize, or humanize inequality and hierarchy. Inequality and hierarchy embedded in *lianmian* have been unmasked by Lin Yutang (1935) who argues that *lianmian* is undemocratic, since it renders all the rules, regulations, and laws ineffective; Zhongtian Lu (1996) who points out that *lianmian*, together with *renqing*, constitutes a form of political governance shrouded in kindness that gives the people of higher *wei* extreme flexibility to deal with inferiors and gives inferiors a sense of extreme uncertainty and insecurity and later Jia (2001) who finds that *lianmian*, "this very conflict-preventive and harmony-building mechanism" (50), "masks and reinforces social hierarchy and in-groupness, which may breed inequality, injustice, and close-mindedness" (50), maintain status quo, block innovation and social mobility since *lianmian* inherently discourages change, challenges, and open competition.

Renqing is the giveaway of the social capital or the giving of a favor for the good of the other using one's *wei* with the trust and expectation that the beneficiary will remember it, develop a relational attachment to the benefactor and pay it back when the benefactor is in need. This is a mutually unspoken assumption that both the parties hold.

In the *wei-ming-lianmian-guanxi-renqing* complex, *wei* and *guanxi* are two philosophical constructs that reflect the Chinese way to know about reality (ontology), the Chinese way to interpret reality (phenomenology), and the Chinese values about humanity (axiology). In other words, the Chinese worldview holds that hierarchy and relationality constitute the substance of humanity. *Ming* is a linguistic/rhetorical construct that reflects the Chinese constructionist view of the role of language and communication in our attempt to understand reality, interpret reality, and in our attempt to ethically cultivate and transform humanity. *Lianmian* is largely a sociopsychological construct that reflects a uniquely Chinese way for social interaction, communication, thinking, emoting, and feeling.

If *wei* is said to constitute hierarchy, *guanxi* can be said to be the very reason for existence of hierarchy; naming can be said to be the process of articulation and symbolic construction of hierarchy, whereas *lianmian* is the dynamic process of communication, realization, and perpetuation of this hierarchy and activation of *guanxi*. It seems that *wei* is the ultimate source of *lianmian*, whereas naming connects *wei* and *lianmian* as the bridge. On the other hand, *lian/mian* dynamics or facework is the open-ended and concrete enactment of the *wei* structure in the lifeworld via proper naming with *guanxi* as the given. *Renqing* is a major tool to establish, maintain, and strengthen civilized relationships among humans. However, facework that is not an accurate enactment of the *wei* structure and/or not represented through proper naming and without using *renqing* as the social capital could more or less change the *wei* structure and disrupt the existing web of relations. *Lianmian* in an ideal sense, both privileges the values of hierarchy and relationship. These five interrelated dimensions constitute a coherent complex and co-construct a unique culture of relational authority—the Chinese culture of the *wei-ming-lianmian-guanxi-renqing* complex.

Confucianism is significantly built upon the ontocosmology of *wei* and *guanxi*. In Confucianism, both the hierarchy of moral positions and the hierarchy of social positions are established. In the moral hierarchy there are three positions. They are *shengren* (sagehood) as the highest moral ideal, *junzi* (gentle personhood) as the typical moral ideal, and the mean personhood (*xiaoren*) as a position to be evaded or discarded. The values for self-cultivation are *ren* (benevolence), *yi* (loyalty), *li* (etiquette), *zhi* (wisdom), *xin* (trust), and *ti* (piety). A folk discourse of social hierarchy also operates in daily interaction. One would hear the idiomatic phrases used in Chinese communities such as "*zuo ren shang ren*" ("to become a person above persons"), "*chu ren tou di*" ("to stand out among people", "*yi jing huan xian*" ("to go back to one's hometown from rags to riches"), and "*zhuo wan ren zhi shang yi ren zhi xia*" ("to become a person only next to the most important one and above all the rest"). All these constitute the daily Chinese discourse of *wei*.

The hierarchy of moral positions helps construct the concept of *lian*, whereas the hierarchy of the social positions help construct the concept of *mian*. Together, they cultivate a strong status or *wei* consciousness among Chinese and in Chinese.

Case Analyses

Current Chinese Political Culture Still as Largely a Culture of Relational Authority

The current Chinese political culture is still essentially defined by the *wei-ming-lianmian-guanxi-renqing* complex. In a sense, without this system, there would be no Chinese politics. In the history of Chinese politics, *wei* determines who has or who does not have the right to think, articulate, and theorize (*ming*). This is evidenced by the two age-old Chinese sayings that go like, "Words do not flow from those without rectified names" (*ming bu zheng yan bu shun*) and "Words from the persons of low positions are futile" (*ren bei yan qin*). It is also confirmed by the classic Chinese adage: "Do not conduct the political affairs unless you are in the position to do so." *Ming* advances and enhances or controls and limits the person's *lianmian*. In the past six decades, only three among billions of Chinese have been allowed to think and articulate their theories/thoughts. All of them occupied the highest *wei* of the political system at different times. They were Mao with the Mao Zedong Thought, Deng Xiaoping with his famous "Black Cat or White Cat" theory, and Jiang Zemin with his "Three Represents." All the other Chinese were/are being requested to study these systems of thought, believe in them, and carry them out. Any other thoughts are regarded cultish. In fact, when Mao's thought was in reign, the kind of ideas by Deng and Jiang were regarded as cultish. Now, with Deng's and Jiang's thoughts in reign, Mao's thought is taking a back seat or is being pushed underground. The one who had the right to speak and the privilege to be listened to and followed enjoyed having the most expansive *lianmian*. The successors, of course, felt too relationally indebted to their boss to challenge his ideas. Not to challenge the boss means to repay the *renqing* back to the boss who had promoted the successors. This case illustrates that a properly named *wei* legitimizes or empowers one to speak or not to speak. It also illustrates the relational loop created by *guanxi-renqing*. This is unlike the modern West in which theoretically every citizen has a right to speak and is entitled to one's opinion regardless of the kind of *wei* one holds.

In www.creaders.net on July 15, 2003, there was a report on the issue of the name order for Hu Jintao and Jiang Zemin after Jiang was retired from the post of chairman of the state and party general secretary while retaining his chairmanship in the Military Affairs Committee at the Sixteenth Party Congress in Spring 2003. There was confusion about who is No. 1 and who is No. 2 in the Chinese communities around the world. The issue also caught the most attention from China watchers. Now after several months' trial and error, it has become clear that Hu has the final say about nonmilitary affairs with Jiang next to Hu but above all the standing members of the Political Bureau, and Jiang is No. 1 with Hu as No. 2 in military affairs. This case illustrates that proper *weis* (here it refers to the specific positions in the name order of the political system) with proper names would designate specific areas of power, influence, and kinds of privileges (which constitute the essence of *lianmian* here). This practice would further deliver a sense of political and social stability and even ensure the political and social order. The confusion about the name order and scope of power and influence is illustrated by two scenarios. One is that before Hu Jintao left for the Summit of the Nine Nations, he released his military theory of great-leap type of development with no reference to Jiang Zemin and his "Three Represents" theory as vice-chairman of the Military Affairs Committee. This gave the public a reason for speculation that Hu was beginning to take over the first seat in the Military Affairs Committee from Jiang. The second scenario is a dramatic episode of Hu and the Wen-led campaign against SARS this past spring. After Zhang Wenkang, Jiang's political protégé, was fired from his post of the Minister of Health by Hu and Wen for Zhang's lying about the seriousness of the SARS epidemic, Gao Qiang, the senior vice-minister admitted at the press conference that it was Zhang's fault. It was reported that after a few weeks, the same Gao Qiang, after the alleged intervention of Jiang, corrected himself by saying that Zhang was not to blame. It was further reported later that the same Gao Qiang recorrected himself by saying that Zhang was to blame. The two cases attracted special attention from the public primarily because Hu stepped into Jiang's scope of military powers and Jiang stepped into Hu's scope of civic powers. This confusion compounded the public's already serious sense of insecurity due to SARS with a sense of political volatility and insecurity. It could have helped speed up China's deglobalization process during the SARS outbreak. Perhaps the insiders like Jiang and Hu and their aides found out about the negative consequences due to the conflicting messages about the name order of Hu and Jiang with reference to each other and corrected themselves. That is why there was the report on July 15, 2003 at www.creaders.net titled "Hu Jintao and Jiang Zemin's name order has been clarified." This case illustrates that the existence and proper function of a given *wei* depends on the daily acts and interactions consistent with the given *wei*. Any inconsistency between the *wei*/title and the occupant's acts/words and interacts/conversations would carry risks such as confusion, insecurity, and lack of credibility among the public towards the government, which in turn could lead to political chaos. This is illustrated by the confusion about the scope of powers of Zhao Ziyang and Deng Xiaoping in deciding what to do about the student demonstration in 1989, which led to the ouster of Zhao and the removal of the student demonstrations. Zhao, the then party general secretary, revealed to Gorbachov, the then USSR party general secretary who was visiting Beijing and meeting Zhao, that Deng was the one who had been making the final decisions about important national affairs in China. Gao Qiang shifted his positions back and forth, since he was locked in striving for double loyalty for Hu and Jiang who were almost equally powerful over him. Between truth and *guanxi-renqing*, he chose to cater to the latter. Apparently Zhao chose the truth, did not repay *renqing* to Deng who had promoted Zhao, and made Deng lose face in front of the global media. The result was the broken relationship. The cost for the truth was Zhao's lifelong house arrest.

To avoid similar confusion and subsequent undesirable social consequences, the Chinese Communist Party Committee Office and the Mayor's Office of Ankang City in Northwest China issued a public announcement on June 25, 2003, on how to standardize the management of name plates by the gate of the buildings where each of the CCP and government agencies as well as and other related organizations at all levels under the jurisdiction of the city are located. The following is a translation of the announcement, which was downloaded on July 11, 2003, at www.ankang.gov.cn/news/zwxx/20030525132935.mtml:

> To All County/District Chinese Communist Party Committees, All County/District People's Governments, the Chinese Communist Party Ankang City Committees and City Mayoral Departments, and All the People's Bodies:
>
> The name plates hanging on the gate of every building of all CCP agencies, administrations and the people's bodies and their affiliates at all levels are important symbols of the scopes of the powers and natures. In recent years, with the changes of the structure of the administration and its subsequent changes of the agencies in Ankang, the name plates used by these agencies are not standardized in shape, size, type of character used, hanging position, and the order of the different name plates on the shared gates and

so on. In order to strengthen the management of the name plates of all these agencies/bodies, the following rules are to be followed:

1. In accordance with "The Approach to the Management of the City of Ankang's Agency Structuration", after the agencies are established, merged or disbanded, registration is to be done in the agency structure office at the appropriate level in order to make, use or destroy a name plate.

2. The name plates of the CCP agencies at city, county and township levels are elongated stripe-shaped, painted in white, with the characters written in red from top to bottom, and are hung vertically. The name plates of the administrations, people's bodies and other agencies at all levels plus the second-tier agencies are elongated stripe-shaped, painted in white, with the characters written in black from top to bottom, and are hung vertically. The name plates of the offices within these agencies are elongated stripe-shaped, painted in blue, with characters written in white from left to right, and are hung horizontally. The name plates of the second-tier agencies can be hung side by side with those of the administration offices on condition that the name plates of the former must be smaller in size. The name plates of the offices within the administrative agencies must not hang their name plates parallel to the name plates of the administrative agencies. Ad-hoc organizations must not hang their name plates. Agencies which have not been approved for operation by the agency structure offices must not hang name plates. Name plates must be hung in highly visible positions, and must look solemn, serious, with no decorations.

3. Name plates of the county/district party, administrative agencies and the departments of the City Party Committee and City Administration must be 240 centimeters in length and 40 centimeters in width. The name plates of the second-tier agencies must be 230 centimeters in length and 38 centimeters in width. The name plates of the township Party committee, people's government and the departments of the county/district Party committee and people's government and the people's bodies at this level are 220 centimeters in length and 36 centimeters in width. The name plates of the second-tier agencies at the township level are 215 centimeters in length and 34 in width. The name plates of the laison offices of the city, county/district, township and neighborhood are 30 centimeters in length and 12 centimeters in width. All the agencies at all the levels within the city must follow the above standards.

4. Name plates must bear legalized names. If the names have too many characters to be on a proper plate, they can be simplified consistent with the word name simplification standards and the approval of the appropriate office of agency structuration. Name plates must use the simplified Chinese characters released by the State Council. The calligraphic style must be Sung style. The paint used to write names can be picked on the basis of need by the appropriate office of agency structuration.

Issued by the Office of The Chinese Communist Party Ankang Committee, Office of the People's Government of City of Ankang

The print-out indicates that the document was issued online at www. ankang.gov.cn at 1:29 p.m. on June 25, 2003, China time.

In the above case, all the artifacts, such as name plates, their different sizes and different colors, their hanging positions, different colors of Chinese characters, the order and directions of the flow of the characters, and so on are all translated into symbolic building blocks or a system of naming constituting and displaying the city's hierarchy of power and authority. This document also dictates occupants of different *wei*s within this hierarchy to communicate with one another in the ways consistent with the different *wei*s. The document also expects people within and outside the city to communicate with the different occupants of these *wei*s in the ways consistent with their *wei*s. People who hold the highest *wei*s like the party secretary of the Chinese Communist Party City Committee who is assigned the most power and the mayor who is assigned the second most power next to the party secretary in the city are expected to communicate with the rest of the officials and people dominantly in both business and social contexts. In front of the provincial officials, these two most powerful city officials are expected to communicate submissively. On the other hand, the officials who have less power than these two and the people in the city are expected to communicate with the two submissively. If such rules are violated either realistically or perceptually, it means the code of *lianmian* is broken, and loss of face occurs. The violators will be either overtly or covertly penalized by the more powerful. However, since people within this system of hierarchy are all emotionally interrelated or in a web of *guanxi* (*guanxi wang*), they can pull *guanxi* and give *renqing* (in the form of bribery, showing loyalty) to be excused from such penalty or to be promoted to an even more important *wei*.

Because occupying an important *wei* allows the occupant so much freedom, privilege, power, and loyalty, Chinese political culture of relational authority has cultivated people's strong love of *wei*. A friend of mine told me on the phone the other day (personal communication with Xingan Xu, 2003) that one of his friends had spent a bribe of Y200,000.00 (an equivalent of $200,000.00 US in terms of spending power in respective countries) and bought a department director's position in a county in Northwest China. The amount of money would be an equivalent of his ten years' salary as the department director. But his love of a position is more than his love of money, since the position would make him more respected than the money he had. In other words, the director's position made him a person above persons *(ren shang ren)*, but the money alone could not have been able to garner so much respect and power for him. He is truly a man of *wei*, by *wei*, and for *wei*. Naming, *lian-mian-guanxi-renqing* are all more or less implicated in this case.

The Current Education Reform in China is Quite an Effort to Perpetuate the Culture of Relational Authority, Contrary to the Intended Goal

In recent years of China's educational reform to enhance competition and make universities market oriented, there has been a growing trend for universities in China, especially flagship universities from China, such as Peking University and Tsinghua University, to hire high-profile government officials to be affiliated professors as part of the education reform effort. Peking University's School of Journalism and Communication, for example, has hired about a dozen government officials from the Department of Culture, Department of Propaganda, etc. to be affiliated professors. Tsinghua University's School of Journalism and Communication has hired Wang Daohan, the former boss of Jiang Zemin in Shanghai, as a professor. Zhu Rongji, the former premier, was dean of the School of Management of Tsinghua University. Qian Qisheng is still dean of the College of International Relations of Peking University and Li Zhaoxin, foreign minister, is a professor of the English Department of Peking University. However, overseas Chinese scholars and students, lower in rank than those, are ignored or neglected, even though they are more knowledgeable in the respective fields as researchers and educators than the above-mentioned government officials. The underlying assumption of this practice is that authority or a high *wei* is not only the source of power and influence, but also is regarded as a major source of knowledge by these institutions of higher learning. This kind of practice seems to propose that what is truth is determined by one's *wei* more than one's academic training or specialization; the higher one's *wei* is, the more knowledge and truth one is assumed to possess. The purpose of education in this context seems to legitimize and hallow authority, rather than remain skeptical of and challenge authority. Intended as an instrument to reform education and make it more innovative, this effort ends up with an opposite result. It has strongly affirmed the value of authority in Chinese culture and may be making Chinese higher education less competitive and innovative rather than more competitive and innovative. What the universities got in exchange with these big *wei*s and big names was primarily access to the means to curry favors (*renqing*) from higher-ups and more expansive *lianmian*, which do not directly translate into a competitive edge in teaching and research.

In job ads aimed at luring Chinese students and scholars to go back and work in China published in *People's Daily* (Overseas Edition), one would read the different guidelines for male applicants and female applicants. For male applicants, the age limit is 45 years old and below. But for females, the age limit is 40 years or below. For applicants who are Ph. D. advisors, the retirement age is 65 years old; but for those who are not Ph. D. advisors and male, the retirement age is 60 years old. For those who are not Ph. D. advisors and female, the retirement age is 55. This means that the higher your current position is, on condition that you are male, the more years you are permitted to work; the lower your current position is, on condition that you are female, the fewer years you are allowed to work. This is a policy that perpetuates the age and gender hierarchy that have been in practice for thousands of years in China. The erroneous assumption is that females have less worth than males. To a typical person of Western culture, this is a policy of double discrimination—age discrimination and gender discrimination.

The Returned Overseas Chinese students and scholars are asked to communicate in the Chinese way instead of the Western way in order to survive and flourish in the contemporary Chinese society or *jiaoji bentuhua*, while at the same time the Chinese official discourse calls for China's further globalization (*yu guoji jiegui*). This means that overseas Chinese students and scholars who have returned need to communicate according to the norms and rules and rituals of the culture of relational authority instead of using the norms, rules, and rituals of the Western culture of equality and individuality. What is the use of spending money and time studying the Western culture, if these students and scholars are expected to fit into the culture of authority instead of acting as mediators between the two conflicting cultures and as agents of change for both cultures?

There Have Been Signs of Change in the Culture of Authority

In the field of technology industry in China today, most of the CEOs are young people. This is a major change with regard to age in Chinese culture in the past ten some years. In this sector in China, like the United States, youth is respected as a symbol of innovation and competition. In the Chinese cyberspace showcased by www.amazon.com, walls of political, social, and economic hierarchy are crumbling for the first time in Chinese history. Chinese netizens are enjoying equality in expressing themselves, to be read and valued like never before. The value of competition is also entering into educational administration. Peking University's current effort to institute the American type of tenure system has a potential in revolutionizing Chinese organizational behavior and in extension, the Chinese culture of relational authority. These are growing cracks of change in the culture of relational authority that could hopefully contribute to a pervasive transformation of Chinese culture of authority into a hybrid of relational equality. Current Chinese politics, education, and social and organizational life are truly relational and authoritarian in practice, with growing cracks for change.

Conclusion

In this complex of *wei-ming-lianmian-guanxi-renqing, wei* and *guanxi* are ontocosmological, while *ming* is rhetorical and communicative, and *lianmian* and *renqing* are primarily social-emotive. Together, they constitute the grammar for understanding Chinese politics, communication, sociology, and psychology. From the historical perspective, the aura of authority in Chinese culture has been becoming thinner and thinner. The practice of relational authority has become less formalized and less overt and more covert, compared with the past. The practice of bound feet is no longer. *Koutou* is no longer. However, the above case analyses show that the practice of authority in the form of the *wei-ming-lianmian-guanxi-renqing* complex is powerfully maintained in most sectors of the contemporary Chinese society, such as Chinese political culture and education, despite the economic reform and social change. Therefore, China still has a long way to go before it transforms itself into a culture of relational equality.

References

Brown, Penelope, and Levinson, Stephen. 1987. *Politeness.* Cambridge: Cambridge University Press.

Chang, Huiqing, and Richard Holt. 1994. "A Chinese Perspective on Face as Inter-relational Concern." In S. Ting-Toomey (Ed.), *The Challenges of Facework.* Albany: State University of New York Press.

Chen, Victoria. 1990–1991. "Mien tze at the Chinese Dinner Table: A Study of the Interactional Accomplishment of Face." *Research on Language and Social Interaction, 24*: 109–140.

Cheng, Chung-ying. 1986. "The Concept of face and its Confucian Roots." *Journal of Chinese Philosophy, 13*: 329–348.

———. 1996. "*Zhouyi* and Philosophy of *wei* (positions)." *Extreme-Orient, Extreme-Occident, 18*: 150–175.

Creaders.net. July, 2003. "Hu Jintao and Jiang Zemin's Name Orders Are Set." Retrieved on July 15, 2003 at: www.creaders.net.

Goffman, Erving. 1967. "On Face-work." In E. Goffman, *Interaction Ritual* (pp. 5–45). New York: Pantheon.

Ho, David. 1976. "On the Concept of Face." *American Journal of Sociologists, 81*: 867–884.

Hwang, Kwang-Kuo (1987). "*Face and Favor: The Chinese Power Game.*" *American Journal of Sociology*, 92: 944–974.

Jia, Wenshan. 2001. *The Remaking of the Chinese Character and Identity in the 21ˢᵗCentury: the Chinese Practices.* Westport, CT(?): Ablex.

Kipnis, Andrew. 1995. "'Face': An Adaptable Discourse of Social Surfaces." *Positions, 1*: 119–147.

Lin, Yutang. 1935. *My Country and My People.* New York: Reynal & Hitchcock.

Lu, Zhongtian. 1996. "Insights into the Worldly Affairs Constitute Knowledge and Experience in Dealing with Issues Concerning Human Feelings Is as Good as the Ability to Write Good Articles (*Shishi dongming jie xuewen, renqing lianda ji wenzhang*): On the Psychology of *renqing* and *mianzi*." In Z. Lu, *Zhong Guo Ren de Chuan Tong Xintai* (*The Social Psychology of Chinese Tradition*) (pp. 141–152). Hongzhou, Zhejiang, China: Zhejiang People's Press.

Office of Chinese Communist Party Angkang City Committee and Office of the Ankang People's Government (June, 2003). "Zhonggun Ankang Shiwei Bangongshi, Ankangshi Renmin Zenfu Bangongshi Guanyu Gueifan Geji Dang de Jigou, Guojia Xengzheng Jiguan, Renmin Tuanti Jiqisuoshu Shiyedanwei Biaopai Guanli de Tongzhi (The Anouncement on the Management of the Name Plates of the Agencies of All Levels of the Chinese Communist Party, Government, People's Bodies and their Affiliates by the Office of the Chinese Communist Party Ankang Committee and Office of Ankang City Government)." Retrieved on July 11, 2003, at: http://www.ankang.gov.cn.

Scollon, Ron, and Suzanne Scollon. (1994). "Face parameters in East-West Discourse." In S. Ting-Toomey (Ed.), *The Challenges of Facework* (pp. 133–158). Albany: State University of New York Press.

Smith, Arthur. 1894. *The Chinese Characteristics*. New York: Fleming H. Revell Company.

Ting-Toomey, Stella. 1988. "Intercultural Conflict Styles." In Y. Y. Kim and W. B. Gudykunst (Eds.), *Theories of Intercultural Communication* (pp. 213–238). Newbury Park, CA: Sage.

Ting-Toomey, Stella. 2003. "Managing Intercultural Conflicts Effectively." In L. A. Samovar and R. E. Porter (Eds.), *Intercultural Communication: A Reader* (pp. 385–405). Belmont, CA: Wadsworth Publishing Company.

Xu, Xingan. (July, 2003). Personal communication. Gardiner, NY.

Zai, Xuewei. (1995). *Zhongguoren de Lianmian Guan (The Chinese Perspective on Lianmian)*. Taibei, Taiwan: Guiguan Press.

Creeping Absolutism: Parental Authority as Seen in Early Medieval Tales of Filial Offspring

Keith N. Knapp

Introduction

The influential Tang Code, which was drafted around AD 650 and established the legal framework for later Chinese dynasties as well as those of imperial Japan, Korea, and Vietnam, paints a picture of inviolable parental authority. It designates unfilial conduct as one of the Ten Abominations (*shie* 十惡)—crimes so venal that their authors were neither released under general amnesties nor were their executions delayed until ritually appropriate times. Moreover, the Code deals stiff penalties for any unfilial acts: sons who curse or beat their parents or report their crimes to the authorities should be executed; those who disobey their parents' orders or materially support them in a deficient manner should serve two years of penal servitude; those who have separate household registers (i.e. live apart) from their parents or keep private goods should serve three years of penal servitude; and those who fail to marry according to their parents' wishes should receive one hundred strokes with a heavy stick. The state even makes sure that a son should respect his dead parents' authority; hence, if he conceals his parents' death and does not mourn, he should be exiled; if he ends his mourning before the appropriate time or forgets his grief and makes music, he should serve three years of penal servitude; if he has children while mourning, he should serve one year; and if he marries, three years.[1] Ch'ü T'ung-tsu has noted that parents could have the state prosecute their children for the most trivial of matters and also determine their children's penalty. As a result, he concludes that, "parents in China had absolute power to control and punish their children."[2] Sun Xiao likewise notes that, in the Han dynasty, patriarchs could legally sell their children, freely dispose of family property, and in some cases, even kill their children.[3] These alleged privileges have led a number of Western and Chinese scholars, beginning with Max Weber, to compare the Chinese "family head" (*jiazhang* 家長) with the powerful Roman *paterfamilias*.[4]

Since these characterizations of the patriarch's authority are largely based on prescriptive sources, such as law codes and ritual manuals, one ponders whether, in reality, parents wielded so much power? And if so, was this true for the entire imperial era? In two seminal articles, the sociologist Gary G. Hamilton has already underlined the fallacy of equating Chinese patriarchalism with its Roman counterpart. He notes that, in the West, by definition, patriarchs were male, and due to the patriarch's unique relationship with the divine, his power was personal, absolute, and oftentimes arbitrary. Thus, Roman law often emphasizes *patria potestas*, the father's power.[5] In contrast, the closest Chinese equivalent of *patria potestas* is *xiao* 孝 (filial piety), which stresses sonly obedience, rather than parental authority. Due to the Chinese emphasis on the duties of children rather than the power of the father, Chinese patriarchy depersonalizes power and instead emphasizes the roles that family members must fulfill to maintain household harmony. In other words, instead of submitting to the patriarch's power, children adhere to their own prescribed familial role. Finally, in China, the family head could be either male or female.[6] Hamilton's findings are significant because they indicate that Chinese patriarchy was of a very different sort, one which relied less on the ability of a parent to punish and more on a child's willingness to "do the right thing," by carrying out the patriarch's orders in the interests of enhancing the family's welfare.

Building on Hamilton's insights, this paper seeks to plumb the nature and extent of paternal authority in the early medieval period (AD 100–600). First, by comparing filial piety tales from this era with their earlier counterparts, this essay will indicate that early medieval authors were in an unprecedented way attempting to persuade sons and daughters-in-law to unconditionally follow their parents' orders. Second, by underlining the fears that the stories disclose, it will further show that the patriarch's hold over subordinate family members was far from overwhelming. To corroborate this conclusion, the third part of the essay will document the prevalence of the custom of *shengfen* (dividing the patrimony while one's parents are still alive). Instead of the Roman *paterfamilias*, this essay will conclude that Chinese family heads resemble much more the fathers of ancient Athens who demanded filial respect and support, but who had no choice but allow their adult sons a certain amount of independence and wealth.[7]

Conditional Parental Authority in Early China

Although anecdotes about filial piety from early China are not plentiful, they exist in sufficient numbers to suggest how *Ru* 儒 ("Confucian") writers envisioned familial authority. These anecdotes plainly indicate that normally sons and daughters must follow their parents' orders. A statement that Liu Xiang 劉向 (77–6 BC) attributes to the crown prince of Jin best sums up what obedience to a parent entails: "I have heard that he who is a son exhausts himself in being obedient to his lord (i.e., father), does not pursue his own desires, respectfully and solemnly undertakes his orders, and does not disturb his lord's tranquility (*an* 安)."[8] In a nutshell then, being a good son means obeying commands, foregoing desires, and insuring a parents' happiness. Hence, many early descriptions of filial sons emphasize how they always obeyed their parents' commands and never exercised their own personal authority. For instance, as a son, the Duke of Zhou 周公, "had nothing arbitrary about his conduct and nothing self-willed about the affairs he managed"[9]—his behavior was always in accord with his father's will. Furthermore, truly filial children not only obey their parents' explicit commands, but also their unspoken wishes. A story from the *Mengzi* 孟子 illustrates this point: every time his father asked whether there were leftovers from his meal, whether or not there were, Zengzi 曾子 (c. 505–436 BC) would always answer positively because, by doing so, he fulfilled his father's unspoken wish that his grandsons enjoy the dainties from his table. When Zengzi's own son would consistently tell him that there were no leftovers from his meal, Zengzi felt that his son's filiality was only superficial.[10]

That is not to say, though, that filiality necessarily required that children had to obey all of their parents' orders. In fact, early *Ru* texts make it clear that there are times when they must disobey their parent's instructions. As Xunzi 荀子 (ca. 313–238 BC) put it, there are three circumstances under which a son will not follow a parent's order: if it puts the parent's life in danger, if it disgraces the parent, or if it makes him or her no better than birds and beasts.[11] Clearly, for Xunzi, a child could decline to perform any order that endangered the parent's safety or reputation, or that was inhumane. The following anecdote provides us with a clear case in which a son should remonstrate. Once while hoeing a field, Zengzi mistakenly cut the root of a melon plant, which caused his father to nearly beat him to death. Upon recovering, Zengzi's first concern was to make sure his father did not injure himself in administrating the beating. The *Shuoyuan* 說苑 (Garden of Persuasions) version of this story adds that, after the beating, Zengzi played the lute and sang to make sure his father knew that he was neither hurt nor angry. Nevertheless, Kongzi 孔子 (Confucius) severely rebuked Zengzi for allowing his father to perform a criminal act that might have resulted in public punishment (if the beating caused Zengzi's death). Kongzi further reminded him that, even though the sage-king Shun 舜 always did his father's bidding, he was nowhere to be found when his father wanted to kill him.[12] Similarly, even though it was clearly an affront to parental authority, Mengzi justifies Shun's marrying Yao's 堯 daughter without obtaining his father's approval, by stating that he did so because he had to make sure that his family had descendents.[13] In other words, continuance of the patriline was more important than obeying his father's wishes. In a similar vein, when his father was about to divorce his stepmother for mistreating him, Min Ziqian 閔子騫 (fl. 520–480) vigorously protested by pointing out that, by doing so, his father would make three children (his two half brothers and himself) suffer, rather than just one.[14] Hence, in narratives from before the Eastern Han (AD 25–220), a parent's authority was by no means unconditional. Although a son had to submit to righteous commands, he could circumvent those that were not.

Absolute Submission in the Early Medieval Tales

Early medieval filial piety accounts differ from their predecessors in that they lay even greater stress on sonly obedience. According to these tales, no matter how inappropriate or inane a parent's request might be, children should always do their parent's bidding. Hua Bao 華寶 (sixth century AD), for instance, neither married nor served in office because, before leaving for the frontier where he would die, his father told him that he would arrange those matters upon his return.[15] Unlike Shun who married without his father's approval, Hua rigidly adhered to his father's spoken command, even though it is doubtful that the elderly gentleman would have wanted his son to forego increasing the lineage's fame through serving in office or producing heirs for the patriline. In some tales, filial children even obey their parents' orders when they ask the impossible. In the story of the *Sanzhouren* 三州人 (Men of the Three Regions), three strangers who were orphans, met and decided to become a "family." As soon as the eldest of the three was designated as "father," he began to issue orders. He commanded that the two "sons" build a hut in the marsh. Just as they were about to complete it, he ordered that they build another near the river. Just as they were about to complete that one, he ordered that they should build the hut in the river itself. The "sons" agreed to all of these requests without hesitation, doubt, or opposition. Moved by the sons' filial piety, Heaven intervened and created for them an island in the river's middle.[16] This narrative implies that, since even this makeshift family could vest a pseudoparent with unquestioned authority, how much more should natural families do so! Notice too that Heaven sanctions both the father's absolute say-so and the sons' eager submission.

As this last tale indicates, to emphasize the imperative of absolute obedience, many of the tales feature protagonists who follow the orders of a fictive parent who has no means to enforce his or her authority. For example, even though his "mother" was nothing more than a wooden statue, before either Ding Lan 丁蘭 (first century AD?) or his wife lent out any household goods, they would ask for its consent. That is to say, he and his wife were so filial that even though his real mother was dead and his surrogate mother was a block of wood, they still did not dare treat the family's wealth as their own.[17] Since Qin legal texts from Shuihudi 睡虎地 in Hubei province indicate that fathers and sons often had separate wealth while residing in the same household,[18] this tale was probably directly aimed at redressing this social deficiency. At the same time, it illustrates the *Ru* principle that, while their parents are alive, children have nothing that they can call their own: the *Li ji* 禮記 (*Book of Rites*) states, "A son and his wife should have no private goods, nor animals, nor vessels; they should not presume to borrow from, or give anything to, another person."[19] That children possess nothing calls attention to their inferiority and their parents' superiority. Thus, the same texts tells us that, "While his parents are alive, a son neither dares to hold his body as his own, nor does he dare to use his wealth for his own private ends. This is to show the people that there is hierarchy (*you shangxia* 有上下)."[20]

The tale of Li Shan 李善 (fl. 25–75), the filial servant, even more vividly makes this point that a son/inferior must act submissively no matter the condition of his parent/master. Li saved his master's infant son from death, but had no way to feed him milk. Heaven eased Li's distress by providing his male breasts with milk. Although he was suckling his young master, Li would still "serve him no differently than he would an adult lord. If there were a matter to be dealt with, he would kneel [before the infant] and ask for guidance. Only after doing so would he act."[21] Despite that he was, in fact, parenting the infant, Li never forgot that he was inferior in status to his young charge. Early medieval men regarded Li as epitomizing filiality because he treated his baby master exactly as an adult filial son should treat his elderly and decrepit parents: despite fulfilling the role of a nurturing parent to his helpless, and in many ways infantile, parents, he still subjugates his actions to their wishes, though, he could easily follow his own.[22]

In the early medieval narratives, sons even accede to their parents' wishes to kill them, which directly contravenes Xunzi's teaching that children should not carry out immoral orders. The following narrative about Wang Xiang 王祥 (185–265) indicates how much attitudes towards a parent's authority had shifted from the days when the story of Shun escaping his parents' murderous plots was written.

> Xiang once was sleeping on a separate bed when his stepmother came over and stabbed at him in the dark. As it happened, he had gotten out of bed to relieve himself; consequently, she only vainly skewered his bedclothes. After returning to the room, he realized his stepmother bore him an implacable resentment; kneeling before her, he then begged her to end his life. His stepmother then for the first time came to her senses and loved him ever afterward as her own son.[23]

Since Wang had committed no wrong and his stepmother was trying to murder, rather than punish him, without a doubt, her actions were not only unethical, but also illegal. Yet, rather than seeking a way to stay alive like Shun, Wang asks to be put to death to fulfill her wish. Likewise, in a Chinese Jonah story, a crown prince named Chen Xuan 陳玄 is slandered by his stepmother, which causes his father to order his suicide. Chen thereupon jumps into a river. A huge fish emerges to allow Chen to escape on its back, but he replies, "I am a sinner (*zuiren* 罪人) and merely seek to die." The fish thereupon allows him to do so.[24] Although both Wang and Chen knew their parents were doing wrong, neither one offered the slightest objection; on the contrary, each willingly accepted death at his parent's hands. This passive attitude towards a parent's unrighteous behavior is a far cry from Kongzi berating Zengzi for allowing his father to almost beat him to death. Incidentally, an early medieval version of this same story relates the narrative element of Zengzi playing the lute after his beating to show his father that he was not harmed, but leaves out that of Kongzi condemning Zengzi's behavior.[25] The early medieval narrative praises Zengzi precisely because his father nearly killed him, yet he was still concerned about his father's happiness. In short, according to the early medieval tales, a parent's wish must be fulfilled, even if it is unjustified and unrighteous.[26]

The Lordly Father

The absolute character of the submission advocated in the early medieval tales perhaps stemmed from the fact that parents were now supposed to be viewed as rulers within their own homes. Whereas texts from before the Eastern Han, such as the *Xiaojing* 孝經 (*Classic of Filial Piety*) and the *Lushi chunqiu* 呂氏春秋 (*Mr. Lu's Annals*) urge sons to serve their sovereign as they would their father,[27] early medieval accounts, on the contrary, want sons to serve their father as they would their sovereign. Consequently, a number of filial piety stories depict the ideal family as having the atmosphere of a court: sons treat their parents as they would their ruler.[28] The filial piety story of Gu Ti 顧悌 (third century) best exemplifies this phenomenon.

> Every time Gu Ti received a letter from his parents, he sprinkled the floor with water, swept it, and straightened his clothes. He set out a long table and placed the letter on top of it. He then bowed and read it while kneeling. He acknowledged each sentence. Upon finishing it, he again bowed twice. When his father had a question about him being sick or fatigued, Gu Ti moved towards the letter shedding tears and choking back sobs.[29]

Note that the ritual acts that Gu performs in receiving his father's letter are comparable to those taken by a magistrate upon receiving an imperial edict.[30] Watanabe Shinichirō has astutely pointed out that the word *chi* 敕, which usually designates the emperor's orders or edicts, was often used in early medieval anecdotes to describe the commands that a patriarch gave to his family members.[31] In early medieval times, then, the *Ru* normative sources go from stressing ruler as father to father as ruler.

This leaves one wondering why the early medieval tales put so much more stress on parental authority than their predecessors. This emphasis was related to two early medieval phenomena: namely, the weakness of central government and the growth of extended families. The early medieval period in China witnessed the collapse of strong effective government. Whereas the Qin and Western Han governments appear to have had a high degree of control over localities, by the second half of the Eastern Han, this was no longer the case. Strong central control did not reappear until the Sui government reasserted the center's power in the 580s. Emblematic of the state's decline was the abandonment of the Avoidance Rule and the fact that local officials often worked without pay. When the Qin and Western Han governments were at their height, they often diligently endeavored to curb the growth of large, powerful families. With the waning of central government power in the Eastern Han, though, affluent families grew larger in size and more complex in structure. It was precisely these increasingly large and rich families that filled the power vacuum at the local level that the decline of central authority created. Large families were advantageous because they furnished a ready supply of manpower to fight off enemies or attackers, cultivate (or supervise the cultivation of) reclaimed land, and create a network of political agents. Thus, family heads had much at stake to keep these valuable political and social units together and coherent. The authors of the tales realized that one means of doing so was to elevate the status of father to that of ruler. Thus, just as a vassal should be willing to sacrifice his life for his lord, so too should a child be willing to sacrifice everything for his lordly father.[32]

Submission to Roles

A feature common to both early medieval stories and their predecessors is that, no matter how their parents treat them, filial offspring fulfill their parents' orders without resentment. Narratives from both periods portray many fathers as being short-tempered and gullible, and their second wives as scheming, resentful, and cruel. Consequently, both fathers and stepmothers perpetuate all sorts of brutal acts on their sons. We have already mentioned that Shun's father and stepmother tried to kill him several times; Zengzi's father nearly beat him to death; Min Ziqian's stepmother intentionally provided him with shoddy clothing; and Wang Xiang's stepmother attempted to stab him. Nevertheless, in all of these stories, a parent's malicious actions in no way diminish the filial son's love for him or her.

The Han skeptic and philosopher Wang Chong 王充 (27–79?) explains this motif of cruel parents by saying that children's filiality only becomes noticeable when they have an unkind father, hence these anecdotes show parents in an unflattering light to throw their children's exemplary devotion into sharper relief.[33] However, since the behavior of parents in many anecdotes is irrelevant to a son or daughter's acts of filial piety, this is, at best, only a partial answer. The answer, then, lies in the nature of the obedience that children owed to their parents. This obedience is one in which a son's love for his parents cannot be affected by their faults. This is because his filiality is not contingent upon his parents' actions; it is merely the type of behavior that his role demands. Thus, we are here a far cry away from "Antigone" in which the Athenian

Sophocles justifies Haemon's rebellion against his tyrannical and unreasonable father Creon.[34] These stories thereby confirm Gary Hamilton's point that Chinese patriarchy is depersonalized and stresses obedience to one's role, rather than to the patriarch's personal authority. In short, a son submits to whoever fills the role of household head; the patriarch need do nothing to merit this obedience.

Fear of Losing Authority

The authors of the early medieval tales felt it necessary to stress that filial children should, no matter what the cost, immediately and fully comply with their parents' orders because, in real life, children might only selectively follow their parents' wishes, or ignore them altogether. In other words, by stressing the importance of immediate and unwavering obedience, the stories imply that parental authority is not nearly as formidable as it should be. This insecurity concerning the family head's power arose from several sources. First, by growing old, parents became more dependent upon their sons' for sustenance. By doing so, they risked losing their sons' respect and becoming viewed as a burden.[35] This unfilial notion that the elderly are an encumbrance is plainly evident in the story of the filial grandson Yuan Gu 原穀. As soon as his grandfather could no longer work, Yuan's father and mother viewed him as useless and intended to abandon him. His father only desisted when Yuan reminded him that he would have to do the same to him when he became old.[36] Significantly, the story does not refute the notion that the elderly are worthless; instead, it appeals to the reader's self-interest about how he or she will be treated upon aging. Sun Gui's 孫晷 (fourth century) biography gives us an even more palpable sense of the treatment that the elderly poor might receive.

> Among the relatives and long-time friends of Sun's family, there were several who were destitute and old. They always came around seeking handouts. Most people loathed them and treated them rudely. However, when Sun met them his respect and appreciation for them intensified. When it was cold, he would sleep with them under the same quilt; when they ate, he would eat out of the same vessels. Sometimes he would disrobe and give his clothing to them to relieve their suffering.[37]

In short, unlike most people, when Sun met poor kinsmen, he valued them for their age and their past contributions to his family; he did not despise them because they were no longer of practical use. Both these stories suggest that early medieval parents were well aware that their authority might vanish with age.

Even though Sun Gui's elderly relatives had neither authority nor wealth to command his attention, he still venerated them, which is what made him so special. In real life, a parent's authority was based on the fact that he or she still had the ability to punish or reward his or her children. One should note that one can render nearly all of the classical Chinese words for respect or reverence, such as *jing* 敬, *su* 肅, *gong* 恭, and *shen* 慎, as to be careful or cautious. That is, to be cautious around those one fears or holds in awe. Thus, just as subjects follow their ruler's orders because they fear the penalties for not doing so, children follow their parents' orders for fear of their punishment. The *Han Feizi* 韓非子 points out that a mother usually fails to raise her son properly because she relies on love rather than fear, whereas a father usually succeeds because the punishment he metes out produces fear, that is, respect.[38] In early medieval times, Yan Zhitui 顏之推 (531–591) repeats this rationale: "When parents are imposing and stern, but show a bit of solicitude, their children will then fear them, which will produce filiality." Note that he baldly states that fear induces filial behavior. He then praises Lady Wei 魏夫人 who continued to physically discipline her son, a general, even though he was in his forties.[39] Since in practice parents' authority was in part dependant upon their ability to punish or inspire fear, if they could no longer do so, their power, as well as the special privileges that accompanied it, was in danger. The filial exemplar Han Boyu 韓伯瑜 cried when his mother's blows with the bamboo rod no longer hurt him.[40] Of course, he was bemoaning the fact that she was growing old; nevertheless, it was her loss of the means to assert her authority that alerted him to the fact.

The problem of weak authority seems to have particularly afflicted mothers.[41] It is most plainly apparent in stories in which daughters-in-law or slaves mistreat helpless, elderly mothers. For example, in one version of the Ding Lan tale, Ding's wife got tired of waiting on her wooden "mother-in-law" hand and foot, so one day, out of spite, she burnt the statue's face. In another tale, Sheng Yan's 盛彥 (d. ca. 285) female slave became tired of waiting on his sick, blind mother, so while her master was away she fed maggots to the old crone.[42] A mother's frail authority as family head was doubtlessly related to the prevalence of remarriage and concubinage, which made it so that, after her husband's death, a mother would most likely govern over many children that were not biologically her own, and thus emotionally distant from her. Some stepsons might have been even older than their putative mothers.[43] Perhaps due to their weak authority, many tales describe how a filial son would do anything to fulfill his stepmother's wishes, even to the extent of endangering his life. One of the best examples of this is Wang Xiang who, in the depths of winter, exposed his skin to the ice to get his stepmother fish and weathered a withering storm to carry out her orders to protect her crab-apple tree.[44] The common inclination to not submit to a stepmother and the consequent need to bolster her authority within the family would also explain why stepmothers are featured in so many of the early medieval tales.

Another reason for the weakness of the mother's power is that the Classics themselves do not offer a clear picture of her authority. According to the ritual codes, children should treat their stepmother just as they would their biological mother; thus, even if stepsons were older than their stepmother, they should still treat her like they would their normal mother; i.e., they should obey all her commands and strive to fulfill all of her unspoken wishes. Nevertheless, the Classics put forth a contradictory notion in the form of *sancong* 三從 (The Three Obediences); that is, while young, women should obey their father's directives, when married, their husband's, and when old, their son's. As a result, after one's father dies, the Classics provide contradictory messages about whom should fill the role of family head. Most sons probably meekly followed their biological mother's orders and treated her with the same filial piety as their fathers. Other more aggressive sons might have asserted their own authority with *sancong* in mind. Since stepsons' relations with their stepmothers were often strained, they were even less likely to give their full obedience to a woman who was not their biological mother. Yan Zhitui (531–591) advises men not to remarry after the death of their first wife because of the ugly tensions that often crop up between stepmothers and stepchildren. He states that stepsons often insultingly call their stepmother "concubine" and their half brothers "hired laborers."

The Prevalence of *Shengfen*

Needless to say, the filial piety stories can only furnish indirect hints of what the early medieval family was like. Other evidence, though, particularly the ubiquity of the custom of *shengfen* 生分 (splitting the patrimony while one's parents are alive), corroborates the tales' impression of weak parental authority. This custom is often credited to the Qin laws that discouraged fathers and sons or brothers from living together,[45] which remained in effect until the Wei Kingdom (220–265) deemed it illegal for fathers and sons to have separate finances.[46] Although the Han practice of *shengfen* probably was a continuance of Qin custom,[47] Luo Tonghua suggests there were many economic reasons for its popularity.[48] Biographies of Eastern Han upright officials, such as those of Xu Jing 許荊 (fl. 90–140) and 何廠 He Chang (fl. 80–110), provide us with a sense of how widely this custom was practiced in some areas.

> Xie Hong 謝弘 and others who are from Chen [in Hunan] did not nurture their parents and lived apart from their brothers. [Because of Xu Jing's teachings] the people that returned home to reverently care for their parents became more than a thousand.[49]

> He Chang's kindness and his attention to the rites transformed the behavior of commoners. Of those who departed with their portion of the inheritance while their parents were still alive, more than two hundred returned home to reverently nourish their parents, belatedly wear mourning clothes [for their deceased parents], or to yield their inheritance to (their siblings).[50]

In regard to the first anecdote, Luo points out that, since Chen prefecture's average household size was 3.7 members per family, and it had nearly 500,000 residents and over 120,000 households, Xie was successful in reuniting only a token number of split families. Luo further indicates that *shengfen* was current throughout Han China.[51]

During the Northern and Southern Dynasties (220–589), this custom continued to be widespread, particularly in the south. The *Sui shu's* 隋書 (*History of the Sui*) "Treatise on Geography" claims that in Liangzhou 梁州 (Sichuan) and Yangzhou 揚州 (Jiangsu, Anhui, Zhejiang, Fujian, Jiangxi, and Guangdong) fathers and sons often live separately.[52] A memorial by a Liu-Song official, Zhou Lang 周朗 (424–460), confirms that the "Treatise on Geography" was not merely perpetuating a northern stereotype of the south.

> The withering of the moral teachings has brought us to this. Nowadays, among gentlemen-grandees and those below them, in seven out of ten families, even while their parents are still alive, brothers have separate finances. Likewise among commoners, in five out of eight families, fathers and sons have separate wealth. Extreme cases in which close relatives do not even know when each other is in danger or has died, do not aid each other when they are hungry or cold, or who slander or defame each other out of jealousy are too numerous to count. We should emphasize the prohibitions (of living separately from one's

parents and brothers) in order to change this custom. To those
who already excel in family affairs, attention should be devoted
to rewarding them. From now on, those who do not change
should have their wealth confiscated.[53]

Since having separate finances meant to establish an independent household, this memorial suggests that many southerners, no matter what their
social class, were financially independent from their parents and brothers.[54] This type of southern division usually took the form of brothers
splitting the patrimony and functioning as financially independent units,
while still living within the same compound. This phenomenon was generally called *yimen shuzao* 一門數灶 (several stoves existing in one gate).
Since all family members were supposed to eat from the same kitchen,
separate stoves meant the existence of distinct family units.[55] The family
of a southerner named Pei Zhi 裴植 (466–515), who served as an official
for the Northern Wei, furnishes a specific example of this type of southern family division:

> Even though Zhi sent his salary from the regional government
> to support his mother and aid his younger brothers, each one of
> them had his own distinct wealth and finances. They lived
> together but had separate stoves. They had one gate (*men* 門),
> but it had several kitchens. This is probably because they were
> contaminated by the customs of Jiangnan.[56]

As Li Binghai points out, the central emotional relationship at the heart
of these newly created families within the same compound was that of
husband-wife, rather than parent-child.[57] Consequently, as Zhou Lang
suggested, once brothers split the patrimony they neglected their parents
and treated each other with indifference. As Six Dynasties sources would
say, relatives would treat each other as *xingluren* 行路人 (strangers on
the road).[58] Interestingly, works called *Xiaozi zhuan* 孝子傳 (*Accounts
of Filial Offspring*) that circulated filial piety stories are almost entirely
southern in origin; in other words, the tales that preached family unity
and the importance of the patriarch's authority were being created and
propagated in the areas where *shengfen* was most current.

As the last line of the passage concerning Pei Zhi indicates, many
northern literati viewed *shengfen* as a distasteful southern practice, which
their cousins undoubtedly learned from the uncivilized aborigines.[59]
Nevertheless, documents from Dunhuang signal that *shengfen* continued
to be practiced in the northwest during this period.[60] Moreover, as a
subcommentary to the Tang Code indicates, since the Code only punishes

parents who order their children to have a separate household registration, not parents who order their children to have separate finances,
shengfen was still legal. In other words, as long as it was done at the
parent's initiative and it did not affect household registration, the state
was indifferent to this practice. Hori Toshikazu thinks that this southern
style of family division was a compromise between having a complex
family ruled by a strong patriarch and a family being split completely
apart by *shengfen*.[61]

Reasons behind the Practice of Shengfen

Luo Tonghua has insightfully argued family division usually came
about due to economic reasons. Often it happened when an adult son
perceived that his brother was unfairly doing less work or using more
than his share of the family's resources. Furthermore, he states that such
large families usually needed to be wealthy to sustain so many family
members and mollify conflicts that might occur between them.[62] The
following tale of Li Chong 李充 (fl. 121) indicates both the economic
pressures that might lead to *shengfen* and the manner in which it was
formally undertaken.

> Li Chong's family was poor. He and his six brothers ate together
> and handed down clothes to each other. Chong's wife secretly
> said to him: "Since we are so poor now, it will be difficult for
> tranquility in this family to last long. I have my own wealth, so
> I hope you will consider splitting off from the family and living
> apart." Chong pretended to agree by saying, "If you want to live
> separately from the family, you should distill some wine and
> make preparations for an assemblage, and invite and beckon our
> close and distant kin from the village, so we can deliberate on
> this matter." His wife, obeying his commands, laid out the wine
> and feasted the guests. Chong kneeled down among those
> summoned and told his mother, "This wife, for no reason, has
> instructed me to leave and distance myself from my mother and
> elder brothers. Her crime deserves the punishment of being
> driven away." He thereupon berated her loudly, and then ordered
> her to leave the compound. His wife held back her tears and left.
> Those summoned were surprised and reverent, and thereupon
> withdrew and dispersed.[63]

Note that Li's wife believes that the family's extreme poverty will lead
to discord. To prevent this from happening, she thinks the more prudent

economic course is for her and her husband to establish an independent household. Tellingly, rather than express shock and indignation at Li's wife's request for *shengfen*, his kin were surprised and impressed by his willingness to divorce her because of it. Apparently, gathering kin together to arrange *shengfen* was far from unusual—what was unusual was declining to split the patrimony. Significantly, the person who saves the day is not the family head, in this case Li Chong's mother, but rather one of her sons.

The rationale that Li Chong's wife gives for wishing to divide the family estate suggests another reason why *shengfen* might occur—it was a practical means to avoid disharmony within the family. Hence the household head might use it whenever he or she could not control an unruly offspring or pacify personality clashes within the family. For instance, in the filial piety story of Xue Bao 薛包 (fl.110–140), since his stepmother loathed him, his father gave him a portion of the estate and forced him out of their home.[64] In another anecdote concerning the exemplary woman, Li Mujiang 李穆姜, her four stepsons detested her, which prompted a neighbor to suggest that she live separately from them.[65] In each of these cases, when there is no obvious means to resolve a domestic problem, the protagonists resort or are advised to *shengfen*. Moreover, in neither of these cases is *shengfen* itself seen negatively.

The common practice of *shengfen* indicates that early medieval family heads were far from having the unconditional authority that the filial piety stories hoped they would. If family heads did have the sway of a Roman patriarch, then we would expect them to control the patrimony until their death. That they allowed division of the patrimony, and might do so to quell family disputes, indicates that their ability to control family members was in fact limited.

Concluding Remarks

Scholars have overestimated the power of Chinese early imperial patriarchs because they have taken prescriptive sources as reporting historical fact. When describing the powers that family heads wielded within the home, they have largely relied on ritual instructions from the *Li ji* and laws from various legal codes.[66] By doing so, they have confused how the authors of these documents wanted families to function with how they actually did so. Since overwhelmingly sources from the early medieval period are prescriptive rather than descriptive, a student of the period has no choice but to read between the lines. My interpretation of the normative filial piety stories suggests that patriarchs were often worried that their adult sons would subvert parental authority by using family property for their own benefit, making their own decisions, questioning the family head's commands, or regarding him or her as a cumbersome burden.

This by no means suggests that early medieval family heads did not wield considerable power within their households. As legal documents from Shuihudi indicate, even during the non-Confucian Qin, a family head could, with a considerable degree of confidence, expect that officials would accede to his or her request to have a child killed for unfilial behavior. Nevertheless, the tale's authors' emphasis on parental authority and their anxiety over its weakness, combined with the prevalence of *shengfen*, indicate that early medieval family heads had much less power than their Roman, or even their late imperial, counterparts. The patriarchs of early medieval China, thereby, seem much more akin to fathers in Athenian society—although they usually expected obedience and in their old age sustenance from their sons, they understood that their power could not be wielded unreasonably, and that circumstances existed under which a certain degree of authority and the freedom to act had to be ceded to their adult sons.

Although the filial piety narratives unknowingly reveal the relative frailty of Chinese household heads, they also indicate that their upper-class authors perceived the need for and desperately wanted to strengthen parental authority. We should bear in mind that not long after these authors advocated that parents should have more power within the household, other educated Chinese established laws to do exactly that, such as statutes that outlawed fathers and sons from having separate finances. In other words, the long march to the point where it was proverbial that a parent could never be wrong begins in the early medieval period.

Notes

This paper was initially presented at the 1999 Association for Asian Studies meeting in Boston. I would like to thank the following people for their instructive comments on earlier drafts of this paper: Roger Ames, Anne Behnke Kinney, Mark Edward Lewis, Karen Turner, Robin Yates, and the participants in the Cultures of Authority in Asian Practice On-line Conference.

1. See articles # 6, 120, 155, 156, 179, 188, 329, 345, & 348 in Changsun Wuji 長孫無忌 et al. *Tanglü shuyi* 唐律疏議 (Taipei: Hongwenguan chubanshe, 1986) and Wallace Johnson, trans. *The T'ang Code* (2 vols. Princeton, NJ: Princeton University Press, 1979 & 1997). See also Wang Yubo 王玉波, *Zhongguo jiazhang-zhi jiating zhidu shi* 中國家長制家庭制度史 (Tianjin: Tianjin shehui kexueyuan chubanshe, 1989), 240–247.

2. See Ch'ü T'ung-tsu, *Law and Society in Traditional China* (Paris: Mouton, 1965), 28–29.

3. See Sun Xiao 孫筱, "Xiao de guannian yu Handai jiating" 孝的觀念與漢代家庭 *Zhongguoshi yanjiu*, 3 (1988), 149–150.

4. See Max Weber, *Economy and Society*, ed. Guenther Roth and Claus Wittich (3 vols. New York: Bedminster Press, 1968), 1: 377, G. Jamieson, *Chinese Family and Commercial Law* (Reprint; Hong Kong: Vetch and Lee Limited, 1970), 4–5, and Shi Fengyi 史鳳儀, *Zhongguo gudai hunyin yu jiating* 中國古代婚姻與家庭 (Wuhan: Hubei renmin chubanshe, 1987), 251–254. The first two of these texts are cited in Gary G. Hamilton, "Patriarchalism in Imperial China and Western Europe," *Theory and Society*, 13 (1984), 406–408. Japanese scholars, on the other hand, tend to stress the weakness of the Chinese patriarch, especially vis-à-vis the state. For example, see Hori Toshikazu 堀敏一, "Kodai Chûgoku no kafuchôsei—sono seiritsu to tokuchô" 古代中國の家父長制—その成立と特徴," in *Ie to kafuchôsei* 家と父長制, ed. Hikaku kazoku shigakukai 比較家族史學會 (Tokyo: Waseda daigaku shuppansha, 1992), and Yoshida Kôichi 吉田浤一, "*Chûgoku kafuchôseiron hihan jôsetsu*" 中國家父長制論批判序說, in *Chûgoku sensei kokka to shakai tôgô* 中國專制國家と社會統合, ed. Chûgokushi kenkyûkai 中國史研究會 (Kyoto: Bunrikaku, 1990).

5. For a discussion of the characteristics and development of the phenomenon of *patria potestas*, see Joseph Plescia, "*Patria Potestas* and the Roman Revolution," in *The Conflict of the Generations in Ancient Greece and Rome*, ed. Stephen Bertman (Amsterdam: B. R. Gruner, 1976).

6. See Gary G. Hamilton, "Patriarchy, patrimonialism, and filial piety: a comparison of China and Western Europe," *British Journal of Sociology*, 41.1 (1990), 77–104, and his "Patriarchalism in Imperial China and Western Europe," *Theory and Society*, 13 (1984), 393–425.

7. For an informative discussion of the relationship between Athenian fathers and sons, see Barry S. Strauss, *Fathers & Sons in Athens: Ideology and Society in the Era of the Peloponnesian War* (Princeton, NJ: Princeton University Press, 1993), especially chapters 2 & 3.

8. D. C. Lau 劉殿爵 and Chen Fong Ching 陳方正, *Xinxu zhuzi suoyin* 新序逐字索引 (Hong Kong: Hong Kong Commercial Press, 1992), 7.10.

9. Lau et al. *Hanshi waizhuan zhuzi suoyin* 韓詩外傳索引 (Hong Kong: Hong Kong Commercial Press, 1992), 7.4; James Robert Hightower, *Han shih wai chuan* (Cambridge: Harvard University Press, 1952), 225–26.

10. *Mengzi* 孟子 (in *Shisanjing zhu shu* 十三經注疏, ed. Ruan Yuan 阮元 [8 vols. Taipei: Yiwen yinshuguan, 1993]), 7B.8a–b; D. C. Lau, trans. *Mencius* (Harmondsworth, Middlesex: Penguin Classics, 1983), 125–26.

11. Lau et al. *Xunzi zhuzi suoyin* 荀子逐字索引 (Hong Kong: The Commercial Press, 1996), 29.141–142.

12. *Hanshi waizhuan zhuzi suoyin*, 8.25; Hightower, *Han shih wai chuan*, 280, and Lau et al. *Shuoyuan zhuzi suoyin* 說苑逐字索引 (Hong Kong: Hong Kong Commercial Press, 1993), 3.7.

13. *Mengzi*, 9a.4b–5b; Lau, *Mencius*, 139.

14. *Shuoyuan zhuzi suoyin*, 21.1.

15. Ouyang Xun 歐陽詢 (557–641), *Yiwen leiju* 藝文類聚 (2 vols. Shanghai: Shanghai guji chubanshe, 1999), 20.371.

16. Li Fang 李昉 (925–996) et al. *Taiping yulan* 太平御覽 (Reprint; Taipei: Taiwan shangwu yinshuguan, 1986), 61.4b and Li Fang et al. *Taiping guangji* 太平廣記 (Reprint; Taipei: Guxin shuju, 1980), 161.322.

17. *Taiping yulan*, 482.4a.

18. See Hori, "Kodai Chūgoku no kafuchōsei," 164–166 & Ota Yukio 太田幸夫, "Suikochi Shinbo takekan ni mieru, 'Shitsu,' 'Ko,' 'Dōkyo,' o megutte" 睡虎地秦墓竹簡にみえる『室』『戶』『同居』をめぐって in *Tōajiashi ni okeru kokka to nōmin* 東アジア史における國家と農民, ed. Nishijima Sadao 西島定生 (Tokyo: Yamakawa Shuppansha, 1984), 86 & 92.

19. *Li ji zhu shu* 禮記注疏 (in *Shisanjing zhu shu*, vol.5) 27.11b. The translation is from James Legge, trans. *Li Chi: Book of Rites* (2 vols. New Hyde Park, NY: University Books, 1967), 1: 458.

20. *Li ji zhu shu*, 51.21b.

21. Fan Ye 範曄 (398–445) *Hou Han shu* 後漢書 (Beijing: Zhonghua shuju, 1965), 81.2679.

22. Wu Hung contends that the story of Li Shan exemplifies righteousness rather than filial piety (see his *The Wu Liang Shrine* [Stanford, CA: Stanford University Press, 1989], 168 & 182). Nevertheless, the inscription over Li Shan's depiction at Wu Liang Ci, which reads "The Loyal and Filial (*zhongxiao* 忠孝) Li Shan" (*The Wu Liang Shrine*, 295), suggests otherwise. That early medieval literati viewed Li Shan as filial can be seen in that his story appears in works entitled "Accounts of Filial Offspring." Moreover, in his *Zhengao* 真誥 (Declarations of the Perfected), Tao Hongjing 陶弘景 (456–536) puts Li Shan forward as an example of a man who perfected filiality. See Mugitani Kunio 麥谷邦夫, *Shinkō sakuin* 真誥索引 (Kyoto: Kyōtō daigaku jinbun kagaku kenkyūjo, 1991), 16.10b.

23. Yang Yong 楊勇, *Shishuo xinyu jiaoqian* 世說新語校箋 (Reprint; Taipei: Taiwan jidai shuju, 1975), 1.14; Liu I-ch'ing, *A New Account of Tales of the World*, trans. Richard Mather (Minneapolis: University of Minnesota Press, 1976), 8. A similar tale is told of Jiang Yi 蔣翊. See Lau et al., *Dongguan Hanji* 東觀漢記逐字索引 (Hong Kong: Hong Kong Commercial Press, 1994), 21.37; and the *Yōmei bunkō Xiaozi zhuan* 陽明文庫孝子傳 (n.d.) and the *Funabashi Xiaozi zhuan*

船橋孝子傳 (n.d.), which are manuscripts that are photographically reproduced in Yōgaku no kai 幼學の會, *Kôshiden chûkai* 孝子傳注解 (Tokyo: Kyuko shoin, 2003), 309–310 & 373–374. Wu Hung translates the *Funabashi Xiaozi zhuan* version of the tale in his *The Wu Liang Shrine* (Stanford, CA: Stanford University Press, 1989), 292.

24. *Yiwen leiju*, 96.1672 and *Taiping yulan*, 935.8b and 416.5b, which has a lengthier version.

25. *Kōshiden chūkai*, 313–314 & 378.

26. The only early medieval exception to this is the tale of the filial grandson Yuan Gu, which will be discussed below. In this story, Yuan subtly remonstrates with his father, but he only does so to prevent his father from committing an unfilial action.

27. *Xiaojing* 孝經 (*Shisanjing zhu shu*, volume 8), 5.5b and Lau et al. *Lushi chunqiu zhuzi suoyin* 呂氏春秋逐字索引 (Taipei: The Commercial Press, 1996), 69–70.

28. For example, "Fan Hong's 樊宏 (d. AD 51) father Chong 重 was warm-hearted and generous, but he also had rules and regulations. Three generations of his family held its wealth in common. During the morning and evening audiences, his sons and grandsons would pay their respect to him, as if they were at court" (*Hou Han shu*, 32.1119). Satake Yasuhiko 佐竹靖彥 makes this same point about the formality of the court being duplicated in the home in his "Chūgoku kodai no kazoku to kazokuteki shakai chitsujō 中國古代の家族と家族的社會秩序," *Jinbun gakuhō*, 141 (1980), 34.

29. *Yiwen leiju*, 20.370 & *Taiping yulan* 412.5a. Pei Songzhi's 裴松之 (372?–451) commentary to Chen Shou's 陳壽 (233–297) *Sanguo zhi* 三國志 (Beijing: Zhonghua shuju, 1982) also quotes this passage (52.1228).

30. See Edwin O. Reischauer, *Ennin's Diary: The Record of a Pilgrimage to China in Search of the Law* (New York: The Ronald Press Company, 1955), 180–182.

31. See Watanabe Shinichirō 度邊信一朗, *Chūgoku kodai shakai ron* 中國古代社會論 (Tokyo: Aogi shoten, 1986), 145.

32. For a discussion of the growth of extended families and their effect on the early medieval view of the family, see Keith N. Knapp, *Selfless Offspring: Filial Children and Social Order in Early Medieval China* (Honolulu: University of Hawai'i Press, 2005).

33. Huang Hui 黃暉, *Lunheng jiaoshi* 論衡校釋 (4 vols. Beijing: Zhonghua shuju, 1990), 27.1109; Wang Ch'ung, *Lun-Heng: Miscellaneous Essays of Wang Ch'ung*, trans. Alfred Forke (2 vols. Reprint; New York: Paragon Book Gallery, 1962), 2: 137.

34. Haemon's rebellion against his father is based on the following grounds: First, since everyone in Thebes thinks Creon's decision to execute Antigone is unreasonable, by remonstrating Haemon is merely trying to safeguard his father's welfare. Second, since giving the dead a proper burial is the sacrosanct law of the gods, Creon's actions are contravening reason itself. Third, Creon mistakenly believes that the city-state exists for his own benefit, rather than the reverse; thus, he unreasonably believes that he does not have to take heed of his countrymen's opinions. For these reasons Haemon believes his father is insane; consequently, his commands no longer need to be followed; indeed, they must be actively opposed. However, from an early Confucian point of view, without even mentioning Haemon's attempt to stab his father, his persistent and angry remonstration would have been sufficient to label him as an unfilial son. That is because, even though a filial child has a duty to remonstrate when his parent is doing wrong, he must never do so in a disagreeable manner. I would like to thank Roberta Adams and Virginia Suddath for their penetrating comments that caused me to look afresh at the text of "Antigone."

35. Twentieth century anthropological studies from China and Taiwan likewise suggest that as soon as an elderly man either loses his ability to work or divides the family estate, his authority as well as his preferential treatment within the family disappears. See Margery Wolf, *House of Lim* (Englewood Cliffs, NJ: Prentice Hall, 1968), 50–51, Sung Lung-sheng, "Property and Family Division," in *The Anthropology of Taiwanese Society*, ed. Emily Martin Ahern and Hill Gates (Stanford, CA: Stanford University Press, 1981), 370–73, Martin C. Yang, *A Chinese Village* (New York: Columbia University Press, 1945), 57, and Francis L. K. Hsu, *Under the Ancestors' Shadow* (Stanford, CA: Stanford University Press, 1967), 116–117.

36. *Taiping yulan*, 519.3a.

37. Fang Xuanling 房玄齡 (576–648), *Jin shu* 晉書 (Beijing: Zhonghua shuju, 1974), 88.2284–85.

38. Wang Xianshen 王先慎, *Han Feizi jijie* 韓非子集解 (In volume 5 of the *Zhuzi jicheng* 諸子集成 [8 vols. Shanghai: Shanghai shudian, 1986]), 18.320.

39. See Lau, Chen, & Ho Che Wah 何志華, *Yanshi jiaxun zhuzi suoyin* 顏氏家訓索引 (Hong Kong: Zhongwen daxue chubanshe, 2000), 2–3.

40. *Shuoyuan zhuzi suoyin*, 3.8. For a discussion of the meaning of this anecdote, see Shimomi Takao 下見隆雄, *Kō to bōsei no mekanizumu* 孝と母性のメカニズム (Tokyo: Kyūbun shuppan, 1997), 35–39.

41. This of course does not mean that all female household heads lacked authority. As Bret Hinsch has indicated, women as de facto family heads sometimes exercised immense power over family decisions and resources. See his "Women, Kinship, and Property as Seen in a Han Dynasty Will," *T'oung Pao* 84 (1998), 10–20, and his *Women in Early Imperial China* (Lanham, MD: Rowman & Littlefield, 2002), 48–57 & 64–65.

42. For the stories of Ding Lan's wife and Sheng Yan's female slave, see respectively Dao Shi 道世 (d. 683), *Fayuan zhulin* 法苑朱林 (Shanghai: Shanghai guji chubanshe, 1991), 49.361 and *Jin shu*, 88.2276–77.

43. For a description of the familial tensions created by the custom of remarriage, see *Yanshi jiaxun zhuzi suoyin*, 6–7, and Teng Ssu-yu, trans. *Family Instructions for the Yen Clan* (Leiden: E. J. Brill, 1968), 12–15.

44. See *Shishuo xinyu*, 1.14.

45. As part of his reform, Shang Yang 商鞅 (ca. 390–338 BC) instituted two laws that encouraged *shengfen*, one of which doubled the tax a household had to pay if a father lived with two or more adult sons; the other of which forbade fathers, sons, and brothers from living in the same room (see Takigawa Kametarô 瀧川龜太朗, *Shiji huizhu kaozheng* 史記會注考證 [Reprint; Taipei: Hongshi chubanshe, 1986], 68.8, 11).

46. See *Jin shu*, 30.925; Ch'ü T'ung-tsu, *Han Social Structure*, ed. Jack Dull (Seattle: University of Washington Press, 1972), 6; and Makino Tatsumi 牧野巽, *Shina kazoku kenkyū* 支那家族研究 (Tokyo: Seikatsu sha, 1944), 316–18.

47. Jia Yi's 賈誼 (fl. 200–168) description of the Qin family states that, upon becoming adults, sons of rich families are sent away with part of the estate, while sons of poor families leave and become marrying-in sons-in-laws. He goes on to say that many characteristics of the Qin family have survived into the Han. See Ban Gu 斑固 (32–92), *Han shu* 漢書 (Beijing: Zhonghua shuju, 1962), 48.2244–45.

48. See his "Handai fenjia yuanyin chutan" 漢代分家原因初探, *Hanxue yanjiu*, 11.1 (1993), 141.

49. *Hou Han shu*, 76.2472.

50. *Hou Han shu*, 43.1487.

51. Luo, "Handai fenjia yuanyin chutan," 140–141.

52. Wei Zheng 魏徵 (580–643), *Sui shu* 隋書 (Beijing: Zhonghua shuju, 1973), 29.830 & 31.886.

53. Shen Yue 沈約 (441–513) *Song shu* 宋書 (Beijing: Zhonghua shuju, 1974], 82.2096–97. For an illuminating example of how relatives who have already split the patrimony might abuse each other, see Ren Fang's 任昉 (460–508) impeachment of Liu Zheng 劉整, which is included in Xiao Tong 蕭統 (501–531), *Wenxuan* 文選 (Reprint; Taipei: Huazheng shuju, 1986), 20.559–563. Victor Mair has translated this text in his *The Columbia Anthology of Traditional Chinese Literature* (New York: Columbia University Press, 1994), 542–547.

54. Zhou Lang's memorial also provides some insight into why small families and *shengfen* were popular in the south. In the memorial Zhou Lang criticizes the current tax system in which monetary and corvée labor taxes are based on

the wealth of the household. The system causes people to keep their households small by not clearing new land, committing infanticide, or by remaining unmarried to avoid having an even heavier tax burden (*Song shu*, 82.2094). For arguments about the effect of southern tax policies on the size and composition of southern families see Tang Changru 唐長孺, *San zhi liu shiji jiangnan datudi suoyouzhi de fazhan* 三至六世紀江南大土地所有制的發展 (Reprint; Taibei: Boshu chubanshe, 1957), 7; Dong Guodong 凍國棟, "Beichao shiqi de jiating guimo jiegou ji xiangguan wenti lunshu 北朝時期的家庭規模結構及相關問題論述," *Weijin Nanbeichao Suitang shi*, 8 (1990), 39. Dong also believes that Southern families were smaller to make the most of commercial opportunities that were available to them. This would be in line with the inheritance customs of medieval European merchant families, in which, at an early age, sons received a portion of the patrimony and left home, so that they would have the freedom and capital to engage in business (See David Herlihy, *Medieval Households* [Cambridge: Harvard University Press, 1985], 91).

55. See Li Binghai 李秉懷, "Nanchao yi men shu zao fengsu de lishi wenhua yanyuan"南朝一門數灶風俗的歷史文化沿源, *Minjian wenyi jikan* 28.4 (1990). For a description of this phenomenon in modern times, see Wolf, *The House of Lim*, 28–29, and Hsu, *Under the Ancestors' Shadow*, 113–122.

56. Wei Shou 魏收 (506–572), *Wei shu* 魏書 (Beijing: Zhonghua shuju, 1974), 71.1571–72.

57. Li, "Nanchao yi men shu zao fengsu de lishi wenhua yanyuan," 117.

58. For example, see *Wei shu*, 85.1873.

59. For derogatory comments about *shengfen* being a southern aboriginal practice, see the biographies of Xue Shen 薛慎 (Linghu Defen 令狐德棻 [583–666], *Zhou shu* 周書 [Beijing: Zhonghua shuju, 1971], 35.625) and Yue Sun 樂遜 (*Zhou shu*, 45.818).

60. For evidence from the northwest that implies *shengfen*'s continued practice, see Yang Jiping 楊際平, Guo Feng 郭鋒, and Zhang Heping 張和平, *Wu–shi shiji Dunhuang de jiating yu jiazu guanxi* 五–十世紀敦煌的家庭與家族關係 (Changsha: Yuelu shushe, 1997), 58–61.

61. Hori, "Kodai Chûgoku no kafuchôsei," 182–183.

62. Luo, "Handai fenjia yuanyin chutan," 143–145. David Wakefield indicates that families divided the patrimony for nearly the same reasons during the Qing. See his *Fenjia: Household Division and Inheritance in Qing and Republican China* (Honolulu: University of Hawai'i Press, 1998), 36–39. Interestingly, according to family division documents, a majority of families divided the patrimony while a parent was still alive (44–52).

63. *Hou Han shu*, 81.2684. The *Dongguan Hanji* contains a more abbreviated version of this story. See 19.27 and *Taiping yulan*, 412.4b–5a.

64. *Hou Han shu*, 39.1294.

65. *Hou Han shu*, 84.2794.

66. For example, see the argument of Liu Houqin 劉厚琴, "Handai fengjian fuquanzhi sixiang yanjiu" 漢代封建父權制思想研究, *Shixue yuekan* 4 (1995), which is largely based on quotations from the *Li ji*.

References

Ban Gu 斑固 (32–92). *Han shu* 漢書. Beijing: Zhonghua shuju, 1962.

Changsun Wuji 長孫無忌 et al. *Tanglü shuyi* 唐律疏議. Taipei: Hongwenguan chubanshe, 1986.

Chen Shou 陳壽 (233–297). *Sanguo zhi* 三國志. Beijing: Zhonghua shuju, 1982.

Ch'ü T'ung-tsu. *Law and Society in Traditional China*. Paris: Mouton, 1965.

———. *Han Social Structure*, ed. Jack Dull. Seattle: University of Washington Press, 1972.

Dao Shi 道世 (d. 683). *Fayuan zhulin* 法苑朱林. Qisha Dazangjing, ed. Shanghai: Shanghai guji chubanshe, 1991.

Dong Guodong 凍國棟, "Beichao shiqi de jiating guimo jiegou ji xiangguan wenti lunshu 北朝時期的家庭規模結構及相關問題論述," *Weijin Nanbeichao Suitang shi*, 8 (1990): 33–42.

Fan Ye 範曄 (398–445). *Hou Han shu* 後漢書. Beijing: Zhonghua shuju, 1965.

Fang Xuanling 房玄齡 (576–648). *Jin shu* 晉書. Beijing: Zhonghua shuju, 1974.

Hamilton, Gary G. "Patriarchalism in Imperial China and Western Europe," *Theory and Society*, 13 (1984): 77–104.

———. "Patriarchy, Patrimonialism, and Filial piety: a Comparison of China and Western Europe," *British Journal of Sociology*, 41.1 (1990): 393–425.

Herlihy, David. *Medieval Households*. Cambridge: Harvard University Press, 1985.

Hightower, James Robert. *Han shih wai chuan* (Cambridge: Harvard University Press, 1952.

Hinsch, Bret. "Women, Kinship, and Property as Seen in a Han Dynasty Will," *T'oung Pao* 84 (1998): 1–20.

———. *Women in Early Imperial China*. Lanham, MD: Rowman & Littlefield, 2002.

Hori Toshikazu 堀敏一. "Kodai Chūgoku no kafuchōsei—sono seiritsu to tokuchō" 古代中國の家父長制—その成立と特徴." In *Ie to kafuchōsei* 家と父長制, ed. Hikaku kazoku shigakukai 比較家族史學會. Tokyo: Waseda daigaku shuppansha, 1992, 155–183.

Hsu, Francis L. K. *Under the Ancestors' Shadow.* Stanford, CA: Stanford University Press, 1967.

Huang Hui 黃暉. *Lunheng jiaoshi* 論衡校釋. 4 vols. Beijing: Zhonghua shuju, 1990.

Jamieson, G. *Chinese Family and Commercial Law.* Reprint; Hong Kong: Vetch and Lee Limited, 1970.

Johnson, Wallace, trans. *The T'ang Code.* 2 vols. Princeton, NJ: Princeton University Press, 1979 & 1997.

Knapp, Keith N. *Selfless Offspring: Filial Children and Social Order in Early Medieval China.* Honolulu: University of Hawai'i Press, 2005.

Lau, D. C. 劉殿爵, trans. *Mencius.* Harmondsworth, Middlesex, U.K.: Penguin Classics, 1983.

Lau & Chen Fong Ching 陳方正. *Xinxu zhuzi suoyin* 新序逐字索引. Hong Kong: Hong Kong Commercial Press, 1992.

———. *Hanshi waizhuan zhuzi suoyin* 韓詩外傳索引. Hong Kong: Hong Kong Commercial Press, 1992.

———. *Shuoyuan zhuzi suoyin* 說苑逐字索引. Hong Kong: Hong Kong Commercial Press, 1993.

———. *Dongguan Hanji* 東觀漢記逐字索引. Hong Kong: Hong Kong Commercial Press, 1994.

———. *Xunzi zhuzi suoyin* 荀子逐字索引. Hong Kong: The Commercial Press, 1996.

———. *Lushi chunqiu zhuzi suoyin* 呂氏春秋逐字索引. Taipei: The Commercial Press, 1996.

Lau, Chen, & Ho Che Wah 何志華. *Yanshi jiaxun zhuzi suoyin* 顏氏家訓索引. Hong Kong: Zhongwen daxue chubanshe, 2000.

Legge, James, trans. *Li Chi: Book of Rites.* Reprint; 2 vols. New Hyde Park, NY: University Books, 1967.

Li Binghai 李秉懷. "Nanchao yi men shu zao fengsu de lishi wenhua yanyuan" 南朝一門數灶風俗的歷史文化沿源, *Minjian wenyi jikan* 28.4 (1990): 112–19.

Li Fang 李昉 (925–996) et al. *Taiping yulan* 太平御覽. Reprint; Taipei: Taiwan shangwu yinshuguan, 1986.

Li Fang et al. *Taiping guangji* 太平廣記. Reprint; Taipei: Guxin shuju, 1980.

Li ji zhu shu 禮記注疏, edited by Ruan Yuan 阮元 (1764–1849). In volume 5 of the *Shisanjing zhu shu* 十三經注疏. 8 vols. Taipei: Yiwen yinshuguan, 1993.

Linghu Defen 令狐德棻 [583–666]. *Zhou shu* 周書. Beijing: Zhonghua shuju, 1971.

Liu Houqin 劉厚琴. "Handai fengjian fuquanzhi sixiang yanjiu" 漢代封建父權制思想研究, *Shixue yuekan* 4 (1995): 48–53.

Liu I-ch'ing. *A New Account of Tales of the World.* Trans. Richard Mather. Minneapolis: University of Minnesota Press, 1976.

Luo Tonghua 羅彤華. "Handai fenjia yuanyin chutan" 漢代分家原因初探, *Hanxue yanjiu*, 11.1 (1993): 135–157.

Mair, Victor. *The Columbia Anthology of Traditional Chinese Literature.* New York: Columbia University Press, 1994.

Makino Tatsumi 牧野巽, *Shina kazoku kenkyū* 支那家族研究. Tokyo: Seikatsu sha, 1944.

Mengzi 孟子. In volume 8 of the *Shisanjing zhu shu*. 1815, rpt. Taibei: Yiwen chubanshe.

Mugitani Kunio 麥谷邦夫. *Shinkō sakuin* 真誥索引. Kyoto: Kyōtō daigaku jinbun kagaku kenkyûjo, 1991.

Ota Yukio 太田幸夫, "Suikochi Shinbo takekan ni mieru 'Shitsu,' 'Ko,' 'Dōkyo' o megutte" 睡虎地秦墓竹簡にみえる『室』『戶』『同居』をめぐって. In *Tōajiashi ni okeru kokka to nōmin* 東アジア史 における國家と農民, ed. Nishijima Sadao 西島定生. Tokyo: Yamakawa Shuppansha, 1984, 75–105.

Ouyang Xun 歐陽詢 (557–641). *Yiwen leiju* 藝文類聚. 2 vols. Shanghai: Shanghai guji chubanshe, 1999.

Plescia, Joseph. "*Patria Potestas* and the Roman Revolution." In *The Conflict of the Generations in Ancient Greece and Rome*, ed. Stephen Bertman. Amsterdam: B. R. Gruner, 1976, 143–69.

Reischauer, Edwin O., trans. *Ennin's Diary: The Record of a Pilgrimage to China in Search of the Law.* New York: The Ronald Press Company, 1955.

Satake Yasuhiko 佐竹靖彦. "Chūgoku kodai no kazoku to kazokuteki shakai chitsujō 中國古代の家族と家族的社會秩序," *Jinbun gakuhō*, 141 (1980): 1–61.

Shen Yue 沈約 (441–513). *Song shu* 宋書. Beijing: Zhonghua shuju, 1974.

Shi Fengyi 史鳳儀. *Zhongguo gudai hunyin yu jiating* 中國古代婚姻與家庭. Wuhan: Hubei renmin chubanshe, 1987.

Shimomi Takao 下見隆雄. *Kō to bōsei no mekanizumu* 孝と母性のメカニズム Tokyo: Kyūbun shuppan, 1997.

Strauss, Barry S. *Fathers and Sons in Athens: Ideology and Society in the Era of the Peloponnesian War*. Princeton, NJ: Princeton University Press, 1993.

Sun Xiao 孫筱. "Xiao de guannian yu Handai jiating" 孝的觀念與漢代家庭 *Zhongguoshi yanjiu*, 3 (1988): 149–154, 167.

Sung Lung-sheng. "Property and Family Division." In *The Anthropology of Taiwanese Society*, ed. Emily Martin Ahern and Hill Gates. Stanford, CA: Stanford University Press, 1981, 361–381.

Takigawa Kametarô 瀧川龜太朗. *Shiji huizhu kaozheng* 史記會注考證. Reprint; Taipei: Hongshi chubanshe, 1986.

Tang Changru 唐長孺. *San zhi liu shiji jiangnan datudi suoyouzhi de fazhan* 三至六世紀江南大土地所有制的發展. Reprint; Taibei: Boshu chubanshe, 1957.

Teng Ssu-yu, trans. *Family Instructions for the Yen Clan*. Leiden: E. J. Brill, 1968.

Wakefield, David. *Fenjia: Household Division and Inheritance in Qing and Republican China*. Honolulu: University of Hawai'i Press, 1998.

Wang Ch'ung. *Lun-Heng: Miscellaneous Essays of Wang Ch'ung*. Trans. Alfred Forke. 2 vols. Reprint; New York: Paragon Book Gallery, 1962.

Wang Xianshen 王先慎. *Han Feizi jijie* 韓非子集解. Volume 5 of the *Zhuzi jicheng* 諸子集成. 8 vols. Shanghai: Shanghai shudian, 1986.

Wang Yubo 王玉波. *Zhongguo jiazhangzhi jiating zhidu shi* 中國家長制家庭制度史. Tianjin: Tianjin shehui kexueyuan chubanshe, 1989.

Watanabe Shinichirô 度邊信一朗, *Chûgoku kodai shakai ron* 中國古代社會論. Tokyo: Aogi shoten, 1986.

Weber, Max. *Economy and Society*. Ed. Guenther Roth and Claus Wittich. 3 vols. New York: Bedminster Press, 1968.

Wei Shou 魏收 (506–572). *Wei shu* 魏書. Beijing: Zhonghua shuju, 1974.

Wei Zheng 魏徵 (580–643). *Sui shu* 隋書. Beijing: Zhonghua shuju, 1973.

Wolf, Margery. The *House of Lim: A Study of a Chinese Farm Family*. Englewood Cliffs, NJ: Prentice Hall, 1968.

Wu Hung. *The Wu Liang Shrine*. Stanford, CA: Stanford University Press, 1989.

Xiaojing 孝經. Volume 8 of the *Shisanjing zhu shu*.

Xiao Tong 蕭統. *Wenxuan* 文選. Reprint; Taipei: Huazheng shuju, 1986.

Yang, Martin C. *A Chinese Village*. New York: Columbia University Press, 1945.

Yang Jiping 楊際平, Guo Feng 郭鋒, and Zhang Heping 張和平. *Wu-shi shiji Dunhuang de jiating yu jiazu guanxi* 五–十世紀敦煌的家庭與家族關係. Changsha: Yuelu shushe, 1997.

Yang Yong 楊勇. *Shishuo xinyu jiaoqian* 世說新語校笺. Reprint; Taipei: Taiwan jidai shuju, 1975.

Yōgaku no kai 幼學の會. *Kôshiden chûkai* 孝子傳注解. Tokyo: Kyuko shoin, 2003.

Yoshida Kōichi 吉田泫一. "*Chūgoku kafuchōseiron hihan jōsetsu*" 中國家父長制論批判序說. In *Chūgoku sensei kokka to shakai tōgō* 中國專制國家と社會統合, ed. Chūgokushi kenkyūkai 中國史研究會. Kyoto: Bunrikaku, 1990, 55–107.

Virtue 德 (*de*), Talent 才 (*cai*), and Beauty 色 (*se*): Authoring a Full-fledged Womanhood in *Lienüzhuan* 列女傳 (*Biographies of Women*)

Robin R. Wang

The prominent Han Confucian scholar Liu Xiang 劉向 (79–8 BCE) compiled 125 biographies of women, from legendary times to the Han dynasty, to evoke and commemorate an ideal of womanhood. Since this ground-breaking effort, the stories of *lienü* 列女 (exemplary women) have permeated all aspects of women's lives throughout Chinese history. From such stories was gradually fashioned a celebrated, sustainable, and enduring tradition, the so-called *lienü* tradition.[1] This *lienü* tradition provides an opportunity to explore the ongoing social construction of female identity and gender roles within concrete social contexts. This essay will embark on a philosophical analysis of these stories to demonstrate how the authority of woman was constructed, comprehended, and contested in the early Chinese thought and culture. This endeavor will focus on three distinctive and culturally significant contexts relating to womanhood: virtue 德 (*de*), talent 才 (*cai*), and beauty 色 (*se*).

It is important to notice that biography is always determined by an act of representation as well as by an act of construction. Liu Xiang defines and constructs a normative standard for women (*what ought to be the case*) through stories of women claiming to be descriptive of real lives (*what is the case*). Three consistent and interrelated themes run through this essay: What kinds of virtues[2] are to be celebrated? How are these virtues related to broader social values? That is, what is the link between the virtues for women and the values generally promoted by Confucian tradition? Finally, could Liu Xiang's narratives still author for us an intellectual space where we can contribute to the development of

gender identities appropriate to an era of globalization? These themes
will verify that there is a strong convergence between the Confucian
ideal of becoming human and Liu Xiang's construction of womanhood:
women are valued and praised for their cultivated dispositions and rational abilities and are given a privileged position in shaping the person,
family, and state. It is the consistency between the Confucian ideal and
Liu Xiang's discourses that explicates how and why women regarded
them as authoritative and thus actually assumed the beliefs and practices
sanctioned in them as their own. By suggesting how these biographies
may be analyzed philosophically, one hopes to show the relevance of the
Lienüzhuan to contemporary deliberations of gender equality and personal identity.

It is not easy to map out systematically the particular female virtues
exhibited throughout these 125 stories. Liu Xiang's own attempt was to
order them into seven chapters/categories. Six of these exemplify desirable virtues, namely, maternal rectitude 母儀 (*muyi*), sagely intelligence
賢明 (*xianming*), benevolent wisdom 仁智 (*renzhi*), chaste obedience 貞
順 (*zhenshun*), pure righteousness 節義 (*jieyi*), and rhetorical competence 辯通 (*biantong*). The last chapter is called "The Vicious and
Depraved" 孽嬖 (*niebi*) and gives cautionary tales against the vices of
women. Each category is supported by fifteen to tewenty stories. To make
the most sense of Liu Xiang's intention, I have arranged a section of the
stories into three perspectives: first, virtue (*de*), which is inclusive of Liu's
reflections on maternal rectitude (*muyi*), benevolent wisdom (*renzhi*),
chaste obedience (*zhenshun*), and pure righteousness (*jieyi*); second,
talent (*cai*), which is comprehensive of his consideration on sagely intelligence (*xianming*) and rhetorical competence (*biantong*); and finally,
beauty (*se*), which is a broad but brief presentation of the relevant por-
tions of his illustrations of rhetorical competence (*biantong*), coupled
with an acknowledgment of the cautionary tales taken from the final
chapter. Consistent with the requirements of this arrangement, the
majority of the stories examined here will be taken up in the first section
on women's virtue. Each section, nevertheless, may add to our appreciation of how women author their own authentic humanity through the
conscious appropriation of their own minds, actions, and experiences.

Part One: Virtue 德 (*de*) as the Foundation of Womanhood

Virtue (*de*) is the most important element of a human being in the
Chinese intellectual tradition. Confucius, seeking to model it in his own
life, acknowledges the magnitude of virtue for realizing one's own

humanity. "The Master said, 'I set my heart upon the Way, base myself on virtue (*de*), lean upon benevolence (*ren*) for support and take my recreation in the arts.'" (*Analects* 7:6). It is *de* that makes someone a human being. In this aspect, one can argue that the human nature is manifest in the *de*. In an essay, "Do Women have a Distinct Nature?" feminist philosopher Nancy Holmstrom contends that

> nature should be understood as underlying structures that explain a range of behavior . . . If we are concerned with human beings as distinct from other biological beings, then their natures are biological. But if we are concerned with humans as social beings, then their natures, i.e., the underlying structures that explain their behavior—must be understood as socially consti- tuted and historically evolving . . . This brings out the point that there are many levels of generating structures, many levels of explanation appropriate to human beings.[3]

Holmstrom alerts us that human nature is not to be construed as some timeless essence derived from biology, but is socially constituted and historically evolving. Her insight is not only consistent with Liu Xiang's biographical demonstration of women's virtues, it is also presupposed in the analysis that follows. Like many Chinese thinkers, Liu Xiang gives special emphasis to *de*, inasmuch as four out of a total of seven chapters are devoted to *de*. Women's *de* is evident in their disposition, character, and behavior. We therefore distinguish three unique patterns from these stories.

Women as Role Models

In the *Yijing* 易經 (*The Book of Change*), the thirty-seventh hexa- gram, *Jiaren* 家人 (family), carries the following interpretation: "The proper place for the woman is inside 內 (*nei*) the family, and the proper place for the man is outside 外 (*wai*) the family. When both man and woman are in their proper places, this is the great appropriateness 義 (*yi*) of heaven 天 (*tian*) and earth 地 (*di*)."[4] Women's function is com- monly understood as operating within the inner sphere (*nei*) of family. Teaching the children and helping the husband 教子相夫 (*jiaozi xiangfu*) are woman's ultimate mandate and responsibility. What is offered in the *Lienüzhuan* is not simply a reaffirmation of this mandate, but an answer to the question of how it is to be appropriated and practiced. The *Lienüzhuan* imparts vivid details about its implementation. First of all, women are not there simply to cook food and clean house as if they were mere servants. In fact, none of the 125 stories even offer any comments on how well women are doing such household chores. The ideal mother, for example, is portrayed as a teacher for her children but more importantly as a role model for them. She presents herself as a living example for her children and shows the way to cultivate the virtues. So significant is her distinctive way of inculcating the virtues through personal example that it has been recognized as a distinguishable pedagogy in Chinese educational theory, namely, the *yisheng shijiao* 以身施教 (educating through a personal living example).

Liu Xiang's retelling of the story of Mencius's mother 孟母 (Mengmu) is a lucid example of the ways in which women are the authoritative teachers of morality for their children.[5] Like Confucius, Mencius was brought up by a single mother. At four different stages of Mencius's life she played a pivotal role. First, when Mencius was young, Mengmu moved her residence three times, from living by a marketplace, and then by a cemetery, but finally near a school, in her search to find the best environment for bringing up Mencius. Second, when Mencius later went to school he complained about the hard work of study and wanted to quit. His mother had him watch her cut the cloth she had been weaving all day long, thereby forcing him to realize how self-destructive it would be for him to cut off his studies. From that time on, Mencius grasped the importance of cultivating himself through hard work. Third, after Mencius was married, he considered divorcing his wife because she had not been properly attired to receive her husband when he barged in on her unannounced. Mengmu confronted him, pointing out that it was Mencius, not his wife, who had violated ritual propriety, for he had failed to knock on the door before entering her room. Mengmu challenged him to rethink his interpretation of the application of rituals. Fourth, when Mencius's opinion was not respected by leaders in his own town, he assumed that honor required him to move away. But he was worried about his mother, and thought that it would be unfilial to leave her. Mengmu sagely reminded him that, just as a woman must follow the ritual, so a man has to do what is right or just. She teaches her son that loyalty and filial piety may require men to search for righteousness not reducible to one's natural instinct for the security of family members.

The story exhibits how the mother decisively influenced Mencius at four crucial stages in his moral education. In each of these stages the function of mother is to be valued, not as a plain caregiver, but as an intricate stimulus to the child's basic moral development. Mencius's mother is not simply a weaver of cloth, but the weaver of Mencius's intellectual, spiritual, and moral mentality. This is the true meaning of motherhood. The story also confirms a strong conviction that the mother employs the primary authority in the shaping of the mind, character, and person of the younger generation.

In the second chapter of the *Lienüzhuan*, titled Sagely Intelligence (*xianming*), we observe many cases where woman as wife has an authoritative position and successfully gives advice and guidance to her husband, thus ensuring that her husband takes the proper path. The King of Xuan 宣王 (Xuanwang), for example, was very lazy, wanting very much to stay in bed all day with his wife.[6] He thus was unable to take good care of the affairs of state. One day, Jianghou, his wife, took off all her jewelry and adornments and asked for forgiveness. She said, "It is my fault for making the King so indolent and desirous only of the company of a woman. I am to blame for his lost virtue and the problems of the state. If a King is too fond of sex 好色 (*haose*), all his other desires will be uncontrollable as well. This will cause disorder in the kingdom. The root of this disorder lies in me, so please forgive me."[7] King was deeply stirred by her words and admits: "I may have lost the *de*, but all this was caused by me. It is not at all your fault."[8] From that moment on, King changed his way of living, got up early and went to bed late, diligently taking care of things for the people. Eventually, his kingdom was flourishing. At the end of each story in the *Lienüzhuan* there is a commentary that authorizes the moral of the story. In the commentary on this story, it states that Jianghou is not simply beautiful, but she also cultivates her virtues. Woman may initially receive affection because of her beauty, but she had better use virtue to cement the relationship.

Like a barometer helping one to anticipate changes in the weather, women also assist men in many situations by interpreting the challenges they face. The King of Chu heard that Yu Lingzi is a good scholar so he sent someone to deliver an invitation to him with 100 *liang* of gold.[9] Yu Lingzi said to the messenger, "My wife is inside, so let me discuss it with her."[10] Yu Lingzi tells his wife that the King wants him to be his officer and has brought along a substantial amount of gold with the invitation. "If I become an officer today there will be a lot of horses and carriages, and good food tomorrow. Should I accept the King's invitation?" The wife answered, "Although you only make shoes for a living, the *qin* 琴 (a musical instrument) is on your left and *shu* 書 (books) on your right. You can find a lot of joy within them. An abundance of horses will only bring you some land; and delicious food, after all, is just a piece of meat. Now merely for a little land and a little tasty food, you will have to worry about so many other things. Is this worth it? This is a chaotic time and many disasters will occur. I'm afraid that you will be unable to save even your own life."[11] So Yu Lingzi declined the offer and went back to his ordinary life. The moral of the story points out that the wife is adored for her virtue. She prefers peace and contentment to riches and higher social status.

These stories evoke an observation made by the first feminist philosopher, Mary Wollstonecraft (1759–1797). In her powerful work *A Vindication of the Rights of Woman* she well claims: "Connected with man as daughters, wives, and mothers, their [women's] moral character may be estimated by their manner of fulfilling those simple duties; but the end, the grand end of their exertions should be to unfold their own faculties and acquire the dignity of conscious virtue."[12] Wollstonecraft thus stresses that however restricted the social roles of women may seem to be, in fact they may supply an appropriate context in which women's own dignity and self-worth still stand fully revealed. Being a daughter, wife, or mother need not be seen as a restriction or imperfection. Liu Xiang's stories have made this point clearly.

Autonomous Being: Personification and Practitioner of the Confucian Virtues

As we have seen so far, the common Confucian virtues, such as 忠 *zhong*, 信 *xin*, 仁 *ren*, and 義 *yi*, are highlighted in many of Liu Xiang's stories. His narratives authorize models for women seeking to practice Confucian virtues culminating in a rendering of the ideal person 君子 (*junzi*) epitomized now as a woman. They also authorize a special type of autonomy that seems to foresee the hopes of many contemporary feminists. "Feminist writers in recent decades have been seeking to set out an alternative self-understanding which begins with the assumption of being-in-relation, and which attends to the networks of relationship in the context of which meaningful personal life is to be found."[13] A distinctively Confucian view of personal identity, constituted in the sociality of human being, formed in relationships with others as well as transformed through them, can be discerned in the type of moral autonomy celebrated in the *Lienüzhuan*.

Let's examine some stories. Consider, for example, the case of Jienu.[14] Someone hates Jienu's husband and wants to murder him. But this unnamed assailant cannot find an opportunity. He has heard that Jienu is a woman noted for her humanity, filial piety, and righteousness 仁孝有義 (*renxiao youyi*), so he captured her father as a hostage in order to extort information about the husband from his wife. Jienu learns about it and starts to deliberate what must be done. "If I don't give in to the kidnapper's demand, my father will be killed. This is unfilial 不孝 (*buxiao*). If I cooperate, my husband will be killed. But this is not righteous 不義 (*buyi*). If I am not *xiao* and not *yi*, I cannot go on living in this world."[15]

So she decides to sacrifice her own life to make both her father and her husband safe. She told the assailant that she will help him murder her husband. "I'll open the window for you, and the one lying on the east will be he." That very night Jienu opens the window and lies down on the east side. The assailant comes and murders the one lying on the east, only later to find out that the person he killed was the wife, Jienu. He was so deeply moved by Jienu's self-sacrificing behavior and overcome with such remorse that he gives up the idea of pursuing the husband any further. The commentary observes: "Jienu has *ren* (benevolence) and *xiao* (filial piety), and values *renyi* more than life itself. This is a highly praise worthy and noble action."[16] It also specifically refers to the action celebrated in the *Analects*, despite the fact that the *Analects* presents no mention of women's virtues as such: "The Master said, 'For gentlemen of purpose [*junzi*] and men of benevolence [*ren*] while it is inconceivable that they should seek to stay alive at the expense of benevolence, it may happen that they have to accept death in order to have benevolence accomplished" (*Analects*, 15:9).[17] The *Lienüzhuan* illustrates a connection between Confucian teaching and the practice of exemplary women like Jienu. It entails that when it comes to actually honoring these virtues and ideals, women are equal to men.

There is another story that bears comparison with the *Analects*. A stepmother and stepdaughter named Chu and her one son live on the coast, where pearl cultivation is a common occupation.[18] The stepmother wears them for decoration. One day they have to cross the border going inland. According to the policy at the time, no one can carry pearls to the other side of the border, with the penalty for violation being death. So naturally when they approach to the border, the stepmother takes off all her pearls and leaves them in a basket at the border. Her nine-year-old son, however, was very curious. He picked up the pearls and put them back into his mother's make-up bag without anyone's knowledge. When they pass the border the officers find the pearls in the stepmother's baggage. They announce: "This is against law! Who is responsible for it?" The stepdaughter Chu, immediately responds, "I am responsible for it. Please punish me!" The stepmother also steps forward, "No, she is not the one, I am. I put these into my box." Both accept responsibility and are willing to take the death penalty in order to save each other's life. Everyone surrounding them is deeply moved, and they all start to cry. The officer about to write out the criminal charges cannot hold a pen to the paper. "This mother and daughter have such strong bond. This is truly righteous (*yi*)! I can't find anyone guilty!"[19] So he decides to let them both go because morality is much more important than merely following the regulation. The commentary depicts that this is analogous to what the *Analects of Confucius* have to say about what it means to be true or faithful in a relationship 正直 (*zhengzhi*). When the father steals a sheep the son will not report it to the authorities. "Fathers cover up for their sons and sons cover up for their fathers. Straightness is to be found in such behavior." (*Analects*, 13:18). In the case from the *Lienüzhuan*, stepmother and stepdaughter cover up for each other. This, too, is *zhengzhi*. This case of mother and daughter relationship may be helpful for clarifying the argument of the story in the *Analects* 13:18, as its meaning is debated even today among scholars.

Defending Self-Respect: Facing Moral Dilemmas

As the core of the new kind of socially constituted, relational autonomy that feminists are seeking these days, self-respect is a rich complex of beliefs, attitudes, and behaviors that begs for philosophical clarification. Indeed, proper appreciation of one's own moral worth is clearly an indispensable dimension of the fully virtuous person, no matter how that ideal is conceptualized. John Rawls, for example, repeatedly insists that self-respect is "the most important primary good."[20] He also articulates its two basic aspects. First, self-respect "includes a person's sense of his own value, his secure conviction that his conception of his good, his plan of life, is worth carrying out."[21] Second, "self-respect implies a confidence in one's ability, so far as it is within one's power, to fulfill one's intentions."[22] Rawls's view suggests that the sense of self-respect springs from one's values system.[23] What is perceived as the good and right will not only maneuver one's actions but also shape one's basic self-understanding. Such an interpretation of self-respect casts light on the way women defend their self-respect, self-esteem, and the sense of their own worth in the *Lienüzhuan*. Women are more likely to face various situations as moral dilemmas and experience stressful tensions between conflicting moral obligations. In Liu Xiang's stories women from empresses to maids have their own unique ways of responding to these predicaments. Most of them are venerated for being willing to resign their very lives in order to preserve their dignity, character, and self-respect. They all take their own behavior incredibly serious, for they recognize how their actions may impact one way or another on their own sense of self-worth.

The practices commended in the *Lienüzhuan* are rooted in the teachings of *Analects* and *Mencius*. Later the accounts of these virtuous actions evolved and the qualities celebrated in them were applauded in the cults of various female martyrs 烈女. In chapter four, "Pure Righteousness" (*jieyi*), women have to deal with the toughest predicaments of life. For example, while walking in the country of Lu, Luyi is observed carrying a little child in her arms while holding hands with an older child.[24] Then the invaders descend on them. Luyi puts down the younger child and grabs the older one and starts to run down the hill. The younger child cries, "Mommy, Mommy!" But Luyi does not even turn around and continues running ahead. The soldier asks the little child, "Who is your mother holding?" The little child answers "I don't know." Soldiers command Luyi to stop or else they will use the bow to shoot her. Finally Luyi stops and talks with the soldiers. A soldier questions her, "Whose is the child you are holding?" Luyi says, "It is my brother's child. I saw you coming and, knowing that I have no ability to protect two, I dropped the one and picked up the other one." The soldiers are very confused with Luyi's action. "A child is naturally the most cherished by its own mother. Mothers will be affected deeply if anything happens to their own child. How could you leave your own child and take another's child?" Luyi explains, "Love for my own child is a private love 私愛 (*siai*), but taking care of my brother's child is public righteousness 公義 (*gongyi*). I can't act against public righteousness for the sake of a private love. Even if I saved my own child by doing this no one will accept me in the future. I will have no place to stay. So I am willing to endure the pain of losing my own child, if that is what it takes to follow righteousness. I can't survive without righteousness."[25] When the military commander heard Luyi's reasoning, he reported it to the King and urged him to stop the invasion of Lu. He said, "We can't invade Lu. Even the women in Lu know how to preserve virtue and act according to righteousness. They are not selfish and they do protect the public righteousness. If the women in Lu can do this, then their leaders must be exemplary too. Please withdraw our troops."[26] The King accepted this request and rewarded Luyi with a hundred cloths and named her the "righteous sister." 義姊 This story also displays how women exercise their public responsibilities primarily by maintaining their virtue in the immediacy of family life.

Other stories also reveal the tension between private love and public righteousness. Two stepbrothers were arrested for fighting with other people and were held liable for one person's death.[27] The investigation proved that one of these two must have actually killed this person. The Judge asked both brothers who killed him. Both of them confessed, "I did it, not my brother." One year passed by and the judge still cannot decide. The King said, "If we let both go that will allow the badness to go without punishment; but if we execute them both, we'll murder one innocent person." So he decided to ask their mother, since mothers usually know their children better. The mother was solicited whom the authority should execute for the crime. The mother suggested, "Execute the younger one." The King, though willing to follow her idea, remains a little probing about this. He inquires, "Everyone has special affection for the younger child. So why do you want to have your younger child killed?" The mother elucidates, "The younger one is my child and the older one is my stepchild. When his father died I made a promise to take good care of his son. I made this promise and so I must carry it out. If I allow the older one to die but let the younger one live, I will break my promise and favor my own private love while giving up the public righteousness. What will I rely on to live in this world if I don't have righteousness? I know I will be deeply saddened by the death of my own child but will this affect me to practice righteousness?"[28] The King was stimulated by her words and was highly impressed with her virtue. He ordered the release of both boys and honored the mother as "the righteous mother" 義母.

These two stories demonstrate women's value system, and how they may make priorities among conflicting values. In each case the women draw a clear distinction between their own feeling or sentiment and the righteous action. Yet the stories are also truly puzzling. The question is reasonably posed, why do these women do such things? What did they actually have in mind? A possible answer might emerge from a feminist lens. According to Robin S. Dillon, any feminist conception of self-respect must be built on a foundation of relatedness.

> For recognition of self-respect involves recognizing one's place in the moral community, as a person among persons, understanding that and how one is related to all other persons. It is this more encompassing vision of the self-in-relation-to others that distinguishes self-respect from the more narrowly focused self-love.[29]

This conception of self-respect highlights the fact that our ability to comprehend and value ourselves as persons depends on being acknowledged and respected by others. The women in the *Lienüzhuan* attain self-respect because they are honored and esteemed by others. Dillon thus makes it easier to perceive the link between self-sacrifice and a feminist concept of self-respect. She concludes: "Self-sacrifice in and of itself is not oppressive or denigrating or incompatible with self-respect. For it is possible to give up pursuing my self-interest, even to give up myself, in a self-respecting manner—knowing what I am worth and so knowing the extent and meaning of my sacrifice."[30] Such an insight may unravel the enigma contained in these stories. Though deliberately posed in extreme terms, the moral dilemmas faced by these women permit us to glimpse how self-sacrifice may be a significant condition for maintaining their self-respect and self-worth. If they resolve their dilemmas by favoring their private loves, they risk forfeiting not only their public righteousness, but their own basic sense of self as a fully human person. The loss of moral identity, or irreparable breach of self-esteem, at least in these stories, is more painful than any other loss, no matter how close to their natural desires.

It may be useful to point out how these stories about female virtue effectively refute Kant's patronizing observations on women's morality. Declares Kant:

> The virtue of a woman is a *beautiful virtue*. That of the male sex should be a *noble virtue*. Women will avoid the wicked not because it is upright, but because it is ugly; and virtuous actions mean to them such as are morally beautiful. Nothing of duty, nothing of compulsion, nothing of obligation.[31]

Consistent with this assumption Kant describes himself as "hardly [able to] believe that the fair sex is capable of principle."[32] Would Kant have made the same statement if he were lucky enough to read these exemplary stories? For all their difficulty, and precisely because of their nobility, they do in fact anticipate the feminist concern that women and men should be regarded as moral equals.

Part Two: Talent 才 (*cai*) as a Necessary Component of Womanhood

Rousseau articulates an ideal woman, Sophie, who as the result of right education is the perfect complement for Emile, the ideally educated man. The unique skill Sophie possesses is the art of being a woman. But the mind of this ideal woman is of a certain type. "Sophie's mind is pleasing but not brilliant, solid but not deep. She has always something attractive to say to those who talk with her, but lacks the conversational adornments we associate with cultured women."[33] In Western philosophical tradition reason and rationality have been viewed as a special property of men. Feminists have claimed that the problem of subordination of women is the product of this gender dualism. However Liu Xiang's stories presuppose a widely divergent conceptual framework and impart a different practical vision. It is very much expected in the early Chinese tradition that women should be talented 才 (*cai*). Talents do not refer so much to one's innate natural ability as to certain culturally bounded and cultivated capacities. These range from intuitive insight to logical reasoning and noticeably are inclusive of reason or rationality. There are at least thirty stories testifying to ancient Chinese expectations related to the cultivation of female talents (*cai*). They are recapitulated in following two aspects.

Epistemological Proficiency: Knowing the Dao

Philosophers have always exhibited a great fondness for the concept of knowing. Yet what is viewed philosophically as knowing tends to be reduced to what can be analyzed epistemologically, which reinforces a bias privileging the experiences of men only. Women's ways of knowing are ignored. Rather than assuming the rational abilities of women to be inferior, the stories of the *Lienüzhuan* call for a positive appreciation for the creative capacities distinctive of women's embodiment and activities. They are much admired, celebrated, and embraced. In these stories, virtuous mothers, wives, and daughters are shown giving an authoritative interpretation of the *dao* 道 (ways) of human occurrence and the course of public events. Not to be confused with witches or fortune-tellers, women are nevertheless relying on their own wisdom to discern the direction of an action or to envisage its likely outcomes.

Let's look at the one of the stories from the chapter on Benevolent Wisdom 仁智 (*renzhi*). Tao is a newly elected officer in the county government.[34] After three years in his post, his land has not improved much. Yet his family's wealth has increased three times over. His wife warns him about this, but he disregards her point of view. After five years, one day Tao brings home 100 four-horse carriages. All of the people in the village come to congratulate him. Only his wife carrying their son is crying. Tao's mother deems this is the bad omen. His wife exclaims, "My husband has little ability but still holds a big post. This must bring on some disaster. He has done nothing to improve his land but our clan gets rich. In the past a good king managed the country. His family was poor but the country was wealthy. People respected this kind of leader, so people were happy and their names and legacies were passed on successfully. Now my husband manages the country. His family is wealthy, but the country is poor. People do not respect him. This is a sign of failure and trouble to come. I want to leave here with my son."[35] So the wife left this house. One year later, robbers invaded their house and killed Tao and his relatives. Because his mother was so old the robbers spared her. The wife came back and took care of her mother-in-law for the remainder of her life. The moral of the story is that the wife knows righteousness and can foresee the dire consequences of unrighteousness. Compared to her husband, she has the deeper insight and wider knowledge.

Here is another story from the same chapter. The daughter of King Wei received two marriage proposals from two different countries, Xiu and Qi.[36] Her father wants her to accept Xiu's proposal, but the daughter believes she should go with Qi. Her reason is that Xiu is a small country and far away, yet Qi is a big country and close by. "If our land is attacked, Qi will be capable of helping us. We should accept their proposal for the sake of the country's long-term benefit."[37] But her father didn't listen to her and married her off to the Xiu. Years later Wei was attacked and Xiu could not come to help, but Qi arrived to assist Wei. Her father very much regretted not following his daughter's suggestion. The moral of the story designates how praiseworthy is the daughter's vision and foresight.

Here is yet another one, making a similar point. One day the young son came home crying, and his mother asked him the reason.[38] The son tells his mother that he saw the two-headed snake and was afraid that it was a bad omen indicating that he will die. The mother reassures him, and uses the occasion to offer him a profound advice. "The virtue of a man can overcome any difficulties and misfortunes. If you have *ren* and *yi*, heaven (*tian*) will assist you. *Tian* only supports those who have virtues. So if you have good virtue you should not fear anything."[39] When the son had grown up he became a county officer. His mother was honored as the one who knew well the natural decree of morality.

Cultivating Rationality: An Aptitude for Argument

Women foster many special abilities. Knowing how to argue effectively and coherently in various circumstances, they artfully employ the rhetoric of persuasion. Their rhetorical abilities are commendable because they have been responsible for the rescue of many human lives. Here are some stories from the sixth chapter: Rhetorical Competence 辯通 (*biantong*).

Gonggong spent three years making a sword for the King.[40] But when the King first used it, the sword could not even go through a single layer of armor 甲 (*jia*). The King was very angry and wanted to kill the sword-maker, Gonggong. Gonggong's wife requested an audience with the King. She pleaded for her husband's life on three grounds. "First, let me recall a legal precedent: none of the past three Kings executed any people even when someone tried to steal their staffs. Each of your predecessors also tried to take good care of people who worked for them. Secondly, my husband has worked really hard to make this sword and fashioned it out of the very best materials. It would be irrational for you to kill my husband just because you can't go through one layer of *jia*.

Thirdly, there is a special way to use the sword."[41] Then she gave the King specific instructions on how to operate the sword. The King paid attention to her and tried again. The sword now went through seven layers of armor. The King discharges Gonggong and rewards his wife with a lot of gold. The wife of Gonggong is praised for coping with her husband's adversity and finding a rational way to save his life.

The other story tells how a daughter rescued her reckless father by means of her reasoning.[42] Duke Qi favored a special tree in the town, so he ordered people to watch over it and had them put up a sign: "The death penalty for anyone disfiguring or damaging this tree." However Yan, the father of Jing, got drunk and injured the tree. He was arrested. Jing is very much concerned about the life of her father, and she went to Duke Qi's house to talk with him. She explained that "My father thought a disharmony of *yin* and *yang* might be the reason why we don't have timely rain and healthy crops these days. So he was praying to heaven for grace and mercy. That is why he drank a little more than he should have. I have heard that past kings all were very kind to their people and did not hurt their people. Today you, the King, will kill my father for the sake of that tree. If you do so, for one thing, you will cause me to become a fatherless child, and people in other countries will talk about this. They will conclude that our King cares more about trees than he does for his people. I am afraid this will affect our legal system and the King's reputation for virtue."[43] The King reconsidered his verdict and realized that favoring certain material things and killing people to suit one's own pleasure are the chief signs of an evil leader. "This is a bad policy about the tree." The King removed the order posted at the tree and released all the offenders. The moral of the story is that the daughter is to be acclaimed for her life-saving rhetorical proficiency.

Many stories revere this kind of woman's special talent. One day a military general has to cross the river.[44] But the boatman was too drunk to do his job. The general is very angry and wants to kill this man. The boatman's daughter appeals to the general to excuse her father's behavior. "My father learned you wanted to cross the river, so he worshipped the god of the river to ensure a safe journey. It is part of worship to drink a little, but the little he drank made him drunk. I propose that you kill me for his fault. Besides, he is drunk and will not know why he is being punished. If he doesn't know why he is being executed, it would be like slaughtering an innocent person. If you really want to eradicate him, you should do so after he has awakened."[45] The general was deeply moved by these words and discharged the father immediately.

Each of these stories presents a celebration of women's capabilities. Women are prized for their talents and are seen acting consistently with both private love and public righteousness. The rationality of their life-saving petitions evidently proves that exemplary women upheld the standard of benevolence and righteousness that the people expected of their rulers. In each of these cases, they also cleverly expound the alleged faults of their husbands and fathers. When it was not possible to erase the offense, the women surrender their own lives as a substitute for their troubled father or husband. Such a dramatic exhibition of filial piety could not but soften the hearts of the offended rulers. As their hearts were inspired, so their minds could see more clearly a solution consistent with their own moral responsibilities as fair-minded rulers. The rhetorical skills established by these women would be the envy of any scholar appointed to make appeal in a court of law. Conventional morality and ritual propriety are preserved, and justice is served. How better to celebrate the role that extraordinary talent may play in authorizing meaningful life for women?

Part Three: Beauty 色 (*se*) as a Constructive Power of Womanhood

The vicissitudes of human desire in and for the female body have been a topic for extended discussion in many cultures. The *Lienüzhuan* makes its own unique contribution to such conversations. Many stories expand upon the point that, while feminine beauty 色 (*se*) can inspire affection from men, women need to have virtue to cement this affection (以色親之, 以德固之 *yise qinzhi, yide guzhi*). This raises certain philosophical issues with reference to the power of moral agency, or the basic and common capacity to act responsibly in fulfilling human desires. Agency, however, is yet another contested terrain in feminist theory, for as Susan Frank Parsons observes, "Modern understandings of agency have been troubled by the dilemma of difference that is gender."[46] This dilemma emerges from the inherited dualist structure that separates the human mind and body, and analogously, men and women. The power of agency, which ought to be common to all human beings, thus is prescribed within the limits of male patterns of thinking and acting on their moral responsibilities. By contrast, the *Lienüzhuan* narratives authorize a view of female moral agency, grounded in the typical character of exemplary women whose behaviors are governed by a rational mind.[47]

Beauty as the Manifestation of Inner Virtue

What makes a woman beautiful? The *Lienüzhuan* in various ways explores the linkage between internal dispositional beauty and external physical beauty. Its central affirmation of beauty as the manifestation of inner virtue is evident in the following pair of memorable stories about physically ugly women who were gifted with special intellectual qualities that eventually conquered the hearts of emperors. Both women ultimately became empresses, and as such were glorified for their inner beauty. Each of these fairy-tale-like narratives, predictably extreme in the situations and responses they depict, validate the inherent bond between beauty and virtue. Beauty is manifested and recognized in the strength of female dispositions, traits, and characters. Thus the power of agency is not only operative in the way women regard their own beauty or lack thereof, it is seen to be constitutive of beauty as such. Agency in a beautiful woman is the capacity for making an authoritative, and hence transformative, impact upon a situation. As the *Lienüzhuan* edifyingly promises, virtuous emperors will naturally honor such a standard of beauty.

Zhong Lichun is an ugly lady who has not yet been married off even at the age of 40.[48] One day she requests an audience with the King. Curious to know the reason why an ugly lady would dare to come to his court, the King agrees to meet her. "I have all the concubines I need. If you can't even be accepted by a common man, how dare you come to me? Do you have some special gift?" Zhong Lichun replies, "No, I don't have any special gifts. But I admire *ren* and *yi*, the virtues you profess." The King asks her what she likes to do for amusement. She admits that she is fond of "metaphors 隱 (*yin*) or riddles." She presents a few *yin* to the King, but he could not solve them even after consulting with the riddle books. The next day, the King summons her again and wants to learn more from her. Zhong warns the King that there are four dangers in the kingdom. "First, King, you are forty years old and haven't really educated your sons to prepare them for their future responsibilities. You spend all your time, instead, with women. Once you die, the country will fall into chaos. Secondly, you spend so much money and energy building luxurious palaces that the people have become very tired of serving you. Thirdly, you have forced all the wise people into exile and have surrounded yourself with malevolent people. Truthful information can't ever reach you. Fourthly, since you spend all your time at parties and banquets, you don't pay proper attention to domestic and foreign affairs."[49] The King reflects that what Zhong has said is correct, and so he amends his policies and practices in each of these four areas. The King also decides to stay close to this ugly lady by marrying her. The moral of this story specifies that physical looks are only skin deep and even a King, especially a wise King, should not be obsessed with them. He should learn to treasure woman's wisdom more than her physical looks.

Here is a second story. In a village there lived a mulberry picking girl who had such a large tumor on her neck that people called her "tumor girl" 瘤女.[50] One day, since the King was passing by the village all the people went out to watch his procession, all except the tumor girl. The King was surprised and requested to meet her. The King said to her, "I come by and all the people have stopped working in order to see me. Why don't you do so as well?" The tumor girl explains, "I am following my parents' instruction to work in the field; I have not been instructed to come to see you." The King declared that this is an unusual girl, but thought it a pity she had a tumor. The tumor girl speaks out, "As a girl I always set my heart to everything I do, and the tumor doesn't bother me at all." The King realizes that she is a superior girl and decides on the spot to marry her and bring her to his palace. But the tumor girl objects, "I have to follow my parents' instructions and can't run away with you. We must follow the proper ritual for doing this." The King acknowledges his fault and agrees to abide by the proper ritual propriety. He sends someone with a lot of gold to arrange a formal offer of marriage. When the tumor girl's parents learn that their daughter is going to the palace, they beg her to put on make-up and decorate herself. But the tumor girl refuses to do so. She reasons, "If I dress up the King will not be aware of my own true self." So she leaves for the palace dressed as she usually is for daily work. When she arrives at the palace all the well-dressed concubines laugh at her. The King is embarrassed and tells them not to laugh. "There is a very big difference between wearing make-up and not wearing make-up. She is just not made-up yet." But the tumor girl retorts, "There may be a big difference between being made-up and not. But all the sage Kings used only *ren* and *yi* to decorate themselves, and they lived very simple lives. Their countries flourished, and people respected them. Other Kings didn't use *ren* and *yi* to decorate themselves, but made themselves up with fancy clothing and jewels. Their countries were defeated and even today people revile their misbehavior."[51] The King and the concubines all felt ashamed, and since then they pay more attention to living simply. The King also named the tumor girl as his empress.

The Correlation Between Beauty (se) and Virtue (de)

The last chapter of the *Lienüzhuan* offers fifteen stories of vicious women. Many of these are about the ways that women's beauty, detached from virtue, causes men to indulge themselves in sensual pleasures, thus losing proper focus in their own lives. Such women have vicious characters, ill motivations, and self-serving agendas that lead to turmoil in families and the breakdown of the state. Beauty per se is not a vice, but its positive correlation with virtue depends on who has it and how she would exploit it. Thus the stories proclaim that as a natural endowment beauty is a two-edged sword. It can empower women or it can annihilate them, and the people with whom they are related. It all depends on the possessor's virtues. This brings to mind why throughout Chinese history female virtue is put on a pedestal to be admired, championed, and lived by consistently. The disastrous consequences of departing from female virtues are thus dramatized in the stories from the seventh and final chapter of the *Lienüzhuan*, The Vicious and Depraved (*niebi*). Thus the proper Way for women is transmitted through concrete examples of how and how not to act in their roles and relationships as daughters, wives, and mothers.

Conclusion

No exploration of the concept of authority would be complete without a consideration of how certain texts acknowledged as authoritative actually succeed in shaping people's lives in a particular cultural setting. The *Lienüzhuan* has communicated an ideal of full-fledged womanhood to generations of Chinese women and assisted them conceptually and practically in authoring their own lives. This is the sense in which women's lives become authoritative, as they grow to be the authors of their own life journey. They are indeed subjects in their own rights, and thus moral agents in the fullest sense. The stories considered here also protest that the ideal of authenticity should avoid the pitfalls of fragmentation and abstract individualism and, instead, be situated in a social context that grant the significance of human roles and relationships. These narratives reveal that Chinese women, even in ancient times, were encouraged to cultivate the fullness of their own humanity.

In many ways, Western philosophical traditions have affirmed man as the center of a woman's life, on the assumption that "biology is the destiny." Good womanhood will be understood and embraced only in the context of connections with men. This can be observed either in Aristotle's assertion of woman's nature as "misbegotten or imperfect man"; or Aquinas's conviction that women were created only to be helpmates for men; or in Rousseau's suggestion that the glory of a woman consists in mastering the art of pleasing men. Liu Xiang's stories, however, accentuate other possibilities for construing the relationships between women and men. The exemplary women that he celebrates shine by their own merits and not necessarily by subordinating themselves to men's all-too-often-mistaken guidelines. These stories open up a space where women can expand and sustain their own individuality. In this regard, the virtues exercised are not simply exclusive to the female, as if she were capable of excellence only in "gendered virtues," but rather she excels in all human virtues, as cherished and honored in the Confucian tradition. Liu Xiang challenges us to reaffirm the indivisible unity of virtue, in theory, which should lead us in practice to promote the cultivation of virtue by humanity as a whole, unfettered by the limitations of gender biases. His project may steer us to rediscover the vision of John Stuart Mill, who claims the greater good can be achieved by giving women's nature a "free play."[52]

It is indisputable that Confucians declare there is a primordial difference 別 (*bie*) between men and women. However this difference need not be taken as a justification for the subordination of women. The goodness of the human being is grounded in qualities that express themselves in distinctive forms that men's and women's reasoning and actions may take. Men and women may manifest different qualities under various conditions. What is good is not found therefore in some abstract generalization about human beings, but in a careful and detailed consideration of the differences emanating from men's and women's common aspirations toward becoming fully human. The *Lienüzhuan* underlines a sound and persuasive case that becoming a woman fulfills the Confucian standard of becoming a human. There is no separation between these two achievements. This insight could be valuable for contemporary feminist theory in its effort toward a philosophical reconstruction of womanhood. It also may be of significance in contemporary debates over gender equality, personal identities, and a host of other issues involing the comparative study of moral philosophy today.

Notes

1. Documenting historically the process by which the stories of *lienu* become an identifiable "*lienu* tradition" is beyond the scope of this essay. Nevertheless, the following points should briefly be noted: the process involves both the formation of a specific narrative genre, namely, *lienu* stories, and patterns of cultural transmission by which the stories were written down by an author, with his own intent in doing so, and read by people, who had their own reasons for doing so. If one is to argue that these acts of writing and reading gradually fashioned a tradition that had significant impact on the moral education of men and particularly women in premodern China, one must also assume that the stories once read and learned were also spread through oral transmission, since women were normally illiterate and only exceptionally able to read and write. The impact that

these stories had on the ongoing social construction of female identity and gender roles in no way depends on whether the stories themselves represent fact or fiction, or whether women in sufficient numbers could read them on their own. In either case, as this philosophical analysis is meant to show, the stories constitute a significant plausibility structure by which an ideal of womanhood resonant with the basic Confucian ideal of being human (*ren*) was transmitted to generations of Chinese men and women. The fact that for the most part the scholars who sustained this tradition were males is hardly surprising. What is surprising is the extent to which the actual content of that tradition seems to celebrate an integrated set of moral, spiritual, and aesthetic ideals for women that transcend the logic of patriarchal domination. Opening a philosophical discussion of those ideals is the point of this paper.

2. In what follows, the term "virtue" will be used to describe the cultivated dispositions that are celebrated in the *lienu* tradition. Despite the fears of some scholars that "virtue" may be hopelessly tied to Victorian prudery and a generally repressive notion of women's moral education, the term still seems preferable, since "virtue" is the common translation of the Chinese term "*de*" (德). Moreover, in recent decades the field of moral philosophy has witnessed the recovery of classical Western perspectives on virtue and their positive reassessment in the discourses of contemporary "virtue theory." In that context, the Victorian legacy has proven to be no more contributory toward confusion than it should prove to be in this case.

3. Nancy Holmstrom, "Do Women have a Distinct Nature"? in *Women and Values: Readings in Recent Feminist Philosophy*, edited by Marilyn Pearsall, (Belmont, CA: Wadsworth Publishing Company, 1999), p. 55.

4. "The Classic of Changes," in *Images of Women in Chinese Thought and Culture: Writings from Pre-Qing to Song Dynasty*, edited by Robin R. Wang, (Indianapolis: Hackett, 2003), p. 41. It is important to recall the significance of the *Yijing*'s placing the "*nei/wai*" distinction in the context of *yinyang* cosmological correlations. This context emphasizes the fact that these ostensibly physical spaces are in fact interrelated spheres of relationship whose meaning for men and women will vary according to context. One such context is developmental, insofar as before the onset of puberty boys are free to roam the *nei* and girls are free to roam the *wai*. Another is the fact that in Confucian thinking the relationship between a ruler and his subjects was thought to be within the sphere of *nei*, insofar as a ruler must relate to his subjects as a parent relates to his or her child. Though there are well-defined boundaries to be observed in negotiating the passage from the one sphere to the other, these boundaries must be understood contextually. I am grateful to Peter Hershock for his insightful comments on this point at the online discussion.

5. Liu Xiang: *Biographies of Women* 列女傳 (*Lienüzhuan*), Commentary by Zhang Tao (Jinan, China: Shantong University Press, 1990), 鄒孟軻母, pp. 38–43. All of the selections from *Lienuzhuan* are my own translations.

6. Liu Xiang: *Biographies of Women* 列女傳 (*Lienüzhuan*), pp. 52–54.

7. Ibid., p. 52.

8. Ibid.

9. Liu Xiang: *Biographies of Women* 列女傳 (*Lienüzhuan*), pp. 86–88.

10. Ibid., p. 86.

11. Ibid., p. 87.

12. Mary Wollstonecraft: *A Vindication of the Rights of Woman*, in *Philosophy of Woman: An Anthology of Classic to Current Concepts*, edited by Mary B. Mahowald (Indianapolis: Hackett Publishing Company, 1994), p. 119.

13. Susan Frank Parsons, *The Ethics of Gender*, (Boston, Mass.: Blackwell, 2002), p. 154.

14. Liu Xiang: *Biographies of Women* 列女傳 (*Lienüzhuan*), pp. 200–202.

15. Ibid., p. 200.

16. Ibid.

17. *Confucius, The Analects*, translated by D. C. Lau (New York: Penguin Books, 1979, Book 15, 9), p. 133.

18. Liu Xiang: *Biographies of Women* 列女傳 (*Lienüzhuan*), pp. 195–198.

19. Ibid.

20. John Rawls: *A Theory of Justice* (Cambridge, Mass: Harvard University Press, 1971), chapter 67, reprinted in the *Dignity, Character and Self-respect*, edited by Robin S. Dillon (New York: Rutledge, 1995), p. 125.

21. Ibid.

22. Ibid.

23. Rawls' discussion of "self-respect" is embedded in the Kantian moral philosophy as a whole. The invocation of Rawls in this context is meant to emphasize the area of agreement, however narrow, that he shares with Liu Xiang, namely, that the self-respect is a reflection of value-systems, which is emergent from a cultural tradition. Thus there is no contradiction involved in observing the importance of the value of self-respect in the lives of the women portrayed in the *Lienuzhuan*, while also noting the distinct absence of Rawlsian or Kantian presuppositions regarding the notion of self-respect. Needless to say, it is possible to cherish self-respect within a value-system that can be characterized as a "shame-culture."

24. Liu Xiang: *Biographies of Women* 列女傳 (*Lienüzhuan*), pp. 178–180.

25. Ibid., p. 179.

26. Ibid.

27. Liu Xiang: *Biographies of Women* 列女傳 (*Lienüzhuan*), pp. 183–186.

28. Ibid., p. 184.

29. Robin S. Dillon, *Dignity, Character and Self-respect* (New York: Routledge, 1995), p. 300.

30. Ibid., p. 302.

31. Immanuel Kant, "Of the Distinction of the Beautiful and Sublime in the Interrelations of the Two Sexes" in *Philosophy of Woman: An Anthology of Classic to Current Concepts*, edited by Mary B. Mahowald (Indianapolis: Hackett Publishing Company, 1994), p. 105.

32. Ibid.

33. Jean-Jacques Rousseau, "Sophie, The Outcome of the Right Education" in *Philosophy of Woman: An Anthology of Classic to Current Concepts*, p. 99.

34. Liu Xiang: *Biographies of Women* 列女傳 (*Lienüzhuan*), pp. 72–74.

35. Ibid., p. 73.

36. Liu Xiang: *Biographies of Women* 列女傳 (*Lienüzhuan*), pp. 94–95.

37. Ibid., p. 96.

38. Ibid, pp. 98–100.

39. Ibid.

40. Liu Xiang: *Biographies of Women* 列女傳 (*Lienüzhuan*), Commentary by Zhang Tao (Jinan: Shantong University Press, 1990), 晉弓工妻, pp. 209–211.

41. Ibid.

42. Liu Xiang: *Biographies of Women* 列女傳 (*Lienüzhuan*), pp. 212–214.

43. Ibid.

44. Ibid., pp. 220–224.

45. Ibid., p. 221.

46. Susan Frank Parsons, *The Ethics of Gender*, (Boston, Mass.: Blackwell, 2002), p. 99.

47. One way to think about the contrast between the view of female moral agency operative in the *Lienüzhuan* and typically Western philosophical views of the same, is to consider their relational and developmental aspects highlighted in these stories. Agency is consistently correlated with moral maturity, one indication of which is the "wisdom" that comes with aging. Learning wisdom in this context means achieving a degree of relational sensitivity that enhances one's

capacity for creative response to the challenges of real living. Female moral agency, in a Chinese setting, may differ from that expected of males, but the difference does not constitute an essential difference. In cultivating their distinctive virtues, both men and women are seeking wisdom, that is, the enhancement of relational sensitivities that allow them to act in ways that are fully human. Respect for one's elders, especially elderly women, is but one sign of the depth and pervasiveness of this expectation regarding female moral agency. In this context, moral agency carries little of the usual Western assumptions regarding autonomy and self-realization. Once again, I am grateful to Peter Hershock for helping me to clarify what I was trying to convey on this point in the online version of this paper.

48. Liu Xiang: *Biographies of Women* 列女傳 (*Lienüzhuan*), pp. 231–235.

49. Ibid., p. 233.

50. Liu Xiang: *Biographies of Women* 列女傳 (*Lienüzhuan*), pp. 235–239.

51. Ibid.

52. John Stuart Mill, "The Subjection of Women" in *Philosophy of Woman: An Anthology of Classic to Current Concepts*, p. 156.

Aspects of Authority in Wu Cheng'en's *Journey to the West*

Roberta E. Adams

The Chinese folk novel, *Journey to the West (Xiyou Ji)*, attributed to Wu Cheng'en (c.1500–c.1582), was popularized in English through Arthur Waley's abridged translation, *Monkey*, first published in 1943.[1] Waley presents the greater part of thirty chapters of the 100-chapter sixteenth-century novel, omitting most of the poetry as well as the couplets that introduce and often end each chapter. While Waley's accessible version may remain the standard for undergraduate world literature classes, only by reading the full text (four volumes, 2,000+ pages) can we appreciate the complexity and depth of this classic, and the complex appeal of Monkey's character. The novel is a tale of adventure with both worldly and other-worldly elements, full of humor, irony, and satire, but it also has serious underlying meaning. The journey is both temporal and spiritual; the pilgrims form an interrelated community and are yet individuals. While the religious pilgrimage is Buddhist, the novel is infused with Daoism and Confucianism, and a major theme is self-cultivation (*xiu dao*) and integration of the self. In examining the portrayals of authority and challenges to authority in the text, this paper will focus on the interrelationships of the pilgrims, particularly of the two primary characters, Xuanzang and Monkey, whose Master/disciple relationship is central to completion of both the temporal journey and the journey toward enlightenment. Authority is vested in personages (mortal and immortal), laws (worldly and heavenly), things (weapons, magic treasures), and ideas and texts, particularly the Heart Sutra and the Buddhist scriptures. I will examine how various kinds of authority are displayed and challenged, and how, in the ultimate conclusion of the journey, authority is completely dissolved.

Critical commentary on *Journey to the West* has swung from early scholars seeing it as profound allegory or as "a manual for Buddhist, Daoist, or Confucian self-cultivation,"[2] to a reaction in the early 1900s when most critics regarded the text as mere satire or entertainment, to the Communist interpretations that saw Monkey as a rebel against bureaucracy and the monsters as "enemies of the people,"[3] to the more recent return to studies of the religious and allegorical import of the text.[4] Many commentators have seen the novel as incorporating the three major philosophies of China. In his eighteenth-century commentary, "The Original Intent of the *Hsi-yu chi* [*Xiyou yuan-ji du fa*]," Liu I-ming gives an essentially Taoist interpretation of the text, but maintains, "*The Journey to the West* is a book that is permeated through and through with the truth of the unity of the Three Teachings [Buddhism, Daoism, and Confucianism].[5] Recent studies by Andrew Plaks site the novel within China's sixteenth-century intellectual thought, "especially its central focus on what is commonly called the 'philosophy of mind' [*xin xue*]."[6] Plaks, who sees a "Neo-Confucian dimension of meaning" in several sixteenth-century novels, examines certain terms and ideas as compatible among the three schools. "We can speak of the 'convergence of the three teachings' as something more integral than any particular movement of contrived syncretism."[7] Plaks's analyses include a focus on underlying Buddhist and Daoist ideas in the novel, while "restor[ing] the centrality of bedrock Confucian concepts within the constellation of ideas at the heart of late Ming literati culture."[8] Francisca Cho Bantly counters with a wholly Buddhist interpretation.[9]

The underlying factual basis for *Journey to the West* is the sixteen-year journey (629–645 CE) of the Tang Dynasty Buddhist monk Xuanzang to India to bring the Buddhist Sutras back to China. In her study of his trip, Sally Hovey Wriggins notes that he returned with 150 pellets of the Buddha's flesh, seven statues of the Buddha, and 657 books, to which he dedicated the rest of his life to translating into Chinese.[10] On his return, the Emperor Taizong, who recognized the political importance of the journey, asked him to become his adviser on Asian relations. Declining that, Xuanzang did agree to write a book about the regions he passed through, *Record of the Western Regions*, completed in 646 CE.[11] Wriggins notes that Xuanzang would have been gratified by his legacy of the promulgation of Buddhism in China, but probably surprised by the range of his influence—on archaeologists, art historians, and historians—and his transformation into a popular religious folk figure and a character in "an epic Chinese novel."[12]

Xuanzang became famous within his own lifetime, and these transformations from history to legend and myth probably began quite early. As oral stories, folk drama, and written texts[13] were developed and spread, Xuanzang's character changed dramatically, and he acquired a set of Immortal disciples to assist him in his quest. Wu Cheng'en imaginatively used and elaborated the earlier materials in his 100-chapter tale of the adventures of Xuanzang (courtesy name Sanzang or Tripitaka), who with the help of his disciples Monkey, Pig, and Friar Sand, and his dragon-turned-horse, vanquish demons and monsters and overcome innumerable dangers before arriving in the Western Heaven to meet with Buddha, acquire the scriptures, deliver them to the Emperor Taizong, and return to the Western Heaven for their immortal rewards. In the afterward to his translation, W. J. F. Jenner notes that the structure of the novel is "like a pair of book ends," with the journey itself, Chapters 13–97, "a number of booklets,"[14] falling between the first twelve chapters—which describe the history of Monkey, of the Emperor Taizong, and the Buddha's directive to Guanyin to find a pilgrim to undertake the journey—and the last three chapters, which present the culminating events.[15]

Wu Cheng'en creates an important innovation from earlier versions of the story by moving the introduction of Monkey to the beginning.[16] To see the appropriateness of his role as Sanzang's disciple, we must first become acquainted with this "splendid" Monkey's history, actions, and character. The story begins at the beginning:

> Before Chaos was divided, Heaven and Earth were one;
> All was a shapeless blur, and no men had appeared.
> Once Pan Gu destroyed the Enormous Vagueness
> The separation of clear and impure began.
> Living things have always tended towards humanity;
> From their creation all beings improve.
> If you want to know about Creation and Time,
> *Read* Difficulties Resolved on the Journey to the West. (1:1)[17]

After a brief description of creation, the five elements, yin/yang, and the formation of the three powers of Heaven, Earth, and Man, the text quickly moves to the Mountain of Flowers and Fruit in the Eastern Continent, to tell of Monkey's birth from a magic stone (1:2–3).

Both the introductory poem and the description of the birth of Monkey not from parents, but from Heaven and Earth, place the entire work within a mythological and supernatural framework. Monkey is a figure outside the realms of authority, heavenly or earthly. One of Monkey's key features is his far-seeing eyes. He bows to the four quarters and, "As his eyes moved, two beams of golden light shot towards the Pole Star palace and startled the Supreme Heavenly Sage, the Greatly Compassionate Jade Emperor of the Azure Vault of Heaven, who was sitting surrounded by his immortal ministers on his throne in the Hall of

Miraculous Mist in the Golden-gated Cloud Palace" (1:5). When his investigating officers report that a magic egg had turned into a stone monkey whose eyes shot the golden light, the Jade Emperor, "in his benevolence and mercy," dismisses the event: "Creatures down below are born of the essence of heaven and earth: there is nothing remarkable about him" (1:5). But, indeed, Monkey *is* remarkable, and the failure of the Jade Emperor to realize this sets up the possibilities for some of the havoc that Monkey later creates in Heaven.

The Jade Emperor is the first figure of authority we encounter in the text, and the elaborate description of him sitting on his throne surrounded by his ministers mirrors the descriptions of many of the worldly rulers that Xuanzang and his disciples encounter on their journey west. The Jade Emperor in his heavenly authority, and the hierarchies of heaven, parallel the secular authority of the Emperor Taizong and the hierarchies of other secular authorities on earth. Throughout the trip, Monkey challenges the power of all such authorities and hierarchies.

After his birth, Monkey lives in idyllic harmony with the creatures of the Mountain of Flowers and Fruit. Because he is able to jump through a waterfall (go beyond the curtain), he becomes the Handsome Monkey King in the Cave Heaven of the Water Curtain until, after three or four hundred years, he recognizes his mortality (impermanence, *wu chang*[18]) and goes off in search of "the Buddhas, the Immortals and the Sages" so that he can "learn to be free from the Wheel of Reincarnation" (1:14). He learns human speech and manners, and finally finding the Buddhist Patriarch Subhuti, Monkey spends about ten years learning the Way (Dao), seventy-two earthly transformations, and cloud-soaring. The couplet that introduces this chapter reads, "He Becomes Aware of the Wonderful Truth of Enlightenment / By Killing the Demon [Mara] He Realizes His Spirit-Nature" (1:27). Subhuti gives Monkey the name-in-religion of Sun Wukong, Monkey Awakened to Emptiness (1:25–26).

The Immortal Patriarch Subhuti, one of the many earthly and heavenly immortals that people the story, presents a different kind of authority in the text. The respect and gratitude that Monkey shows his teacher, and his delight in learning, are Confucian in character and presage the dedication he later gives to Master Sanzang. But Monkey has not learned self-restraint. After he shows off his transformation abilities to the other students, Subhuti dismisses him, instructing him never to tell anyone who his teacher was (1:41). Returning to find his kingdom terrorized by an evil demon, Monkey puts things to rights, kills the demon, and trains his people in the art of warfare. Lacking a weapon suitable to his powers and symbolic of his authority, Monkey obtains from Ao Guang, Dragon of the Eastern Sea, an iron cudgel, the pillar that had anchored the Milky

Way in place. This As-You-Will Gold-Banded Cudgel weighing 13,500 pounds can change its size at Monkey's bidding; he normally carries it in his ear in the form of an embroidery needle. Through his persistence and coercion, he also obtains from the Dragon's three brothers a pair of lotus-root cloud walking shoes, a phoenix-winged purple gold helmet, and a suit of golden chain mail. When he returns home thus garbed and armed, the monkeys fall to their knees; he radiates authority, combining the inner knowledge gained from Subhuti with the external trappings of power (1:55–59).

However, in obtaining these symbolic and powerful accessories, Monkey antagonized the dragons, and they determine to submit a protest to Heaven. The Dragons' written petition against Monkey arrives before the Jade Emperor about the same time as one from the Bodhisattva Ksitigarbha of the Underworld. In a dream, Monkey's soul had been fetched to the underworld, where he protests, "I have gone beyond the Three Worlds, and I am no longer subject to the Five Elements. I don't come under King Yama's jurisdiction. How dare you grab me, you idiots?" (1:63). Smashing the two fetchers to a pulp, he tells the ten kings who he is. When they find his name on the Register of Life and Death, he demands a brush, crosses out all the names in the monkey section, throws the register on the floor and proclaims, "That's an end of it. We won't come under your control any longer" (1:65). Monkey rejects the authority of the Underworld Kingdom and of death. The next morning, he celebrates this with his followers; what occurs in the dream is reality. He has defied and altered the authority vested in the written Register.

Monkey's dealings with Heaven begin with the responses to these complaints against him. The basic nature of the dynamics is that Monkey feels his great talents are not appreciated in Heaven, whereas the Jade Emperor and others find his mischief-making and arrogance unpardonable, because they flout the authority of Heaven. In response to the complaints, the Great White Planet (Venus) suggests inviting Monkey to Heaven, where they can keep an eye on him, rather than hauling out the military might (1:69); they practice deception on the perceptive Monkey and it works. Monkey enjoys the only position open, Protector of the Horses, until he learns that he's essentially a stable boy, at which point he leaves in a huff (1:77–78). Once home, he takes the title "Great Sage Equalling Heaven" (1:79). When Heavenly King Li Jing and Prince Nezha arrive to reprimand him, he says,

> "Hurry back to Heaven and tell that Jade Emperor that he doesn't know how to use a good man. Why did he make me waste my infinite powers on feeding his horses for him? Take a

look at what's written on my standard. If he's willing to give me
this title officially, I'll call off my troops and let Heaven and
Earth continue in peace; but if he refuses I'm coming up to the
Hall of Miraculous Mist to knock him off his dragon throne"
(1:82–83).

Monkey's comment makes one think of how often in Chinese history
the literati were unappreciated and overlooked for official positions,
Confucius among them. Li and Nezha refuse Monkey's challenge and,
in the ensuing battle, the Heavenly forces find themselves no match for
Monkey. Once again the Great White Planet saves the day; since Monkey
"has no idea about real power," why not give him this empty, meaningless
title and invite him back to Heaven (1:89)? With no position, he wastes
his and others' time until, to end his idleness, he is given the job of overseeing the Peach Orchard. Unable to resist, he eats the Peaches of
Immortality, and enraged that he is not to be invited to the Queen
Mother's Peach Banquet (once again, his merits and authority are unrec-
ognized), he goes to the banquet hall, eats up the delicacies, gets drunk,
then wanders into Lao Zi's Tushita Palace and eats up all of the precious
golden elixir pills of immortality. Sobering up, he realizes what he has
done and returns to the Mountain of Flowers and Fruit, quickly running
back once to steal some jade liquor for his followers to enjoy
(1:94–108).
　　This time, all of Heaven is upset at how Monkey has flouted the
laws, but the forces sent down to subdue him are still no match for him.
King Li's second son, Moksa, returns in defeat, gasping, "What a Great
Sage! What a Great Sage! His magic powers are too much for me. He
beat me" (1:124). The Bodhisattva Guanyin, who hereafter plays a central
role in the novel, suggests they send to Guanzhou for the Jade Emperor's
nephew, the Illustrious Sage and True Lord Erlang: "He will agree to be
sent though he would not obey a summons to come here, so Your Majesty
might like to issue a decree ordering him to take his troops to the rescue"
(1:125). After many wonderful battles that include both Monkey and
Erlang transforming into various birds, and Monkey transforming himself
to look like Erlang, Monkey is finally caught, with the help of Lao Zi's
magic bracelet (Diamond Noose), and returned to Heaven (1:127–38).
Unable to kill him by strokes or burning (the fire of samadhi merely
tempers him), they cast him into Lao Zi's elixir-making Eight Trigrams
Furnace, expecting that after forty-nine days, he will be turned to ashes.
But Sun Wukong squeezes into the palace of the trigram Sun (Wind),
bothered only by the smoke in his eyes (1:141–42). When the furnace is
opened, he bursts out, "like a white-browed tiger gone berserk, a single-

horned dragon raving mad" (1:142), once more creating total chaos in Heaven.

Finally the Buddha is asked to subdue him, which he does with a trick, by appealing to Monkey's self-confidence in his own powers. This self-confidence is one aspect of Monkey's authority that makes him the ideal candidate later to accompany Xuanzang to the West, but his crime here is in using his powers only for his own self-aggrandizement. Monkey tells the Buddha he will accept nothing less than the Jade Emperor abdicating his throne in his favor, so Buddha presents him with a wager:

> "If you're clever enough to get out of my right hand with a single somersault, you will be the winner. . . . But if you can't get out of the palm of my hand you will have to go down to the world below as a devil and train yourself for several more kalpas before coming to argue about it again."

Monkey thinks the Buddha "is a complete idiot. I can cover thirty-six thousand miles with a somersault, so how could I fail to jump out of the palm of his hand, which is less than a foot across?" (1:150). Of course, the Buddha is able to make his hand as big as he chooses to; Monkey jumps, sees some flesh-pink pillars at the end of his jump, marks the spot by urinating against one of the pillars and by writing "THE GREAT SAGE EQUALLING HEAVEN WAS HERE," only to find that the pillars are the Buddha's fingers. The Buddha turns his hand over, turns his fingers into the Five Elements Mountain, and imprisons Monkey under the mountain (1:151–58). All praise the Buddha:

> "An egg learnt to be a man,
> Cultivated his conduct, and achieved the Way.
> Heaven had been undisturbed for the thousand kalpas,
> Until one day the spirits and gods were scattered.
> The rebel against Heaven, wanting high position,
> Insulted Immortals, stole the pills, and destroyed morality.
> Today his terrible sins are being punished,
> Who knows when he will be able to rise again?" (1:152)

Heaven interprets Monkey's wish to take the Jade Emperor's place as a desire for high position; Monkey feels the emperor is inadequate and sees it as talent rising to the top. Two points need to be made about this subduing of Monkey. First, the only warrior able to match Monkey's fighting abilities and strategies, Lord Erlang, does not reside in Heaven and would refuse a summons from the Jade Emperor, though he will agree to a request. Like Monkey, he stands up to the authority of Heaven, but unlike Monkey, he is still part of that community and willing to assist them. While the Jade Emperor is symbolic of the ultimate power of Heaven, his power often seems despotic; authority also rests in the community. Secondly, while Lao Zi is able to contribute a powerful magic weapon to entrap Monkey after Lord Erlang has exhausted him, only Buddha can match wits with him and come out the winner, because Buddha's power is based not on symbols and hierarchies, but on his innate essence. Plaks notes,

> This hubristic challenge to the authority of heaven proves quite unstoppable to all who try to combat the monster of ego on its own terms. It is only after demonstrating the actual smallness of the monkey's bloated self in the shadow of the Buddha's fingers. . . . that the overblown mind-monkey is reduced to finite proportions.[19]

Monkey's physical subjection here prefigures "his ultimate submission to the all-encompassing power of the Buddha nature."[20] At this point, the story of Monkey told in the first seven chapters of *Journey to the West* comes round full circle; he begins as a stone egg in a stone mountain and ends up entrapped under a mountain. Monkey will remain there for five hundred years, until Guanyin visits to tell him that he will be let out by the pilgrim to the West: "You can be his disciple, observe and uphold the faith, enter our Buddha's religion, and cultivate good retribution for yourself in the future" (1:181). Monkey gratefully agrees, becoming a Buddhist on the spot.

In the world of the novel, characters obtain power, and hence one kind of authority, through knowledge, action, and the possession of weapons and magical devices. Monkey gained the powerful knowledge of how to transform himself into other creatures and likenesses and how to travel immense distances through cloud-soaring; he also obtained a powerful magical weapon. While these alone would make him a formidable enemy—or friend—it is Monkey's character and actions that get him in and out of trouble and often determine the course of events, both in his dealings with Heaven, and as a disciple to Sanzang on the journey to the West. Monkey is penetrating in mind and vision, wily, confident to the point of arrogance, courageous, rebellious, obstinate, energetic, quick-tempered, and quick to be offended. He is the human mind/heart.[21] He is also whimsical, childlike, creative, resourceful, and once converted and committed to Xuanzang, he is loyal to his Master and persistent and enduring in the quest. C. T. Hsia describes him as the hero of the work, his character defined "in terms of his spiritual detachment, his prankish humor, his restless energy, and his passionate devotion to his master."[22] Anthony Yu points out that, "to bridle the Monkey of the Mind and Horse of the Will [is] a theme central to the entire narrative."[23] Victor Mair calls these "symbols of restless human intelligence and impetuous self-assertiveness."[24]

The disciples Pig and Friar Sand and the dragon who transforms into Xuanzang's horse (which he had eaten), like Monkey, are Immortals who had offended in some way against Heaven (seemingly minor offenses) and had been banished to punishments on earth. Both Yu and Plaks explore the process of Daoist internal alchemy[25] used by all three disciples, who are so powerful because they have "penetrated the secret mysteries of longevity."[26] Pig and Friar Sand also possess magic weapons, a nine-pronged rake and a demon-quelling staff respectively. Guanyin tells each of them that, in order to gain freedom and retribution, they should reform, wait for the pilgrim, and assist him on his journey to seek the Buddhist scriptures. She gives Friar Sand the religious name of Sha Wujing, Sand Awakened to Purity, and Pig the name of Zhu Wuneng, Pig Awakened to Power (1:171–79), thus complementing Sun Wukong, Monkey Awakened to Emptiness. If Monkey is the mind, Pig is the senses; in spite of their brotherhood, their rivalry during the quest provides much of the humor. As Waley puts it, Pig "symbolizes the physical appetites, brute strength, and a kind of cumbrous patience."[27] Self-centered and always acting on his own desires, Pig frequently ignores Sanzang's authority and Monkey's superior vision, ready to desert the mission when things look bad. Friar Sand, on the other hand, is gentle and obedient, blindly following authority without reflection.[28] Thus, each of the various disciples submit to the authority of the Master in different degrees and kinds.

Wu Cheng'en also uses Five Elements correspondences to characterize both the pilgrims and the demons they encounter. Monkey is associated with metal, Pig with wood, Friar Sand with earth, and the dragon horse with water. Plaks notes that Monkey's "steely gaze" and "the iron hardness of his head, or perhaps his mercurial temperament, do in a sense accord with a metallic nature, while [Pig's] ponderous strength, insatiable appetites, and general superabundance of life-force seem to betoken the generative aspects of wood." Friar Sand's identification with earth reflects "his essentially inert reaction with the other members of the party."[29] But while Plaks finds it difficult to give an elemental label to Sanzang, he notes the connection of fire with the heart, so that Sanzang's constant recitation of the Heart Sutra is one basis for his connection with fire. Interaction of the five elements frequently underlies episodes on the journey; they "can be both components of harmonious integration and forces of mutual destruction."[30] These correspondences of the five pilgrims to the five elements underscore their interrelationships and their ultimate harmony; integration of the self thus connects with the interaction and integration of the elemental forces of Nature.

In addition to providing Sanzang with four immortal disciples, Guanyin assigns him a group of hidden celestial protectors, "the Six Dings, the Six Jias, the Revealers of the Truth of the Five Regions, the Four Duty Gods, and the Eighteen Protectors of the Faith; we shall take it in turns to be in attendance every day. . . . [T]he Gold-headed Revealer will always be with you by day and by night" (1:347). Within the framework of the text, these protectors indicate that for the person seeking enlightenment, celestial help is never far away. However, Monkey and the other pilgrims often call on them only as a last resort—sometimes, almost too late—in part because they take their charge to protect the Master so seriously, and in part because of their confidence—especially Monkey's—that they can overcome any obstacle.

In the transformation of history to legend, the intrepid, diplomatic, historical Xuanzang is hardly recognizable in the literary character, who, as Hsia notes, "often appears as a deliberate caricature of a saintly monk."[31] Chapter 9 of the novel, considered spurious by some,[32] provides the rather fabulous biography of the monk, who, like Moses, is put out on the river by his mother (because his father had been killed by bandits), is retrieved and trained by Buddhist monks, grows up to find his mother, avenge his father (who had been kept by the river dragon king and is brought back to life), and find his grandmother and restore her sight (1:183–206). Xuanzang is the reincarnation of the second disciple of Buddha, The Golden Cicada, who had been cultivating his nature through ten reincarnations, but who, by virtue of letting his mind wander (stray from the proper path) during Buddha's preaching, thus slighting the Dharma (Law), was "transferred to the mortal world to suffer torment" (1:273). The Emperor Taizong is also given a fabulous past, when he dies a premature death for failing to fulfill his promise to spare the life of a dragon, pleads his case in the underworld, is granted twenty more years of life, and returns to build a temple and shrine in honor of the couple whose stored up wealth (good deeds) in the underworld he had borrowed during his ordeal there (Chapters 10 and 11). At this point, the two human stories come together, as Xuanzang travels to Chang'an for the opening celebrations and Great Mass at the Great Xiang Guo Monastery, is selected to be Master of Ceremonies, and captures the eye of Guanyin as a possible pilgrim candidate (1:270–74; 289–90).

Anthony Yu cites a Chinese committee on literature that finds the distinguishing feature of this work that "it is a novel of the supramundane."[33] Creating supramundane biographies for the important human characters in the work is in harmony with the mythic framework of the novel. Distinguishing the human characters with these fabulous backgrounds also adds to their authority, both within the context of the story, and with the audience of the text. That the lengthy and laborious journey to fetch the scriptures is fraught with dangers is at one level preordained; Xuanzang is meant to suffer, as Bantly notes in her examination of karma in the framework of the novel.[34] At almost every stage of the journey, once the entire pilgrim band is assembled, Xuanzang and Monkey announce who they are and the reason for their journey; their fame, the authority of their undertaking, spreads and precedes them, usually to their peril.

The Tathagata Buddha sends Guanyin to find a pilgrim to carry his scriptures back to China because the Chinese "are greedy and lecherous and delight in the sufferings of others; they go in for a great deal of killing and quarrelling. That continent can with truth be called a vicious field of tongues and mouths, an evil sea of disputation. I now have Three Stores of True Scriptures with which they can be persuaded to be good" (1:165). When Xuanzang preaches during the festival, Guanyin challenges him, explaining to Tang Taizong, "That master of yours was only teaching the doctrine of the Little Vehicle, which will never send the dead up to Heaven. . . . I have the Three Stores of the Buddha's Law of the Great Vehicle [Mahāyāna], which can save the dead, deliver from suffering, and ensure that the body will live for ever without coming to harm" (1:291). Taizong agrees that Xuanzang should go to India to obtain the scriptures, adopts him as his younger brother, and gives him the honorary name Tang Sanzang, Tang Three Stores (1:295–97). Waley and Yu translate this as the "three baskets" of Buddhist scriptures and use the name Tripitaka. Guanyin provides Xuanzang with treasures from the Buddha, a brocade cassock and a nine-ringed pilgrim staff (1:168; 285–86); Taizong gives him a purple gold begging bowl, a passport allowing him to travel freely, and a horse to carry him (1:296–7).

While the real Xuanzang was given the honorific Sanzang, it was upon his return to Chang'an.[35] Xuanzang left China without permission or official documents and without support. Waley suspects his application never reached the proper officials,[36] but Wriggins notes that Taizong at that point was unsympathetic to Buddhism, that he saw the western regions as hostile, and that he forbade the monk to go; Xuanzang left China traveling by night, in secret.[37] This change from historical fact is quite explicable in terms of the novel, first, because Monkey is the rebel in the story, not Xuanzang. The monk's whole life is intended for the purpose of this journey, and his deference to the authority of the emperor is total. Secondly, this is an authorized journey, as symbolized by Sanzang's passport, which is perused, stamped, signed, and stolen on a number of occasions. It is one of the authoritative documents in the text. Liu I-ming calls it "in effect the certificate or license of one who practices the Tao,"[38] thus giving it spiritual authority as well. Sanzang's purity and innocence are central to the story, what make him so desirable a prize to the demons they encounter. He is always eager to do everything by the letter of the law, respecting both secular and religious authorities. Waley says he "stands for the ordinary man, blundering anxiously through the difficulties of life,"[39] while Hsia notes how, "as an ordinary mortal undertaking a hazardous journey [he is] easily upset by the smallest inconvenience."[40] He is

> singularly attached to bodily comforts, complaining more than once about the cold and hunger inflicted by the journey. The slightest foreboding of ill or danger terrifies him; the most groundless kind of slander at once shatters his confidence in his most trustworthy follower, Sun Wu-k'ung [Wukong], who has never failed to come to his rescue.[41]

That he does not conform to the picture of the ideal monk is part of the humor and paradox of the novel. Guanyin chooses him because he *is* the ideal monk, and to the demons he meets on the road, he exerts incredible authority in that guise. But he is also human, which provides both a wonderful foil for Monkey and also gives hope to human readers—most of whom would be just as cold, hungry, and fearful as Xuanzang—that it's possible to undertake and complete this journey. Critics have pointed out that Xuanzang is often impatient, stubborn, and irritable (Hsia calls him "peevish"[42]), but these traits are displayed with his disciples, in his authoritative role as teacher/Master, and are often completely appropriate, given their behavior.

Although Monkey becomes totally devoted to Sanzang on the journey, Master and disciple have a rough beginning, and Guanyin needs to intervene before Monkey's rebellious spirit is willing to allow the monk to be the one in charge, in spite of his own superior powers. Happy at his release from five hundred years under the mountain, Monkey is eager to show Sanzang what an excellent protector he will be. He gains respect for his powers by quickly subduing and killing a tiger. But when he then kills six bandits who mean to rob them on the road, Sanzang, totally committed to the Buddhist precept of the sanctity of all life, is furious. This important episode, which occurs prior to the dragon horse, Pig, and Friar Sand joining the pilgrimage, clearly delineates the powers and characters of Monkey and Sanzang. There is general critical agreement that the six bandits, who identify themselves to the travelers as "Eye-seeing Happiness, Ear-hearing Anger, Nose-smelling Love, Tongue-tasting Thought, Mind-born Desire, and Body-based Sorrow" (1:334) represent the Buddhist six *cauras*, the six senses of the body that impede enlightenment. "Monkey's execution of them is intended to portray in an allegorical fashion his greater detachment from the human senses, a freedom of which his master and his fellow pilgrim [Pig] have little knowledge."[43] When Sanzang tells Monkey, "You haven't a shred of compassion or goodness in you. . . . You're too evil, too evil" (1:336), Monkey is so upset that he temporarily deserts Xuanzang, who sits by the road lost, unable to take another step. As Hsia has pointed out, Sanzang "is still obsessed with love and compassion for phenomenal beings,"[44] which prevents him from seeing clearly, whereas Monkey's detachment enables him both to see the demons for what they are and to exert authority over them. When Monkey returns and asks why he's still sitting there, Sanzang says, "I couldn't move without you, so I had to sit here and wait till you came back" (1:341). Later in the narrative, Sanzang twice dismisses Monkey, but Sanzang cannot make progress without him, without the demon-conquering Immortal Sage, without the mind/heart.

Commentators have disagreed on how to interpret the gold headband and spell for tightening it that Guanyin had obtained from the Buddha and provided to Sanzang during Monkey's brief absence; does giving Sanzang the ability to control Monkey take away Monkey's spirit and independence? When Monkey, through vanity, is tricked into putting the band on his head, Xuanzang achieves a way of controlling Monkey-mind. After his initial anger, Monkey accepts the power that Guanyin has provided to Sanzang and says, "You must recite scriptures instead of saying that spell all the time. I promise to protect you, and I shall always be true to this vow" (1:344). But at first, he is easily discouraged. Even though Guanyin had told him always to announce their purpose to fetch the scriptures, Monkey neglects to do so when they meet first the dragon, then Pig, then the River of Sand dragon who becomes Friar Sand, necessitating a confrontation with each one before they realize that Monkey is a disciple of the pilgrim they've been waiting for. When Sanzang's horse is eaten by the dragon, Monkey complains to Guanyin:

> "If you'd let me out to roam around enjoying myself as I pleased, that would have been fine. I was all right when you met me above

the sea the other day, spoke a few unkind words, and told me to do all I could to help the Tang Priest. But why did you give him that hat he tricked me into wearing to torture me with? Why did you make this band grow into my head? Why did you teach him that Band-tightening Spell? Why did you make that old monk recite it over and over again so that my head ached and ached? You must be wanting to do me in." The Bodhisattva smiled. "You monkey. You don't obey the commands of the faith, and you won't accept the true reward, so if you weren't under control like this you might rebel against Heaven again or get up to any kind of evil. If you got yourself into trouble as you did before, who would look after you? Without this monstrous head, you'd never be willing to enter our Yogacarin[45] faith." (1:354–55)

Monkey is somewhat relieved when the dragon turns into Sanzang's horse, but he feels that the trip will be too difficult. Guanyin exclaims,

"In the old days, before you had learnt to be a human being . . . you were prepared to work for your awakening with all your power. But now that you have been delivered from a Heaven-sent calamity, you have grown lazy. What's the matter with you? In our faith, to achieve nirvana you must believe in good rewards. If you meet with injury or suffering in future, you have only to call on Heaven and Earth for them to respond; and if you get into a really hopeless situation I shall come to rescue you myself" (1:357).

She gives him some life-saving hairs, and they work together to quell another troublesome spirit; by the time Monkey meets the last of the pilgrim disciples to complete their band, he is awake to the task and is able truly to say to Friar Sand, "I have turned away from evil and been converted to good. I have given up Taoism and become a Buddhist. I am protecting the Patriarch Sanzang, the younger brother of the Great Tang Emperor, on his journey to the Western Heaven to visit the Buddha and ask for the scriptures" (1:443).

Anthony Yu notes that many modern critics "have found it rather difficult to accept Monkey's subjugation," seeing the "conversion" of Monkey as "a basic flaw in the narrative . . . [seeming] to contradict the magnificent heroic character whose defiance and love of independence we have come to cherish and admire in the first seven chapters."[46] Yu disagrees, based on both the complexity of the narrative and on his view of how Buddha is portrayed.

Whereas the bureaucratic pretension and incompetence of both [the Taoist divinities and Buddhist pantheon in the celestial hierarchy] become frequent targets of the author's biting satire, the wisdom and mercy of Buddha—characteristics hardly shared by any of the Taoist deities, least of all by the Jade Emperor—are constantly emphasized.[47]

The journey, initiated by Buddha, is fully embraced by Monkey; "his unreserved commitment to the journey and to what it seeks to accomplish is, in fact, what sustains the pilgrims through all those overwhelming difficulties."[48] I would further maintain that it is not that Monkey is converted, but that he begins to see clearly, that he has a shift of perspective. Whereas formerly he was the center of every enterprise in which he involved himself, now his Master and the goal of the journey become his central focus; as Plaks notes, he becomes singleminded.[49] This is not, however, a shift away from Self or self-cultivation. Monkey also understands and takes to heart Guanyin's earlier promise that he will be able to cultivate good retribution for himself through this undertaking; he will get where he wants to go (which is *not* to be emperor of Heaven). With the other pilgrims, he becomes part of a brotherhood, an interdependent community; the integrity of this community—often broken—grants them all another kind of authority, for only together can they complete the journey and coauthor an integrated Self. Monkey has changed after five hundred years under the mountain; he no longer has the "tendency of the self to fall into the trap of taking its own scope of vision as the total frame of reference."[50] While there is no question that Sanzang does not always use the band-tightening spell (or threat of it) fairly, when it is used, it invariably causes Monkey to refocus and sometimes to take a more creative rather than destructive approach to a problem or situation. Monkey's redirection of his powerful vision is one of the most potent indicators of the new kind of authority he obtains in becoming Xuanzang's disciple and embracing Buddhism.

Throughout the journey, Monkey does remain independent of spirit and rebellious to authority. He even occasionally badgers Sanzang, when he sees Sanzang's spirits flagging, or when he sees that Sanzang's naiveté, trust, and inability to see evil are going to get them all into more trouble; even then, he defers, with inevitable catastrophe the result. But it is not so much the band-tightening spell that gives Sanzang authority over Monkey as it is Monkey's changed view that allows him to recognize Sanzang as Master. I would maintain that Monkey comes to see him as a Confucian *junzi*, an "exemplary" or "authoritative" person, whose enterprise is founded in *ren*, "authoritative conduct." As defined by

Roger Ames in his introduction to *The Analects, ren* is "one's entire person: one's cultivated cognitive, aesthetic, moral, and religious sensibilities as they are expressed in one's ritualized roles and relationships."[51] Throughout the journey to the West, Sanzang fulfills the role of *junzi*; in his relation to kings, officers, simple people, demons, and celestial beings, he unfailingly acts appropriately, observes ritual (*li*), and is concerned that his actions and the actions of others are ethical, moral, good. The combination of the elements for person (*ren*) and the number two (*er*) in the *ren* graph "underscores the Confucian assumption that one cannot become a person by oneself—we are, from our inchoate beginnings, irreducibly social."[52] Sanzang's social community is that of his disciples; he is also a *junzi* in that he oversees this community through communication.[53] On one level, Sanzang and the journey are one and the same. Without Sanzang, there is no quest for the scriptures, as we are often reminded by Pig's selfish desire to divide up the luggage and go home whenever he thinks the Master has been irrevocably lost to demons. Plaks examines textual references to Sanzang as "the body of the law" (*fa shen*), "original nature" (*ben xing*), or "primal spirit" (*yuan shen*) to posit that "such expressions must be interpreted as signifying not a specific aspect of being—body, nature, or spirit—but rather the entire Self of the party as a whole, or more accurately, of the potential seeker of enlightenment through self-cultivation."[54]

While this view of Sanzang as *junzi* may seem to contradict his characteristics as outlined earlier, we need to keep in mind that this text is always working on more than one level. As a soul seeking enlightenment, Sanzang sometimes backslides, lacks perception, and makes minor slips, but the Tang monk in human communities is consistently upright. In discussing the idea of individual character in the Chinese novel, Plaks notes the implication of

> a disjunction between an outer self or persona—fulfilling or failing to fulfill social roles—and an inner, true Self beyond the reach of external entanglements. Such a view would accord well with the common description of the Chinese [*junzi*] as a Confucian in his external social relations and a Taoist in his innermost heart.[55]

Further, the reader perceives Sanzang and Monkey differently than they as characters perceive each other. Because Sanzang is humorless, straight-laced, and dull, our sympathies lie with Monkey, who carries the burden of protection on the trip, and who is mischievous and fun. Sanzang represents the human, mortal self, among immortal disciples; unlike Monkey, he does not always see very clearly with his mortal eyes. Those instances when he seems less than exemplary are generally when he is demanding from his disciples, who often seem incorrigible, forms of behavior closer to his own, or when he is concerned that the trip may end in failure, because of the tremendous hardships or because his life seems doomed. As readers, we get upset when Sanzang doesn't appreciate the loveable Monkey and his powers. But from Sanzang's point of view, which is centered in his monkish standards, in his concern to fulfill his commitment to Taizong and Guanyin, and in his desire to obtain the scriptures so as to bring the Dharma to China and realize salvation of souls, Monkey does not initially appear as a being in whom he can put his full trust. This may be a kind of spiritual blindness on Sanzang's part, one in which he denies Monkey his proper authority, but it is also quite human. During the course of the trip, Sanzang comes to rely more and more on Monkey, and finally to see him as he really is, to appreciate him, and to recognize his spiritual authority. The Master/disciple relationship is very important to the progress that they make in both the temporal and spiritual journeys. Each is working toward his own self-cultivation and self-authorization, each embodies a kind of personal authority in seeking the scriptures, but only together, and with the other disciples, will they achieve the goal.

Authority resides within persons, within the power derived from weapons, within the laws of rulers and of Heaven, but most importantly within the Buddhist scriptures, the goal of the journey. As a reminder of this, and as an indication of the power of their internalized teachings, Sanzang receives one text as a gift from the Rook's Nest Hermit of Pagoda Mountain: "I have a *Heart Sutra*, a total of 270 words in 54 sentences, and if you recite it when you encounter evil influences you will come to no harm" (1:454). Since Sanzang "had already the origins of enlightenment inside himself, he was able to remember the *Heart Sutra* after only one hearing, and it has been passed on down to this very day. This sutra is the kernel of the cultivation of the truth, and it is the gateway to becoming a Buddha" (1:455). C. T. Hsia comments that "the Heart Sutra is the central wisdom (*prajnaparamita*) text of Mahayana Buddhism," a "spiritual companion" to Xuanzang; *Journey to the West* uses the historical Xuanzang's translation of this sutra. His biographers note that he received it on his way *back* from India, after obtaining the other scriptures.[56] In adapting the earlier versions of *Journey to the West* that place this transmission early on, "Wu Ch'eng-en has done nothing less than make his whole novel a philosophical commentary on the sutra."[57]

Hsia notes that while Sanzang constantly recites the sutra on the journey, "its transcendent teaching that 'form is emptiness and the very emptiness is form' is so far beyond his mortal understanding that every calamity that befalls him demonstrates anew his actual incomprehension."[58] This interpretation takes into account neither the narrative comment that follows transmission of the sutra, nor Sanzang's development during the journey. Wu Cheng'en often uses poetry at the ends or beginnings of chapters to comment on what has just occurred or what is about to occur. Chapter 20, immediately following Sanzang's receipt of the *Heart Sutra*, begins with a poem:

> The Dharma is born in the mind,
> And in turn is destroyed by the mind.
> Who do life and death come from?
> Decide for yourself.
> If it is all from your own mind,
> Why do you need others to tell you?
> All you need to do is work hard,
> Squeezing blood out of iron.
> Thread a silken rope through your nose,
> And fasten yourself to emptiness.
> Tie it to the tree of non-action,
> To prevent it from collapsing.
> Don't acknowledge bandits as your sons,
> Or you will forget the Dharma and the mind. . . .
> When the mind appears it is non-existent,
> When Dharma appears, it ceases. . . . (1:458)

The text goes on, "This *gatha* refers to how the Patriarch Xuanzang came to awareness and understanding of the *Heart Sutra* and thus opened the gate. As that venerable elder recited it constantly, a ray of miraculous light penetrated through to him" (1:458–59). Enlightenment for Sanzang is not immediate; constant recitation helps him to internalize the text and reach understanding. When he becomes bewildered and fearful after difficult encounters with demons, Monkey nudges him back to the sutra. A month after a particularly nasty episode, Sanzang becomes frightened on hearing a river and Monkey asks,

> "Have you forgotten your Heart Sutra?. . . . [Y]ou've forgotten the sentence, 'There is no sight, no sound, no smell, no taste, no touch and no mental process.' We men of religion should not look on beauty, hear music, smell sweet fragrances, or taste good flavours. We should not even notice whether we are hot or cold, and our minds should be free from delusion. This is the way to repel the Six Bandits that attack eye, ear, nose, tongue, body and

mind. Because of your mission to fetch the scriptures you are constantly worrying. You are afraid of evil monsters because you cling to your body. . . . If you will keep on inviting the Six Bandits in over and over again how can you ever expect to reach the Western Heaven and see the Buddha?" (2:972)

Sanzang thinks about Monkey's words, but still expresses concern about completing his mission. At that, Monkey reminds him of the saying, "At the right time the achievement completes itself" (2:972–73).

Much later on the journey, Sanzang worries about another high mountain in their way, and Monkey tells him he's forgotten the quatrain,

> "Do not go far to seek the Buddha on Vulture Peak;
> Vulture Peak is in your heart.
> Everybody has a Vulture Peak stupa
> Under which to cultivate conduct."

"Of course I know it, disciple," said Sanzang. "According to that quatrain the thousands of scriptures all come down to cultivating the heart." . . . "But if you're as scared, frightened and disturbed as this the Great Way is distant, and Thunder Peak is far, far away. Forget those wild fears and come with me." When the venerable elder heard this his spirits were revived and his worries disappeared. (4:1953–54)

Towards the end of the journey, Sanzang once again expresses concern about a high mountain and how far they still have to go. When Monkey asks him if he's forgotten the sutra, he responds,

> "The *Prajnaparamita Heart Sutra* is constantly with me, like my habit and begging bowl. . . . There has not been a day ever since the Rook's Nest Hermit taught it to me that I have not recited it. I have never forgotten it for a moment. I can even recite it backwards. How could I possibly forget it?" "You can only recite it, Master," said Monkey. "You never asked the hermit to explain it." "Ape!" retorted Sanzang. "How can you say I don't understand it? Do you understand it then?" "Yes," Monkey replied, "I do." After that neither Sanzang nor Monkey made another sound. (4:2132)

The other disciples laugh and upbraid Monkey, accusing him of putting on airs, but Sanzang responds, "Stop talking nonsense, Wuneng and Wujing. . . . Wukong understands the wordless language. That is true explanation" (4:2133). Plaks interprets this, "the Master gives him credit as the only one who truly understands its message."[59] I see Sanzang and Monkey here sharing the silence of understanding together, each appreciating the other's enlightenment, from which the other disciples are excluded. Each recognizes the other's spiritual authority, and this passage underscores the power of them both. Monkey recognizes that it is Sanzang's worry about reaching his goal that sometimes keeps him too tied to his mortal body, the goal of bringing the possibility of enlightenment to others; only when they actually reach Vulture Peak is Sanzang able to let it go. Sanzang's and Monkey's commitment to this goal is another aspect of their spiritual authority, even if each occasionally gets distracted, Sanzang by the demons, and Monkey by his concern for Sanzang.

The *Heart Sutra* is an authoritative text, and the importance of reciting it is its ability to protect from evil influences. However, its meaning must be internalized. In the temporal journey, the evil influences are the demons, but in the spiritual journey, the demons are in the mind. "The importance of the Buddhist *Heart Sutra* in the novel highlights the collapsing of the distinction between phenomenal illusion and that true emptiness whose realization is the pilgrims' goal. . . . [T]he demons become, not mere hindrances to the journey, but the very phenomenal matrix in which it is necessary to sojourn in order to achieve the goals of enlightenment, immortality, and freedom, by cultivation of the mind."[60] Beginning his journey, Sanzang says, "When the heart and mind live . . . every kind of evil lives; but when they are extinguished, evil is extinguished too" (1:299). "In other words, all the demons who threaten the life and limb of the travelers are essentially manifestations of the unenlightened state of the mind in its process of cultivation."[61] This two-fold nature of the demons explains why Monkey, who could hardly be overcome in his battles with Heavenly forces, constantly meets demons on the road who are an equal match for him in battle; his cudgel is frequently met with magical weapons of equal or greater power. The demons of the mind are far more formidable than celestial beings, because they reside within. Though when Monkey early on blames Guanyin for allowing an evil spirit to live at a monastery dedicated to her, and she helps him subdue the monster by turning into the likeness of one of the monster's companions, he asks her, "Are you a Bodhisattva disguised as an evil spirit, or a Bodhisattva who really is an evil spirit?" She laughingly replies, "evil spirit and Bodhisattva are all the same in the last analysis—they both belong to non-being" (1:413).

Monkey often saves Sanzang from the clutches of evil demons by killing them, but there is a category of demon made up of celestial beings who have left Heaven, usually because they longed for the freedoms and enticements of earth; they are outside of or have escaped from Heaven's authority. Hsia notes that they usually delight in eating human flesh and "enjoy an unrestrained sexual life;"[62] they "exhibit a remarkable range of human passions."[63] Their lust for life and "ferocious aggressiveness only magnifies the hideousness of craving in every one of us, that craving which, in accordance with Buddhist teaching, is the cause of all suffering."[64] In dealing with these monsters, Monkey must invariably seek assistance from Heaven, often from those he had battled earlier. After their subjugation, these demons are generally returned to Heaven, either for trial, or to continue the role they previously occupied (subject to a celestial master), or in a new role, having been converted, such as the malicious Red Boy, whom Guanyin subdues with another head-tightening band, tonsures, and makes her page, Sudhara (2:966). They are "integrated into cosmic order by being installed in a 'right' position in the cosmic bureaucracy."[65] Such episodes remind us that thoughts and ideas which begin as evil, if applied to certain functions or actions, can be converted to purposes and uses that are ultimately good. That is, behavior and actions often determine morality, relative to particular situations and circumstances; sometimes we can convert or control the demons of the mind, rather than wiping them out entirely. "When knowledge and action are seen to be mutually reliant, then one can return to the origin and unify the soul."[66]

The duplicity of demons is one of their most horrible aspects, their ability to present themselves in a multitude of forms and to seem benign while murderous in intent; when vanquished, they reveal their true form. Sanzang often blunders naively into their grasp; as Monkey tells him quite late in the pilgrimage, "the journey's been held up so long and so much effort has been wasted because you can't tell true from false. All the way along I've told you demons are no good, but you will kowtow to them" (4:2109–10). But some of the most dangerous episodes for the pilgrims involve the disintegration of their unity, either when Sanzang dismisses Monkey, or because of a doubling of themselves and their subsequent inability to recognize each other. Plaks notes that multiplicity (*duo xin*) is "an impediment to the singularity of consciousness demanded for spiritual cultivation."[67] When in the Kingdom of Wuji the blue-haired Lion King of Manjusri turns himself into Sanzang, Monkey can't tell them apart; only when he asks them both to recite the band-tightening spell can they hear which one is reciting the true spell. Monkey exhibits here his selflessness, in his willingness to submit to a painful headache in order to know his true Master (2:896).

Sanzang's first dismissal of Monkey occurs rather early on, when Monkey kills an evil corpse spirit, Lady White Bone, whom Sanzang cannot recognize as evil. When Monkey displays the horror of her true image, Pig, out of selfish spite and jealousy of the Master's favoritism for Monkey, purposely makes Sanzang believe that Monkey is deceiving him. Monkey is angry at Pig's deception, hurt at Sanzang's lack of faith in him, and so concerned that the others will not be able to protect Sanzang properly that he tells him to use the band-tightening spell to summon him back if needed. This makes Sanzang so angry that he gives Monkey a letter of dismissal, the written text thereby adding to the authority of the act (2:628). Of course Sanzang does get in trouble, when the terrible Bull-Headed Demon King changes him into the likeness of a tiger and accuses him of being the evil demon. This episode is the only instance in the story where the modest, obedient horse changes back into his dragon self in an attempt to save his master; unable to do so, he sends Pig to beg Monkey to return. Monkey, who says, "I've stayed with the pilgrim in my mind" (2:696), is the only one with the power to release Sanzang from the spell. At the end of the episode, Sanzang expresses his gratitude to Monkey, the pilgrims are all reconciled, and the band continues, "united in their shared determination" (2:720). In the form of the tiger, Sanzang had been chained and put in an iron cage; without Monkey, he loses not only his mind, but his body as well.

Sanzang's second dismissal of Monkey occurs in the second half of the journey, after Monkey has proven his loyalty on numerous occasions. Again, it is because Monkey has killed human bandits (though in this case, they are not symbolic of the senses). Given everything that has transpired in the many years they have spent on the journey, Monkey is so distraught that he goes directly to Guanyin, who points out to him that Xuanzang "is a monk whose heart is set on kindness. Why did someone of your tremendous powers need to bother with killing so many small-time bandits? . . . [T]hey're human and it's wrong to kill them. It's not the same as with evil beasts, demons and spirits" (3:1299). This incident, in which Guanyin upholds Sanzang's compassionate spirit, and suggests that Monkey could have respected the monk—and human life— by just scaring them away, allows for the intrusion of a False Monkey, determined to create an imposter band to reach the West in their place. Monkey was out of harmony with his Master: "Troubles arise if one has two minds (*er xin*); / Doubts cloud everything from sea to sky" (3:1329). Not even Guanyin can tell the two Monkeys apart, and it remains for Buddha to identify the six-eared macaque, a symbol of the "multiplicity of man's consciousness,"[68] whom Monkey promptly kills, much to Buddha's horror (3:1333). Plaks sees this episode as "an allegorical exemplum of the Neo-Confucian concept of mind cultivation, based on Mencius's definition of true 'learning' [*xue wen*] as 'seeking the lost mind' [*qiu qi fan xin*]."[69] The reunification of the five pilgrims indicates both "integration of separate elements of the self within an organic whole" and "the harmonizing of the self within a network of human relations in society and the world at large."[70]

Even this harmony can create problems, however; as the trip progresses, the spiritually detached Monkey becomes more and more attached to his Master and to achieving the goal of the trip, frequently breaking down in tears when Sanzang's danger is grave and he himself has been captured. When in Chapter 86, Monkey finds Sanzang alive after believing him finally to have been eaten, "he felt an itch in his heart that he could not scratch" (4:1987). For the first and only time in the novel, his mind is so affected that he becomes indecisive in his actions, wavering back and forth as to how to proceed, until he finally decides first to release Sanzang, then to try to subdue the monsters (4:1989). Monkey's loss of control over his mind and actions here indicates the depth of his emotional attachment to Sanzang, which almost undercuts his power to act; it also indicates his commitment to the journey, which he thought could not now be accomplished with Sanzang dead.

Along the road to the West, the male demons want to eat Sanzang because his flesh and *yang* spirit, pure through ten reincarnations, will bestow immortality. For the same reason, the female spirits want to mate with him, and the problem of sexual temptation becomes greater the closer the pilgrims get to their goal. It is almost as though, having made some progress with the mental aspects of reaching enlightenment, and becoming more spiritually detached, they become more attached emotionally, and the physical body becomes more vulnerable. In the episodes in which female demons attempt to seduce Sanzang,[71] the disciples agree that if Sanzang has succumbed to sexual temptation, they will give up the quest for the scriptures and disperse. Plaks notes how sensually appealing the temptation scenes are. "By the time we come to the episode of the Jade Hare in chapters 93–95, the ground has been prepared for the convincing portrayal of [Xuanzang's] apparent submission to demonic designs on his pure essence, right at the point where the goal of the quest comes within sight."[72] But the submission is only apparent; in court before the nuptial banquet, Monkey admires Sanzang's *sangfroid*; "What a fine monk! What a fine monk! Dwelling amid splendour, his heart forms no attachment; / Walking through magnificence, his mind is not confused" (4:2175). "It is not sexuality per se but rather its tendency to throw off the equilibrium of the self that is at issue;"[73] Sanzang is able to maintain his equilibrium, and finally to put the six bandits at bay.

Not long after this, the pilgrims finally reach the foot of Vulture Peak. With their final river to cross, only Monkey can run over the three-mile, narrow, slippery bridge over the mighty rolling waves, and his badgering of the others that "this is the way . . . this is the way" (4:2251) can't assuage their fears. When Ratnadhvaja, the Royal Buddha of Brightness, brings over his bottomless boat to ferry them across, Sanzang is too frightened to get on; Monkey pushes him, he falls in the water, and is hauled aboard. As they push off, they see a corpse floating downstream which is, of course, Sanzang's. They all congratulate him, and Sanzang is able to spring lightly ashore, having completed "the boundless dharma of crossing to the other bank" (4:2255–56). They present their passport to the Buddha, who directs them to select scriptures from his Three Stores to propagate in the East. But because they have no presents for the Arhat, he gives them wordless scriptures; the Ancient Buddha Dipankara sends someone after them, and Sanzang exclaims, "even in this world of bliss evil demons cheat people" (4:2265–66). This is probably the only place in the text where Sanzang falls down in his observance of public, community expectation and ritual; he is perceived as lacking in courtesy, in wanting something for nothing. Of course, as readers, we feel the same indignation as the pilgrims; they were, after all, sent on the journey, and their fourteen years of ordeals should be payment enough. But the Buddha reminds them that "the scriptures cannot be casually passed on. Nor can they be taken away for nothing. . . . You were given blank texts because you came here to fetch them empty-handed. The blank texts are true, wordless scriptures, and they really are good. But as you living beings in the east are so deluded and have not achieved enlightenment we'll have to give you these ones instead" (4:2267). This time, Sanzang gives his purple gold begging bowl, a symbolic gesture of mutual generosity, and promises to have the Tang emperor send them rewards. After one final ordeal, to make up the nine times nine of perfection, they fulfill the mission of delivering the scriptures to Taizong. On their return to the Western Paradise, Sanzang and Monkey are made Buddhas, Pig is made Altar Cleanser, Friar Sand becomes a Golden Arhat, and the horse becomes the Heavenly Dragon of the Eight Classes of Being. "All completed the true achievement and reached their proper places," and the novel ends with prayers to the Buddhas (4:2314–17).

In the various types of authority displayed in the novel, those vested in persons, laws (other than Dharma), hierarchies, weapons, and demons, become insubstantial. The authority, authorization, coauthoring connected with self-cultivation have more import, resulting in the integrity of the pilgrims as one harmonized Self, the "one mind" of Monkey and

Sanzang, and their enlightenment. The rebellious Monkey, Great Sage Equal to Heaven, challenged the authority of Heaven and of death. On the road to the West, he challenged the demons of the mountains and caves and the demons of the mind, saying of his *junzi* Master Sanzang, "Our hearts were both joined and our fates were entwined; / As we studied the Way we shared the same mind" (2:1150). He obtains enlightenment, integration of the self, and Buddhahood. Sanzang respects the authority of rulers, bodhisattvas, Buddha, and the scriptures. He maintains the purity of his essence, incorporates his four disciples with himself into a single integrated Self, internalizes the *Heart Sutra*, and obtains the scriptures, enlightenment, and Buddhahood. C. T. Hsia notes that the novel "ultimately demonstrates the paradoxical character of [Buddhist] wisdom in that its nominal hero is granted Buddhahood at the end precisely because he has done nothing to earn it."[74] Sanzang is seeking the scriptures to help save souls, rather than seeking Buddhahood; he maintains his pure nature from beginning to end, resisting temptations and centering the dedication of his disciples. He is also the reincarnated Golden Cicada, now returned to his proper place. Early on, he had told Monkey, "if a monk acts rightly he will grow daily but invisibly, like grass in a garden during the spring" (2:627). Sanzang's growth during the journey is like grass growing invisibly.

Monkey keeps up his character of flaunting authority till the end, asking Buddha to remove the band from his head and "smash it to smithereens" rather than letting Guanyin make someone else miserable with it. The mind has been freed and this symbol of authority over mind is also dissolved. At the end of the journey, neither authority nor rebellion to authority are necessary. Monkey's transformation in the novel is in his dedication of his powers not to his own self-aggrandizement, but to his Master Xuanzang and to the goals of the journey, through which he, too, will attain Buddhahood. But Monkey's refusal ever to completely submit to authorities throughout the novel, particularly when he punctures hypocrisy and arrogance, may indicate that confronting authority is an integral and critical part of the process of self-cultivation.[75] The five pilgrims, in their pursuit and attainment of their goal, realize their interdependency, their coauthorship of an integrated selfhood.[76] However, whatever the serious Buddhist message of the novel, it is still the loveable mischievous Monkey, with his humor, loyalty, clear-sightedness, fearlessness, and complete confidence in his supernatural and natural powers, who catches the imagination of every reader. He is the journey's companion we would all like to have, who lives today in popular children's books and television series for many who will never read *Journey to the West*.

The authority of written texts is of major importance in the novel; Monkey subverts the Register of Life and Death, the written complaints to Heaven, and Sanzang's written dismissal. The passport given by Taizong is returned to him at the end, the document that authorized their journey now documenting it. Sanzang memorizes the Heart Sutra on one hearing and eventually internalizes it, whereas Monkey understands it wordlessly. Wu Cheng'en in his opening poem to the novel invites us to regard *Journey to the West* as an authority, and some commentators do, Liu I-ming maintaining that "wherever this book resides, there are heavenly deities standing guard over it,"[77] and Bantly suggesting that it be regarded as a Buddhist religious text.[78] And, of course, the entire goal of the journey is to obtain the written texts of the Buddhist scriptures. Plaks sees "the final irony of the 'wordless scriptures' . . . [as] a rather transparent joke" about emptiness, and "a final undermining of the fulfillment of the mission," unless we see the journey "as an internal pilgrimage of the mind."[79] But the historical Xuanzang did fulfill his mission, as did the band of pilgrims in *Journey to the West*. All undertook an internal pilgrimage of the mind as well, a journey that continues as long as the mind is alive. The wordless scriptures are connected both to the *Heart Sutra*, with its emphasis on emptiness, and to the experiences of the pilgrims on their journey on the Way (Dao), through which they become of one mind, and an integrated Self. Sanzang needs to return written scriptures to China to save others and to fulfill his mission; his own spiritual journey is completed when he leaves his body in the waters of Vulture Peak. But what Sanzang learned, and Monkey, awake to the meaning of emptiness, knows, is that books, whether Buddhist scriptures or *Journey to the West*, ultimately have no authority. As Sanzang said, "the thousands of scriptures all come down to cultivating the heart" (4:1953). In and of themselves, as things or goals, they are empty; to have meaning and become immortal, they must be eaten, digested, internalized, and integrated into the mind/heart (xin), where they become wordless.

Appendix: *The Heart Sutra*

When the Bodhisattva Avalokitesvara [Guanyin] was meditating on the profound prajna-paramita, [s]he perceived that all the five aggregates* are void and empty, and was thereupon freed from all sufferings and calamities. Sariputra, matter is not different from voidness and voidness is not different from matter: matter is voidness and voidness is matter [form is emptiness and emptiness is form]. Such is also the case with sensation, perception, discrimination and consciousness. Sariputra, all these things are void in nature, having neither beginning nor end, being neither pure nor impure, and having neither increase nor decrease. Therefore, in voidness there is no matter, no sensation, no perception, no discrimination and no consciousness; there is no eye, no ear, no nose, no tongue, no body and no mind; there is no sight, no sound, no smell, no taste, no touch and no mental process; there is no category of eye nor is there a category of consciousness; no ignorance nor the cessation of ignorance; no old age and death, nor the cessation of old age and death; there is no suffering, no causes of suffering, no cessation of suffering, and no way leading to the cessation of suffering; and there is no wisdom, nor anything to be gained. As nothing is to be gained, a Bodhisattva depending on prajna-paramita becomes free in his mind, and as he is free in his mind he has no fear and is rid of dreamlike thoughts of unreality and enjoys ultimate Nirvana. By means of prajna-paramita, all Buddhas of the past, the present and the future realize anuttara-samyak-sambodhi [utmost, right and perfect enlightenment]. Therefore, we know prajna-paramita is a great, divine spell, a great enlightening spell, a supreme spell, and a spell without a parallel, that can do away with all sufferings without fail. Thus we recite the Prajna-paramita Spell and say: Gate, gate, paragate, parasamgate, bodhi, svaha! [Gone, Gone, Gone beyond, Gone completely beyond, O what an awakening, All Hail!] (Wu Cheng'en, *Journey to the West*, 1:454–55.)

Notes

* *Pañcaskandha*: the five aggregates or constitutive elements of the human being. They are (1) *rūpa*, physical phenomena related to the five senses; (2) *vedanā*, sensation or reception of stimuli from events and things; (3) *saṃjñā*, discernment or perception; (4) *saṃskāra*, decision or volition; and (5) *vijñāna*, cognition and consciousness (Yu, *Journey to the West*, 527, note 36).

1. Attribution of authorship of the sixteenth-century 100-chapter version of the text is still controversial, although the identification of Wu Cheng'en as the author has been generally accepted by most scholars, as noted by C. T. Hsia, *The Classic Chinese Novel: A Critical Introduction* (New York: Columbia University Press, 1968), 116. Arthur Waley entitles his abridged translation *Monkey: Folk Novel of China by Wu Ch'eng-en* (New York: Grove Weidenfeld, 1943). For a discussion of authorship, see Anthony Yu's introduction to his translation, *The Journey to the West*, 4 vols. (Chicago: University of Chicago Press, 1977), 16–21; Andrew Plaks, *The Four Masterworks of the Ming Novel* (Princeton, NJ: Princeton University Press, 1987), 188–96; and Glen Dudbridge, "The Hundred-Chapter *Hsi-yu chi* and Its Early Versions" *Asia Major* n.s. 14, no. 2 (1969): 187–90. While Yu feels that Wu is the most likely author, since there is "lack of indisputable

evidence," (21) he credits no author on his title page. In the translation by W. J. F. Jenner cited in this article, Wu Cheng'en, *The Journey to the West*, 4 vols. (Beijing: Foreign Languages Press, 2001 [1997–1986]), the issue of authorship is discussed in an introduction by Shi Changyu, who notes that "nobody has been able to dislodge Wu Cheng'en from his position as the generally accepted author of *Journey to the West*," 1:5.

2. Yu, *Journey*, p. 35.

3. Hsia, *Classic Chinese Novel*, p. 134.

4. Yu, *Journey*, pp. 33–35.

5. Liu I-Ming, "How to Read 'The Original Intent of the Journey to the West,'" trans. Anthony C. Yu, in *How to Read the Chinese Novel*, ed. David L. Rolston (Princeton, NJ: Princeton University Press, 1990), p. 300.

6. Plaks, *Four Masterworks*, pp. 240–41.

7. Ibid., p. 241.

8. Ibid., p. 501.

9. Francisca Cho Bantly, "Buddhist Allegory in the *Journey to the West*," *The Journal of Asian Studies* 48, no. 3 (1989).

10. Sally Hovey Wriggins, *Xuanzang: A Buddhist Pilgrim on the Silk Road* (Boulder, CO: Westview Press, 1996), pp. 176–77. Wriggins retraced much of Xuanzang's journey in writing her book, which focuses primarily on the journey itself. For more information on Xuanzang's activities after returning to China, see Arthur Waley, *The Real Tripitaka and Other Pieces* (London: George Allen & Unwin, 1952), pp. 78–130. Yu also provides a brief overview in his introduction to *Journey to the West*, pp. 1–5.

11. Wriggins, *Xuanzang*, pp. 170–80.

12. Ibid., p. 185.

13. Yu, *Journey*, reviews the textual antecedents, pp. 5–13. Hsia, *Classic Chinese Novel*, discusses subsequent shorter versions, pp. 122–123; also see Plaks, *Four Masterworks*, pp. 186–87. In the Afterward to his translation, Jenner also discusses various versions of the story, Wu Cheng'en, *Journey*, 4:2325–30. Dudbridge's article, "Hundred-Chapter *Hsi-yu chi*" gives an extensive review of extant versions and their relation to each other.

14. Wu, *Journey*, 4:2324.

15. The structure of the novel is examined by Plaks, *Four Masterworks*, pp. 202–19. He focuses on the use of numerology, ten-chapter and half-point divisions, spatial and temporal schemes, seasonal rhythms, and redundancy.

16. Ibid., pp. 186–87.

17. All citations from Wu Cheng'en, *Journey to the West*, are from the Jenner translation; volume number and page number are noted in the text of the article. In this edition, the introduction in Vol. 1 is paginated 1–22, the table of contents is paginated 1–3, and paging begins again with number 1 in Chapter 1 of the text.

18. Yu, *Journey*, p. 38.

19. Plaks, *Four Masterworks*, p. 271.

20. Ibid., p. 209.

21. Andrew H. Plaks, "Allegory in *Hsi-Yu Chi* and *Hung-Lou Meng*," in *Chinese Narrative: Critical and Theoretical Essays*, ed. Andrew H. Plaks (Princeton, NJ: Princeton University Press, 1977), p. 173. Also see Plaks, *Four Masterworks*, p. 236.

22. Hsia, *Classic Chinese Novel*, p. 130.

23. Yu, *Journey*, p. 59.

24. Victor Mair, "The Journey to the West," in *The Columbia Anthology of Traditional Chinese Literature*, ed. Victor Mair (New York: Columbia University Press, 1994), p. 967n.

25. Yu, *Journey*, pp. 39–42, 45; Plaks, *Four Masterworks*, pp. 230–32. For a study of inner alchemy in Taoism and Neo-Confucianism, see Judith A. Berling, "Paths of Convergence: Interactions of Inner Alchemy Taoism and Neo-Confucianism," *Journal of Chinese Philosophy* 16, no. 3 (1989): 512–24.

26. Yu, *Journey*, p. 45.

27. Waley, *Monkey*, p. 8.

28. Robin R. Wang, e-mail communication to author during the "Cultures of Authority in Asian Practice" online conference, 5 September 2003.

29. Plaks, "Allegory," p. 177.

30. Plaks, *Four Masterworks*, p. 268.

31. Hsia, *Classic Chinese Novel*, p. 125.

32. Chapter 9 is missing in the earliest 100-chapter version of the novel published in 1592 and in some subsequent versions. See Yu, *Journey*, p. 14; Dudbridge, "Hundred-Chapter *Hsi-yu chi*," pp. 170–74 and 183–84; and Plaks, *Four Masterworks*, pp. 202–03.

33. Yu, *Journey*, p. 33.

34. Bantly, "Buddhist Allegory," p. 518.

35. Wilt Idema and Lloyd Haft, *A Guide to Chinese Literature* (Ann Arbor: Center for Chinese Studies, University of Michigan, 1977), p. 208.

36. Waley, *Real Tripitaka*, p. 15.

37. Wriggins, *Xuanzang*, p. 3.

38. Liu, "How to Read," p. 304.

39. Waley, *Monkey*, p. 8.

40. Hsia, *Classic Chinese Novel*, p. 126.

41. Yu, *Journey*, p. 44.

42. Hsia, *Classic Chinese Novel*, p. 126.

43. Yu, *Journey*, p. 59.

44. Hsia, *Classic Chinese Novel*, p. 129.

45. The Yogācāra or Vijñanavada school of Indian Buddhism, Consciousness-Only, represented one of the two main branches of Mahāyāna philosophy. Xuanzang's Yogācāra teachings were known as the *Weishi* or *Faxiang* school. A doctrine of pure idealism, "salvation was to be obtained by exhausting the store of consciousness until it became pure being itself, identical with the Thusness [Tathatā] that was the only truly existent entity in the universe," as noted by Wm. Theodore de Bary and Irene Bloom, "The School of Consciousness-Only," in *Sources of Chinese Tradition*, vol. 1, *From Earliest Times to 1600*, 2nd ed. (New York: Columbia University Press, 1999), p. 442. Yu, *Journey*, p. 3, notes that Xuanzang was "deeply vexed" by the question of whether all of humanity could attain Buddhahood. Xuanzang's school in China was in decline by the ninth century and gradually disappeared. Wm. T. de Bary notes that Chinese scholars have shown a new interest in it in the twentieth century.

46. Yu, *Journey*, p. 54.

47. Ibid.

48. Ibid., p. 55.

49. Plaks, "Allegory," p. 183.

50. Plaks, *Four Masterworks*, p. 271.

51. Roger T. Ames and Henry Rosemont Jr., *The Analects of Confucius: A Philosophical Translation* (New York: Ballantine Books, 1998), p. 49.

52. Ibid., p. 48.

53. Ibid., p. 62.

54. Plaks, "Allegory," p. 184.

55. Andrew H. Plaks, "Towards a Critical Theory of Chinese Narrative," in *Chinese Narrative: Critical and Theoretical Essays*, ed. Andrew H. Plaks (Princeton, NJ: Princeton University Press, 1977), pp. 346–47.

56. Hsia, *Classic Chinese Novel*, pp. 127–28.

57. Ibid., p. 128. Plaks, "Allegory," p. 175, agrees.

58. Hsia, *Classic Chinese Novel*, p. 128.

59. Plaks, "Allegory," p. 183.

60. Rob Campany, "Cosmogony and Self-Cultivation: The Demonic and the Ethical in Two Chinese Novels," *Journal of Chinese Philosophy* 6, no. 2 (1979): 91.

61. Plaks, *Four Masterworks*, p. 245.

62. Hsia, *Classic Chinese Novels*, p. 141.

63. Ibid., p. 143.

64. Ibid., p. 147.

65. Campany, "Cosmogony," p. 89.

66. Liu, "How to Read," p. 303.

67. Plaks, *Four Masterworks*, p. 247.

68. Ibid.

69. Ibid., p. 258.

70. Ibid., p. 264.

71. The Queen of Womanland's proposed marriage to Sanzang and his subsequent abduction by the Scorpion Queen (Ch. 54–55); the advances of the Apricot Fairy (Ch. 64); the spider girls who represent the seven passions who enmesh him in their webs (Ch. 72–73); the Mouse Spirit's enticement and proposed marriage in her Bottomless Cave (Ch. 80–83); and the proposed marriage to the King of India's daughter, really the Jade Hare Spirit (Ch. 93–95).

72. Plaks, *Four Masterworks*, p. 248.

73. Ibid., p. 249.

74. Hsia, *The Classic Chinese Novel*, p. 130.

75. I owe this interpretation to a question raised by James Highland in an e-mail conversation during the "Cultures of Authority in Asian Practice" on-line conference, 5 September 2003.

76. These ideas reflect suggestions of Tao Jiang and Peter Hershock in e-mail responses to my paper during the "Cultures of Authority in Asian Practice" on-line conference, 5 September 2003.

77. Liu, "How to Read," p. 299.

78. Bantly, "Buddhist Allegory," pp. 520–21.

79. Plaks, *Four Masterworks*, p. 243.

References

Ames, Roger T., and Henry Rosemont Jr. *The Analects of Confucius: A Philosophical Translation*. New York: Ballantine Books, 1998.

Bantly, Francisca Cho. "Buddhist Allegory in the *Journey to the West*." *The Journal of Asian Studies* 48, no. 3 (1989): 512–24.

Berling, Judith A. "Paths of Convergence: Interactions of Inner Alchemy Taoism and Neo-Confucianism." *Journal of Chinese Philosophy* 6, no. 2 (1979): 123–47.

Campany, Rob. "Cosmogony and Self-Cultivation: The Demonic and the Ethical in Two Chinese Novels." *Journal of Religious Ethics* 14, no. 1 (1986): 81–112.

De Bary, Wm. Theodore, and Irene Bloom, comps. "The School of Consciousness-Only." In *Sources of Chinese Tradition*. Vol. I: *From Earliest Times to 1600*, 440–44. 2nd ed. New York: Columbia University Press, 1999.

Dudbridge, Glen. "The Hundred-Chapter *Hsi-yu chi* and Its Early Versions." *Asia Major* n.s. 14, no. 2 (1969): 141–91.

Hsia, C. T. *The Classic Chinese Novel: A Critical Introduction*. New York: Columbia University Press, 1968.

Idema, Wilt, and Lloyd Haft. *A Guide to Chinese Literature*. Ann Arbor: Center for Chinese Studies, University of Michigan, 1977.

Liu, I-Ming. "How to Read 'The Original Intent of the Journey to the West.'" Translated by Anthony C. Yu. In *How to Read the Chinese Novel*, edited by David L. Rolston, 299–315. Princeton, NJ: Princeton University Press, 1990.

Mair, Victor. "The Journey to the West." In *The Columbia Anthology of Traditional Chinese Literature*, edited by Victor Mair, 966–80. New York: Columbia University Press, 1994.

Plaks, Andrew H. "Allegory in *Hsi-Yu Chi* and *Hung-Lou Meng*." In *Chinese Narrative: Critical and Theoretical Essays*, edited by Andrew H. Plaks, 163–202. Princeton, NJ: Princeton University Press, 1977.

———. *The Four Masterworks of the Ming Novel*. Princeton, NJ: Princeton University Press, 1987.

———. "Towards a Critical Theory of Chinese Narrative." In *Chinese Narrative: Critical and Theoretical Essays*, edited by Andrew H. Plaks, 309–52. Princeton, NJ: Princeton University Press, 1977.

Waley, Arthur. *The Real Tripitaka and Other Pieces*. London: George Allen & Unwin, 1952.

Waley, Arthur, trans. *Monkey: Folk Novel of China by Wu Ch'eng-en*. New York: Grove Weidenfeld, 1943.

Wriggins, Sally Hovey. *Xuanzang: A Buddhist Pilgrim on the Silk Road*. Boulder, CO: Westview Press, 1996.

Wu, Cheng'en. *Journey to the West*. Translated by W. J. F. Jenner. 4 vols. Beijing: Foreign Languages Press, 1993.

Yu, Anthony C., trans. and ed. *The Journey to the West*. 4 vols. Chicago: University of Chicago Press, 1977.

Establishing Authority through Scholarship: Ruan Yuan and the Xuehaitang Academy

Steven B. Miles

Studies of authority in late imperial China have often emphasized that a single individual, the emperor, held a monopoly on legitimate authority.[1] While it was certainly the case that all formal political authority derived from the emperor, recent scholarship on local society has drawn attention to the practice of authority in arenas outside the court and bureaucracy. Some scholars, for example, have examined the exercise of authority according to customary laws or procedures among elites and middlemen in villages, and among clerks and runners in county yamen, or offices.[2] Other scholars have drawn attention to the exercise of moral or cultural authority among the literati, often in opposition to the emperor's claim to such authority.[3] Likewise, studies of women in late imperial China have emphasized the role of patriarchal authority within the family and lineage.[4] Refocusing attention away from the court toward local society, and away from exclusively political authority toward social, moral, and cultural authority, has greatly enriched our understanding of the dynamics of the practice of authority in late imperial China. This chapter attempts to further this trend by examining the practice of authority in scholarship, education, and, more broadly, cultural competition. Nevertheless, such an analysis can never completely be divorced from the notion of political authority. "The Chinese," R. Bin Wong reminds us, "more than any other state in the early modern world, made the principle of instruction (*jiao* 教) basic to its conception of political rule."[5]

In this chapter, I explore the practice of authority in education and scholarship in a particular local context in order to illustrate this relationship between political and cultural authority. My focus will be on a segment of the male elite in one region of the Qing empire, specifically, the group of literati who associated themselves with the renowned

Xuehaitang 學海堂 academy, established in the 1820s in the empire's southernmost metropolis, Guangzhou. Because the academy was created in order to promote a particular scholarly agenda, I will begin with a brief overview of the two main "styles" of Confucian scholarship during the Qing dynasty (1644–1911)—Song Learning and Han Learning—as they relate to issues of authority. The remainder of the paper, drawing on extensive primary research that appears elsewhere, describes the founder's construction of authority through the creation of the Xuehaitang and the appropriation of authority by the scholars who associated themselves with the academy. The founder of the Xuehaitang, Ruan Yuan 阮元 (1764–1849), used his dual status as a political and cultural authority to establish this academy. That is, Ruan Yuan was assigned to Guangzhou as the governor-general of Guangdong and Guangxi from 1817 to 1826, and he was also an influential patron and practitioner of evidential research (*kaozheng* 考證) and Han Learning, the type of scholarship that was all the rage in Ruan's native Jiangnan region and that he sought to promote in Guangzhou. Viewed from a local perspective, however, both during Ruan's tenure in Guangzhou and after his departure, the scholars who associated themselves with the Xuehaitang academy drew on the authority of the academy and its founder to enhance their own status in local Cantonese society.

Authority in Song Learning and Han Learning

It is important to have some grasp of the two major styles or schools of Confucian scholarship prevalent during the early nineteenth century— Cheng-Zhu Neo-Confucianism and evidential research—because Ruan Yuan created the Xuehaitang academy explicitly for the purpose of promoting the latter. Both Cheng-Zhu Neo-Confucianism (referred to as Song Learning by many scholars in the early nineteenth century) and evidential research (in its more narrow version known as Han Learning) made theoretical claims about cultural and moral authority, and were closely intertwined with political authority in practice. Because much has been written about Song Learning and Han Learning, the following discussion attempts to distill from the secondary literature those characteristics that most closely relate to issues of authority: authoritative interpretations of the Classics, the locus of moral/cultural authority, and relations to political authority.

In the early nineteenth century, Song Learning referred to what is known today among Western scholars as Neo-Confucianism, which in its narrow definition designates the version of Confucianism that emerged during the Song dynasty (960–1279) under Cheng Yi 程頤 (1033–1107) and Zhu Xi 朱熹 (1130–1200). Thus, it is also commonly referred to as Cheng-Zhu Neo-Confucianism. Generally speaking, like all Confucians, Cheng Yi and Zhu Xi asserted that ultimate value could be found in the Way of the sages of antiquity; however, they believed that this was most often revealed through philosophical insight or moral charisma.[6] Neo-Confucians argued that this Way had been passed down from the ancient sage-kings to Confucius and Mencius via the *daotong* 道統, or transmission of the Way. Yet this transmission had been severed after Mencius, and was not recovered again until, depending on the specific version, it was realized by any one of several Neo-Confucian scholars in the late Tang dynasty (618–907) or early Song. Subsequently, the *daotong* passed from Cheng Yi through his disciples to Zhu Xi and on through his followers.[7] The *daotong*, then, represented what might be called a "Neo-Confucian lineage of authority."[8]

Beginning in the late Song, but especially in the Ming (1368–1644) and Qing dynasties, Cheng-Zhu Neo-Confucianism was closely connected to political authority in the sense that the Cheng Yi and Zhu Xi commentaries to the Confucian Classics were taken as the standard for the civil service examinations. While Han Learning interpretations began to appear in some sections of the examinations in the eighteenth century, Cheng-Zhu interpretations remained the standard for questions on the Classics and, more broadly, the court continued to appeal to Neo-Confucianism as the basis of its political legitimacy.[9] Despite its "orthodox" status throughout the late imperial era, however, Neo-Confucianism could also work against the claims of the state in the realm of social and cultural authority. Peter Bol suggests that one component of the "Neo-Confucian position" was a denial that political power in the person of the emperor had authority over moral and cultural values, locating this authority "instead in literati who cultivated their moral selves."[10]

This rejection of the emperor's authority in the moral and cultural realm did not prevent Neo-Confucian educators and activists from making use of political authority to sponsor such local projects as the construction of schools and shrines.[11] Likewise, most of the larger provincial and prefectural academies in Qing China were founded under the auspices of officials, and the largest ones in Jiangnan were personally patronized by touring emperors. While Alexander Woodside rightly points out that the Qing state was never capable of implementing centralized control over the academy curricula, the main function of most academies was to prepare students for civil examinations, and this meant education in Cheng-Zhu Neo-Confucianism. With occasional exceptions, this was also the case for major academies in Guangzhou, such as the Yuexiu Academy (Yuexiu shuyuan 粵秀書院).[12]

Like Neo-Confucians, advocates of evidential research during the Qing believed that ultimate value was to be found among the sages of antiquity. But, for them, this was to be found in texts, the Confucian Classics, and was to be verified through detailed textual analysis.[13] By appealing to the authority of texts, many practitioners of evidential research came to believe that commentaries produced by Confucians during the Han dynasty (206 BCE–220 CE) were more authoritative than the later Cheng Yi and Zhu Xi commentaries because they were much closer in time to the writing of the Classics. In particular, they promoted the commentaries and scholarly style of the Han Confucian Zheng Xuan 鄭玄 (127–200). As a result, evidential research was often identified as Han Learning. In contrast to the *daotong* of Song Learning, Han Learning scholars emphasized the passing on of particular exegetical traditions from teachers to students. This practice, alternatively referred to as *shicheng* 師承 (transmissions of the teachers) or *jiafa* 家法 (schools method), might be characterized as a "Han Learning lineage of authority."

While Cheng-Zhu Neo-Confucianism has been viewed as "orthodox" because it was the basis of the civil service examinations, there were also close connections between Han Learning and political authority in the form of imperial sponsorship of evidential research projects. The most famous of these was the compilation of the massive *Siku quanshu* 四庫全書 collectanea in the 1770s and 1780s. This project was largely carried out by Han Learning scholars, employed the methods of evidential research, and reflected a Han Learning scholarly orientation. At the same time, Han Learning concerns began to appear in some of the civil service examinations. Consequently, by the end of the eighteenth century Han Learning was in many ways perceived as being in greater favor at court than was Song Learning.[14]

In addition to its ties with imperial political authority, Han Learning also played a role in bolstering the cultural authority of literati at the local level. Angela Zito draws attention to the way in which evidential research functioned as a class marker.[15] Whereas the spread of literacy and commercial printing in the late Ming had allowed a large number of the socially ambitious to increase their status in local society, the practice of evidential research during the Qing raised the bar for entry into the very upper levels of the cultural elite. Full mastery of evidential research—to become authoritative—required years of painstaking study and hence could only be achieved by a tiny minority of the elite. It also served as a regional marker because, in the eighteenth century, evidential research was essentially limited to Beijing and especially to the Jiangnan region. There were no centers of Han Learning in eighteenth-century Guangzhou. In creating the Xuehaitang in Guangzhou, Ruan Yuan thereby not only sought to raise the level of scholarship in the region, but also in doing so asserted the authority of Jiangnan evidential research.

Constructing Authority: The Xuehaitang Founder

While it was not uncommon for provincial officials, whether they favored Song Learning or Han Learning, to devote some attention to the construction and maintenance of academies in the areas under their jurisdiction, Ruan Yuan exerted an unusual amount of energy in creating the Xuehaitang. Ruan Yuan began presiding over examinations in "ancient learning" in the spring of 1821. These were regularly held on a quarterly basis on the temporary premises of another academy in Guangzhou, but the building where examination questions were announced and the answers collected was decorated with a plaque that read "Xuehaitang" (Sea of Learning Hall). In 1824 Ruan personally selected a permanent site for the Xuehaitang, on a hill overlooking the city, and construction was completed early the following year. Ruan Yuan also compiled the first collection of Xuehaitang examination essays and poems, the *Xuehaitang ji* 學海堂集, in 1825. In 1826, just before he was transferred out of Guangdong, Ruan appointed eight codirectors of the Xuehaitang; as they retired or passed away, future governors-general would appoint replacements.

One reason that Ruan Yuan was able to play such a central role in the creation of the Xuehaitang is that he enjoyed a unique position as someone who was both "an authority" and "in authority."[16] That is, his authority was derived both from demonstrated expertise in Confucian scholarship and from the office he held by imperial appointment. While a Qing emperor and by extension his officials were ideally portrayed as both wise and powerful rulers, in reality high-ranking officials were only occasionally able simultaneously to exert a great deal of influence in scholarship or literature. Like Zeng Guofan 曾國藩 (1811–1872) in the middle of the nineteenth century, however, Ruan Yuan was one of those rare provincial officials who excelled in both roles.

In his role as an authority, Ruan Yuan had already earned a reputation not only as a practitioner but also as a great patron of evidential research and Han Learning in his role as a provincial official. In Shandong province in the 1790s Ruan had promoted construction of a shrine in honor of Zheng Xuan, while as a provincial governor based in Hangzhou city in 1800–1801 he had founded the Gujing jingshe 詁經精舍, an academy with an innovative curriculum that reflected Ruan's scholarly predilections. As governor of Jiangxi in 1814–1816, Ruan organized the printing of the *Shisanjing zhushu* 十三經注疏 ([Han and Tang] Commentaries to the Thirteen Classics). In all of his postings, as well as in his native Yangzhou in Jiangnan, Ruan was a tireless promoter of on-site evidential research, searching out stone inscriptions and artifacts, interviewing village elders, and comparing his findings with historical texts.[17] Ruan Yuan also commanded authority by virtue of his regional native-place: the evidential research and Han Learning movement had been centered in Jiangnan during the eighteenth century, and Ruan cast himself in the role of proselytizer in bringing what he saw as a more advanced form of scholarship to Guangzhou.

One reason that Ruan Yuan would eventually prove successful in this regard is that, as governor-general, he was also someone in authority. As the largest metropolis on the southern edge of the Qing empire, Guangzhou was a city of officials, ranging from provincial administrators down to county magistrates. Most of these officials were involved in academy education, some sponsoring academies and others being responsible for formulating questions for monthly "officials' examinations" at the larger academies. Occupying the post of governor-general, however, Ruan Yuan was the highest official in the city. He was thus able to utilize his position of political authority to mobilize resources to organize and fund the construction of a new academy. Moreover, Ruan employed his authority as a deputy of the emperor in celebrating the scholarly production at the Xuehaitang, proclaiming in his 1825 preface to the *Xuehaitang ji* that "the cultured rule of the Great Qing, [has spread] from the north to the south."[18]

Ruan Yuan's dual position as someone who was both an authority and in authority heightened the importance of his role as the founder— or "author"—of the new academy. Consequently, the Xuehaitang curriculum reflected his scholarly agenda of evidential research and radically differed from the largely Cheng-Zhu curricula of other Cantonese academies by introducing new sources of scholarly authority. For example, scholars at the Xuehaitang ritually observed Zheng Xuan's birthday, and, while the academy curriculum was fairly eclectic, Zheng Xuan was promoted as the authority (*zong* 宗) in classical exegeses.[19] In contrast to examinations at other academies, Ruan Yuan asked examinees at the Xuehaitang to produce examinations (*kao* 考) or explications (*jie* 解) of the Classics, and to question such accepted Neo-Confucian philosophical concepts as "nature" (*xing* 性). For example, the first item in the

Xuehaitang ji was a set of three essays explicating judgments (*tuan* 彖) in the *Yijing* 易經 (Classic of Change). Significantly, an "appended" essay by Ruan himself appeared first, serving as model for the other essays.[20] Elsewhere in the collection, a lengthy essay assessed the similarities and differences between the Mao preface and Zheng Xuan commentary to the *Shijing* 詩經 (Book of Poetry).[21]

In addition to redirecting local scholarship on the Classics by introducing the new methods of evidential research, Ruan Yuan also compiled and printed texts that would provide indispensable tools for conducting this type of scholarship. Most notably, Ruan initiated the compilation and printing of the *Huang Qing jingjie* 皇清經解 at the Xuehaitang between 1825 and 1829. This 1,400-*juan* collectanea contained what Ruan Yuan judged to be the most important masterpieces of classical exegesis produced during the Qing up to that time. Significantly, it contained numerous works composed by Yangzhou natives, including Ruan himself, and thereby solidified Ruan's native-place as the center of evidential research. The *Huang Qing jingjie* was meant to serve as an authoritative model for Xuehaitang scholars to follow. The printing blocks of the collectanea were stored in a specially constructed building adjacent to the Xuehaitang, symbolically and practically asserting the academy's control over this type of scholarship.[22]

Ruan Yuan meant to push a literary as well as a scholarly agenda at the Xuehaitang. As can be seen throughout the *Xuehaitang ji*, he favored pre-Tang poetry and parallel prose, the best examples of which were to be found in the sixth-century anthology, the *Wenxuan* 文選. Thus, in one Xuehaitang examination, Ruan asked examinees to conduct an "examination of [Li Shan's 李善 (d. 689)] commentary to the *Wenxuan*." Similarly, in four essays included in the *Xuehaitang ji*, Ruan had examinees analyze the difference between "literary prose" (*wen* 文) and "utilitarian prose" (*bi* 筆). This distinction goes back to the centuries between the Han and Tang dynasties, when certain scholars argued that only prose that was parallel and rhymed could be considered true prose. Other prose, of less literary value, lacked these refined qualities and characterized plain styles used in historical annals. This was a critical issue for Ruan, who preferred pre-Tang parallel "ancient prose" (*guwen* 古文) to the Tang-Song "ancient prose" popular among Neo-Confucian advocates in the Qing. Like many Han Learning enthusiasts who tended to favor parallel prose, Ruan Yuan perceived the greatest scholarly and literary accomplishments aside from those of his own age as having been achieved in pre-Song times.[23]

As with the Xuehaitang examinations that he designed, Ruan Yuan's selection of a permanent site for the academy exemplifies the importance of his involvement in making the Xuehaitang a source of cultural authority. A short descriptive handbook or "gazetteer" of the Xuehaitang, first printed in 1838 and later updated in 1866, informs readers that Ruan Yuan personally selected the site, choosing to locate it on a hill just inside the city wall on the north side of Guangzhou. Situated on the hill and facing south over the city toward the raucous life of the Pearl River, where people of both sexes and all classes mixed with relative ease, the Xuehaitang redirected the gaze of Cantonese high society from the river toward the more refined heights of the academy grounds. Craig Clunas notes in his study of Jiangnan gardens during the Ming dynasty that height was equated with enlightenment and the more "elevated" pursuits of the cultured elite.[24] Likewise, in choosing a site for the Xuehaitang, Ruan Yuan and his Cantonese literati marked off an area that could be appreciated exclusively by those members of the larger cultural elite who had been recognized for their mastery of difficult scholarly and literary pursuits. Clearly distinguishing this space from the rest of the urban hubbub, access to the Xuehaitang was limited.[25]

Ruan Yuan's Xuehaitang quickly became an important site in the cultural life of the local Cantonese elite. Once again, this was due in large part to Ruan Yuan's personal involvement. Thus, on his birthday—the twentieth day of the first lunar month—in 1825, Ruan carried on a private tradition of avoiding guests and making tea, but this year chose the Xuehaitang as his refuge. Two days later, he invited the Cantonese literati to a banquet at the new academy.[26] During the rest of his tenure as governor-general, Ruan Yuan hosted gatherings of Cantonese literati at the Xuehaitang on several occasions, and the academy continued to attract members of the local elite after his departure.[27] In short, availing himself of his status both as a scholarly authority and a political authority, Ruan Yuan actively inserted himself and his new academy into local cultural circles. Through the institution of the Xuehaitang, he introduced new models of scholarship and literature, and, more importantly, created the means for perpetuating his authority in Cantonese society after his departure.

Appropriating Authority: The Xuehaitang Scholars

As we have seen, Ruan Yuan was able to achieve a great deal because he was both in a position of political authority and was recognized as a cultural authority. But because his cultural authority in Guangzhou was bolstered by his political power, there was a possibility that the authority of his legacy would quickly dissipate after 1826, when

Ruan left his post as governor-general. Yet, unlike most provincial officials who sought to transform local scholarly practice through academy education, Ruan had a lasting impact in Guangzhou. In addition to his charismatic authority while in Guangzhou, this was largely due to the institutionalization of his legacy in the Xuehaitang's curriculum, rituals, and physical space.[28]

One reason for the longevity of the Xuehaitang, and by extension of Ruan Yuan's legacy, was that the academy had a particular appeal for a certain segment of the larger cultural elite of Guangzhou and the surrounding Pearl River delta. Most of the scholars who chose to associate themselves with the Xuehaitang belonged to the urban elite, and, of these, a large number consisted of new arrivals to the region. In other words, most of the literati who identified themselves as Xuehaitang scholars were either members of families that had relocated from the delta hinterland to urban Guangzhou or had recently migrated to Guangzhou from such provinces as Zhejiang and Fujian. Moreover, most of these urban literati, or "gentry," were the recent offspring of merchants or private secretaries (*muyou* 幕友) who had moved to Guangzhou to seek their fortune. Therefore, the scholars and writers who responded with the greatest alacrity to Ruan Yuan's examinations in ancient learning at the Xuehaitang represented a geographically and socially mobile urban elite.

While numerous examples of Cantonese literati who emerged from such families may be found in local gazetteers and genealogies, for present purposes a single example should suffice to illustrate this trend. Chen Li 陳澧 (1810–1881) was the most famous scholar associated with the Xuehaitang throughout the academy's history. Like many families in nineteenth-century Guangzhou, Chen Li's family traced its roots to Shaoxing prefecture in Zhejiang province. Early in the Ming dynasty, an ancestor moved from Shaoxing to Nanjing, and his descendents were registered as residents of one of the two counties that shared jurisdiction of Nanjing. In the eighteenth century, Chen Li's grandfather was the first in the family to migrate from Nanjing to Guangzhou. When he died, he was buried at Guangzhou; his two sons, including Chen Li's father, Chen Dajing 陳大經, remained in Guangzhou. As a nonresident sojourner, Dajing was ineligible for the civil service examinations. Nevertheless, he received a classical education from a Shaoxing native who had attained the licentiate degree in Guangzhou as a merchant-registered student in the Qianlong reign (1736–1795). Despite this early classical education, Chen Dajing served for a time as a yamen secretary and then became a merchant. Members of the growing Chen family were beginning to establish themselves in their new home, but they also maintained ties to fellow sojourners. Chen Li's formal mother was the daughter of a Shaoxing man who had purchased rank, suggesting that he was a merchant, while his sister married the son of a Shaoxing family in the salt trade in Guangzhou. Chen Li was the first in his immediate family to register as a Guangzhou resident, and his family ensured that he would receive a classical education. In addition to preparing for and passing the provincial examinations in 1832, Chen Li also took Xuehaitang examinations in the 1820s and 1830s, and served as a codirector of the academy for several decades after 1840.[29]

Why did the Xuehaitang academy particularly appeal to people like Chen Li who belonged to urbanized, in-migrating, and socially ambitious families? It is my contention that literati produced by such families had an interest in maintaining the authoritative legacy of Ruan Yuan and his academy because it bolstered their own status in the local competition for cultural capital. In-migrating and socially ascendant urban families such as the Chens lacked certain cultural resources available to lineages in the prosperous Pearl River delta hinterland. That is, they neither could claim the authority of long-term settlement in the region or the prestige of successful local ancestors, nor did they possess the accouterments of local cultural authority such as the ornate ancestral halls that dotted the delta hinterland. In other words, they lacked cultural legitimacy as *Cantonese* literati. Association with the Xuehaitang and its scholarly agenda offered a means for these urbanized or in-migrating families to gain and maintain local cultural authority in the absence of these kinds of cultural resources. This was achieved through a dual strategy of appealing to the authority of Ruan Yuan's legacy and by employing the scholarly tools Ruan introduced to claim for themselves the role of arbiters of local culture.

The first strategy entailed appealing to the authority of Ruan Yuan as founder of the academy and promoter of evidential research, in effect institutionalizing his charismatic authority in the form of the academy's curriculum and rituals. In order to understand this process, it is necessary to make clear that the Xuehaitang did not function in the same way as most academies (*shuyuan* 書院) during the Qing. This was reflected first of all in its name: the Xuehaitang was literally a "hall" (*tang* 堂) rather than an "academy." Unlike other academies such as the Yuexiu shuyuan, the Xuehaitang did not have dormitories to house students. Likewise, Xuehaitang examinations were not administered on the academy grounds; instead, examinees were allowed to compose their essays and poems at home. Thus, the Xuehaitang was not so much a school as it was a prestige-granting mechanism. By ranking examinees and publishing exemplary essays and poems in the *Xuehaitang ji* and subsequent collections, first Ruan Yuan and later the codirectors recognized mastery of meticulous evidential research and difficult pre-Tang literary forms. In effect the activities of the Xuehaitang certified the cultural authority of a small segment of the larger elite.[30]

When innovations were made to the Xuehaitang curriculum, they were presented in a manner that appealed to the authority of Ruan Yuan. In 1834 Lu Kun 盧坤 (1772–1835), the current Guangdong-Guangxi governor-general and a follower of Ruan Yuan, recruited ten "specialized students" from among the regular Xuehaitang examinees to select one text in which they were interested from among any of the *Thirteen Classics* (with Han and Tang commentaries), the first four Standard Histories, the *Wenxuan* anthology, Du Fu's 杜甫 (712–770) poetry, Han Yu's 韓愈 (768–824) prose, and the collected works of Zhu Xi. A student would keep daily records of his progress, which would be appraised quarterly by the codirector whose expertise most closely matched the student's interest.[31] In his preface to the *Xuehaitang ji*, Ruan had presented a vision of the "specialized courses" in embryonic form, describing students specializing in pre-Song classical exegeses, etymology, the works of Zhu Xi, historical studies, *Wenxuan*-style literature, and Tang-Song poetry and prose.[32] In later commemorations of the specialized students system, provincial officials such as Lu Kun and Xuehaitang scholars such as Chen Li portrayed Ruan Yuan as the ultimate "author" of the specialized courses.[33]

Nancy Rosenblum's assertion that authority "has both an instrumental and a symbolic face" can be usefully applied to an analysis of the Xuehaitang, because the preservation of Ruan Yuan's authority after his departure depended to a large extent on symbols incorporated into the design of the academy and into the academy's rituals.[34] For example, the Xuehaitang gazetteer notes that one of the annual "refined gatherings" at the academy was to mark Ruan Yuan's birthday on the twentieth day of the first lunar month. This was the only birthday observed in addition to Zheng Xuan's. Furthermore, Ruan's presence was literally inscribed throughout the academy. His image was engraved on a stele at the academy, as explained in an accompanying inscription by one of the first codirectors, "in order to [express] our determination [to follow] the transmissions of the teachers."[35] Another stele contained Ruan's preface to the *Xuehaitang ji*. One of the academy's brick walls was adorned with an inscription that read, "the Xuehaitang established by Grand Guardian of the Heir Apparent Ruan [Yuan]."[36] These commemorations of Ruan Yuan were transformed into apotheosis with his enshrinement in 1863. The Xuehaitang had been used as barracks for British and French forces when they occupied Guangzhou from 1857 to 1861, and it was badly

damaged in a typhoon in 1862. When it was reconstructed in 1863, one
of the old buildings on the academy grounds was converted into a shrine
in honor of the "Grand Tutor [of the Heir Apparent] Ruan."[37]

In addition to invoking the authority of Ruan Yuan, a second strategy consisted of employing the new, "authoritative" scholarly methods
and literary styles promoted at the Xuehaitang to study and write about
local Cantonese culture. In the process, Xuehaitang scholars made a
claim to be the rightful arbiters of local culture, even though many of
them had much more shallow roots in the region than did literati from
the dominant lineages of the delta hinterland. For example, evidential
research crept into their poetry on local sites. Likewise, in the spirit of
Ruan Yuan's emphasis on epigraphy and on-site investigation, some
Xuehaitang scholars produced new kinds of local histories. Both in
composing poetry and in writing history, literati associated with the
Xuehaitang presented themselves as the authoritative interpreters of
local culture.[38]

But this process of producing new, authoritative texts that displaced
others is best seen in another genre of text, the anthology. In order to
illustrate this, let us briefly compare two anthologies, one produced in
the delta before the establishment of the Xuehaitang, and a later anthology compiled by one of the most important Xuehaitang scholars.[39] The
representative delta-based, pre-Xuehaitang anthology is Luo Xuepeng's
羅學鵬 *Guangdong wenxian* 廣東文獻, printed in installments in the
1810s. Luo belonged to a powerful lineage in the Pearl River delta hinterland, and he compiled and printed his anthology at his studio largely
with his own funds. In his editorial principles, Luo informs the reader
that he compiled the anthology for the purpose of celebrating the great
Neo-Confucian philosophers, statesmen, and poets of the Cantonese
tradition, but stresses that all of their achievements ultimately stemmed
from their Neo-Confucian foundation. While Luo opens his anthology
with the works of the Tang poet and statesman Zhang Jiuling 張九齡
(673–740), the rest of the anthology is largely centered on the works of
the great Cantonese philosophers of the Ming dynasty and several prominent Cantonese poets who were martyred during the Ming-Qing transition. Their achievements are proof, Luo asserts, of the moral vigor of
Cantonese literati and the brilliant spirit of the land.[40] In the *Guangdong
wenxian*, Luo Xuepeng thus constructs a particular type of Cantonese
literati identity, one firmly situated in the delta hinterland and appealing
to the authority of Neo-Confucianism as exhibited by the ancestors of
the dominant delta lineages.

Tan Ying's 譚瑩 (1800–1871) *Lingnan yishu* 嶺南遺書 anthology,
printed in six installments between 1831 and 1863, appeals to a very

different type of authority. Tan was hired to compile the anthology by the wealthy maritime monopoly, or Cohong, merchant Wu Chongyao 伍崇曜 (1810–1863), whose family had migrated from Fujian to Guangzhou in the early Qing. Like Wu Chongyao, a relatively recent arrival to Guangzhou, Tan Ying belonged to an urbanized family that had moved from the delta hinterland to work as merchants in the city.[41] Though the Xuehaitang did not directly sponsor the anthology, Tan Ying was closely associated with the academy before and after his appointment as codirector in 1838. Moreover, the *Lingnan yishu* was in fact compiled through the cooperative sharing of books among a group of sojourning Jiangnan literati who first came to Guangzhou with Ruan Yuan and Cantonese literati who were associated with the Xuehaitang. The end product reflected its origins—this was a bibliophile's anthology. Whereas previous local anthologies sought to provide a comprehensive overview of the Cantonese written canon, the *Lingnan yishu* would offer only a selection of rare works. Therefore, in contrast to the coherent moral hierarchy implicit in the organization of the *Guangdong wenxian*, the arrangement of texts in the *Lingnan yishu* does not reflect any particular chronological or moral order.

Tan Ying's 1831 preface to the *Lingnan yishu* further indicated the unique nature of this new anthology. Written in very ornate parallel prose, it was unlike anything else produced in Guangdong in recent times. The preface was a display both of erudition and of literary skill, combining Ruan Yuan's scholarly agenda of evidential research with his literary ideal of parallel prose. Furthermore, through the inclusion of some obscure eighteenth-century works on mathematics, astronomy, and philology, much of the scholarship found in the *Lingnan yishu* looked quite similar to the type of evidential research conducted at the Xuehaitang. Finally, the *Lingnan yishu* was a celebration of the scholarship produced by the scholarly elite associated with the Xuehaitang. The fifth and sixth installments included the works of six early codirectors, and thereby affirmed the stature of the academy as Guangzhou's new cultural hub.

While both the *Guangdong wenxian* and the *Lingnan yishu* celebrated the achievements of Cantonese literati culture, the former centered that culture in Neo-Confucian practice and delta ancestors, while Cantonese culture as portrayed in the latter appeared to culminate in the Xuehaitang and its scholarly and literary ideals. In order to be incorporated into the *Guangdong wenxian*, a text not only had to have been produced by an exemplary Cantonese author, but also had to contain something of moral value that would be relevant to a wide audience among the delta elite. For inclusion in the *Lingnan yishu*, a text had to have scholarly value that would be recognized by a specialized audience among the urban elite in Guangdong and elsewhere. Most important, a text must not be spurious, as was, according to several Xuehaitang scholars, a putative Zhang Jiuling text included in the *Guangdong wenxian*.

The fact that most Cantonese anthologies produced after the establishment of the Xuehaitang were compiled by scholars associated with Ruan Yuan's academy indicates the degree to which urban Cantonese literati at the Xuehaitang came to dominate local cultural production. Their command over a certain type of scholarship and literature allowed them to make claims as authorities on local culture and to achieve a partial monopolization of the region's cultural resources.[42]

Conclusion

This chapter has attempted to expand current notions regarding the social practice of authority in late imperial China by focusing on a space somewhere between the imperial court and the patriarchal family. This brief account of the activities of one charismatic official, Ruan Yuan, and the scholars who associated themselves with his Xuehaitang academy has hopefully highlighted some dynamics of authority in practice. First, while "pure" scholarship completely divorced from political authority is not possible in any society, Confucian scholarship in late imperial China was very intimately intertwined with political authority. Moreover, in this society, even Confucian "eremitism" was a political stance. Thus, Craig Clunas has shown that the "reclusive" garden of the late Ming was in fact an important space for social interaction and intense social competition, or "politics" on a local scale.[43] Political authority was even more salient in the case of the late-Qing academy examined here. Ruan Yuan utilized his unusual combination of political authority and cultural authority to create an academy that had a lasting impact on local culture. Through the Xuehaitang, Ruan effectively instilled new standards of authority in local scholarship and literature.

The case of Ruan Yuan and the Xuehaitang also highlights the importance of symbolic appeals to lineage in scholarship and literature. While the importance of symbol in late imperial Chinese political authority has long been taken for granted, symbolic appeals to Ruan Yuan were equally important in maintaining continuity in the academy's scholarly and literary agenda. Ruan Yuan's authority was literally inscribed on walls and stelae throughout the Xuehaitang, reminding future generations of Xuehaitang scholars about the source of their own power as cultural authorities in Guangzhou. After Ruan Yuan left Guangzhou, scholars at the Xuehaitang continued to invoke his authority, whether in making curricular reforms or constructing a shrine in his honor. The extent to which the Xuehaitang continued to be identified as Ruan Yuan's academy suggests the importance of being able to locate oneself in a lineage of scholarly or literary authority.

Nevertheless, it must be kept in mind both that the scholarly-literary authority proclaimed by the Xuehaitang particularly appealed to one segment of the local cultural elite and that the symbols of that authority were malleable and could be applied creatively. Thus, while the creation of the Xuehaitang stemmed from Ruan Yuan's assertion of his political and scholarly authority for the sake of uplifting what he saw as a backward region, his academy was utilized by a segment of that region's elite to increase its own authority and prestige in the local competition for cultural capital. For many members of this elite, identity with the Xuehaitang became an important strategy for social advancement. Other members of the larger Cantonese cultural elite could rely on other sources of cultural authority, and therefore largely ignored the new academy. In other words, some Cantonese literati, in particular those who lacked other claims to legitimacy, benefited from articulating an identity with the authority of the Xuehaitang and its founder; they appropriated Ruan Yuan's authority for their own purposes.

Thus, a focus on local practice reveals that, while symbols of authority may have a tendency to be perpetuated, in their application there is much more room for negotiation than may seem possible from an analysis of a founder's vision alone. Just as local scholars at the Xuehaitang could appropriate the founder's authority for their own purposes, perhaps subjects under an emperor or dependents under a patriarch could find similar room for movement within the late imperial Chinese court and family.

Notes

1. Lucian W. Pye, *Asian Power and Politics: The Cultural Dimensions of Authority* (Cambridge: The Belknap Press of Harvard University Press, 1985).

2. Prasenjit Duara, "Elites and the Structures of Authority in the Villages of North China, 1900–1949," in Joseph W. Esherick and Mary Backus Rankin, ed., *Chinese Elites and Patterns of Dominance* (Berkeley: University of California Press, 1990), pp. 264–268; Bradly W. Reed, *Talons and Teeth: County Clerks and Runners in the Qing Dynasty* (Stanford, CA: Stanford University Press, 2000), pp. 10–12.

3. Peter K. Bol, "Neo-Confucianism and Local Society, Twelfth to Sixteenth Century: A Case Study," in Paul Jakov Smith and Richard von Glahn, ed., *The Song-Yuan-Ming Transition in Chinese History* (Cambridge: Harvard University Asia Center, 2003), p. 281. Lucian Pye recognizes that such local systems of authority as families and clan associations "were decisive in shaping Chinese society," but he maintains that "they were content to protect their particular interests through informal and often devious means without trying to reshape national authority in order to make it supportive of those interests." Pye, *Asian Power and Politics*, p. 184.

4. Patricia Buckley Ebrey, *The Inner Quarters: Marriage and the Lives of Women in the Sung Period* (Berkeley: University of California Press, 1993), pp. 267–270.

5. R. Bin Wong, *China Transformed: Historical Change and the Limits of the European Experience* (Ithaca, NY: Cornell University Press, 1997), p. 114.

6. R. Kent Guy, *The Emperor's Four Treasuries: Scholars and the State in the Late Ch'ien-lung Era* (Cambridge: Harvard University Press, 1987), p. 155.

7. Thomas A. Wilson, *Genealogy of the Way: The Construction and Uses of the Confucian Tradition in Late Imperial China* (Stanford, CA: Stanford University Press, 1995), pp. 82–97.

8. Bol, "Neo-Confucianism and Local Society," p. 253.

9. Benjamin A. Elman, *A Cultural History of Civil Examinations in Late Imperial China* (Berkeley: University of California Press, 2000), pp. 519–520.

10. Bol, "Neo-Confucianism and Local Society," pp. 245, 281.

11. Bol, "Neo-Confucianism and Local Society," p. 256.

12. Alexander Woodside, "State, Scholars, and Orthodoxy: The Ch'ing Academies, 1736–1839," in Kwang-ching Liu, ed., *Orthodoxy in Late Imperial China* (Berkeley: University of California Press, 1990), pp. 168–170.

13. Guy, *The Emperor's Four Treasuries*, p. 155. Elaborating on the work of Benjamin Elman, John Henderson describes the historicist vision of some Qing scholars who challenged the view of the Classics as a unique source of value by relegating them to a status equal to other genres of writing. See John B. Henderson, *Scripture, Canon, and Commentary: A Comparison of Confucian and Western Exegesis* (Princeton, NJ: Princeton University Press, 1991), pp. 214–215.

14. Guy, *The Emperor's Four Treasuries*, pp. 155–156; Elman, *A Cultural History of Civil Examinations*, pp. 504–520.

15. Angela Zito, *Of Body & Brush: Grand Sacrifice as Text/Performance in Eighteenth-Century China* (Chicago: University of Chicago Press, 1997), p. 69.

16. On the distinction between being an authority on some subject and being in a position of authority in an organization, see Richard E. Flathman, *The*

Practice of Political Authority: Authority and the Authoritative (Chicago: The University of Chicago Press, 1980), pp. 16–17. In an article on the ideal of authority in the *Lunyu* (Analects), Herbert Fingarette suggests a type of authority in Confucian thought absent in Western models: that is, that "the exercise of authority will rest crucially on an authoritative person's acting as a model." Herbert Fingarette, "How the Analects Portrays the Ideal of Efficacious Authority," *Journal of Chinese Philosophy* 8 (1981), p. 30. This calls into question the extent to which the dichotomy between "an authority" and "in authority" may be applied to a Chinese emperor or his officials. Also see Roger T. Ames, "A Response to Fingarette on Ideal Authority in the Analects," *Journal of Chinese Philosophy*. 8 (1981), p. 55.

17. Tobie Meyer-Fong, *Building Culture in Early Qing Yangzhou* (Stanford, CA: Stanford University Press, 2003), pp. 118–120.

18. *Nanhai xian zhi* 南海縣志, 1872 edition, 12:24a.

19. Lin Botong 林伯桐, comp., *Xuehaitang zhi* 學海堂志, 1866, reprint (Taipei: Guangwen shuju, 1971), 39a. The name of the Xuehaitang was inspired by the Han "New Text" Confucian He Xiu 何休; however, the rituals and curriculum at the Xuehaitang clearly show a preference for the "Old Text" scholar Zheng Xuan.

20. Ruan Yuan 阮元, *Xuehaitang ji* 學海堂集, 1825, reprint, in *Zhongguo lidai shuyuan zhi*, volume 13 (Nanjing: Jiangsi jiaoyu chubanshe, 1995), 1:1a–3b.

21. Ruan, *Xuehaitang ji, juan* 3–4.

22. Lin, *Xuehaitang zhi*, 48a.

23. Ruan Yuan, *Yanjingshi ji* 揅經室集 (Taipei: Shijie shuju, 1982), *sanji*, pp. 657–663.

24. Craig Clunas, *Fruitful Sites: Garden Culture in Ming Dynasty China* (Durham, NC: Duke University Press, 1996), p. 152.

25. Lin, *Xuehaitang zhi*, 44a.

26. Ruan Yuan, *Yanjingshi ji, xuji*, p. 199; Xie Lansheng 謝蘭生, *Changxingxingzhai riji* 常惺惺齋日記, 1819–1829, manuscript, Beijing Library, 1/22/DG5.

27. Xie, *Changxingxingzhai riji*, 6/13/DG5, 8/15/DG5, 9/23/DG5, 5/15/DG5, 8/15/DG6.

28. This process might be described, following Weber's categories, as one of the founder's charismatic authority through a process of routinization being transformed into traditional authority. See Max Weber, *Max Weber: The Theory of Social and Economic Organization*, translated by A. M. Henderson and Talcott Parsons (New York: Oxford University Press, 1947), p. 328. Herbert Fingarette,

however, dismisses the applicability of Weber's conception of charisma to the "charismatic" Confucian. See Fingarette, "How the Analects Portrays the Ideal of Efficacious Authority," p. 39.

29. Chen Li 陳澧, ed., *Jiacheng* 家乘, undated manuscript, Zhongshan Library, Guangzhou; Chen Li 陳澧, *Dongshu ji* 東塾集, in Shen Yunlong, ed., *Jindai Zhongguo shiliao congkan*, volume 461 (Taipei: Wenhai chubanshe, 1970), 5:17a–19a, 6:12a. Chen Li's birth mother was a concubine of Chen Dajing.

30. Pierre Bourdieu, *The Logic of Practice*, translated by Richard Nice (Stanford, CA: Stanford University Press, 1990), p. 132; Pierre Bourdieu and Jean-Claude Passeron, *Reproduction: In Education, Society and Culture*, translated by Richard Nice (Beverly Hills, CA: Sage Publications, 1977), p. 108. In contrast to the credentials granted in modern education systems or in the Qing civil service examinations, success at the Xuehaitang did not guarantee cultural capital once and for all; rather, mastery of scholarship and literature had to be repeatedly demonstrated through successive examinations and literary outings.

31. *Xuehaitang zhuanke zhangcheng* 學海堂專課章程, Guangxu era, Zhongshan wenxianguan, Guangzhou, 3a–b; Lin, *Xuehaitang zhi*, 25b–26a.

32. *Nanhai xian zhi*, 12:24a.

33. In this context, Hannah Arendt's interpretation of "authority" as the augmentation of a foundation laid by an "author" is instructive: "The author in this case is not the builder but the one who inspired the whole enterprise and whose spirit, therefore, much more than the spirit of the actual builder, is represented in the building itself." Arendt, "What Was Authority?" in Carl J. Friedrich, ed., *Authority* (Cambridge: Harvard University Press, 1958), p. 100.

34. Nancy L. Rosenblum, "Studying Authority: Keeping Pluralism in Mind," in J. Roland Pennock and John W. Chapman, ed., *Authority Revisited* (New York: New York University Press, 1987), p. 109.

35. Lin, *Xuehaitang zhi*, 34b–35a.

36. Lin, *Xuehaitang zhi*, 35b.

37. Lin, *Xuehaitang zhi*, *tushuo*:3b.

38. Steven B. Miles, "Rewriting the Southern Han (917–971): The Production of Local Culture in Nineteenth-Century Guangzhou," *Harvard Journal of Asiatic Studies* 62 (1) (June 2002), pp. 64, 66–72.

39. The following discussion is largely drawn from Steven B. Miles, "Local Matters: Lineage, Scholarship and the Xuehaitang Academy in the Construction of Regional Identities in South China, 1810–1880," Ph.D. dissertation, University of Washington, 2000, pp. 122–157.

40. Luo Xuepeng 羅學鵬, *Guangdong wenxian: chuji-siji* 廣東文獻初集四集, 1863, editorial principles, 5b.

41. Tan Zongjun 譚宗浚, *Licun caotang shichao* 荔村草堂詩鈔, 1892, 6:12b–13b; Wu Chongyao 伍崇曜, *Lingnan yishu* 嶺南遺書, 1831–1863.

42. Bourdieu, *The Logic of Practice*, p. 125.

43. Clunas, *Fruitful Sites*, pp. 96–97.

Intellectual and Political Controversies over Authority in China: 1898–1922

Lawrence R. Sullivan

"We do not live by virtue of the monarch."

Wu Yu, 1919

The problem of transforming political authority in late nineteenth and early twentieth century China was intimately related to the quest for a new state form and political order. As the "moral administrative reformism" of Qing "practical statesmanship" (*qingshi*) of the late nineteenth century proved increasingly inadequate to the country's mounting political and economic problems, attention shifted to reorganizing the political system and legitimizing it with different principles.[1] But replacing the imperial autocracy and bureaucratic state with alternative institutional arrangements based on new concepts of authority proved enormously complicated and politically divisive. From the late 1890s onward, Chinese intellectuals and politicians clashed over the country's political future, yet with little agreement on the basic principles and structures of authority.

Political Authority: A Definition

Altering political structures in China reflected the inherent difficulties of consciously transforming something so fundamental and deep-seated as political authority. In this article, authority is defined as an imperative command binding people to unifying common action.[2] Authority is the core of the political order, a set of absolute principles compelling uniformity that both precedes power and imbues it with morality. Authority makes possible the effective exercise of power, augmenting it from a mere act of will to legitimate action. Power without authority is reduced to pure coercion with no overarching moral obligation to sanction it.[3] Authority is "not an external force commanding an individual against his will," but an accepted dependence and obedience

171

in which men retain a sense of personal freedom without resort to fear and coercion.[4]

This willful compliance is not a mere response, however, to reasoned discourse or a "rational demonstration" of the authoritative act. Neither enlightenment nor empirical verification constitutes necessary prerequisites of authority. The authoritative judgment is instead a "substitute for objectivity" bringing about united action when two (or more) equally rational and possible options exist for achieving the "common good."[5] As Hannah Arendt notes: "The authoritarian relation between the one who commands and the one who obeys rests neither on common reason nor on the power of the one who commands; what they have in common is the hierarchy itself, whose rightness and legitimacy both recognize . . ."[6]

The strength of a secure authority for any political order is that it draws on innermost preferences that are stamped on the human character over generations and largely accepted as self-evident.[7] Authority in this sense is the constitutive element of any society and reflects an accepted standard of "right" against which the exercise of power can be evaluated and checked.[8] Specifically, authority is grounded in historical traditions, community values, and/or religious-scientific definitions of "the truth" that form the basic consensual framework for the concrete application of the authoritative act. As one commentator notes: "All authority is rightful authority" with community, tradition, religion, and/or science serving as the "higher source" of values validating political acts and structures.[9] "The most essential function of authority is the issuance and carrying out of rules expressing the requirements of the common good materially determined."[10] The creation of a new authority involves much more, therefore, than just the establishment of new political organizations and the appointment of new officeholders to command the state. As the preexisting authority weakens, the very foundation of community and individual identity are critically examined as conditions once accepted as an intrinsic part of the perceived "natural order" undergo radical alteration. Fundamental values of culture, historical tradition, and epistemology are redefined and reconceptualized, often through intense debate and civil conflict. Nothing is indeed more provocative of uncompromising, internecine struggle than competing and fundamentally contradictory visions of political authority.

Redefining Political Authority in China

The problem of transforming political authority in China during the modern era was compounded by the country's two thousand years of unbroken monarchical absolutism. The "mandate of heaven" (*tianming*) was an expression of a universal moral order: eternal, immutable, and beyond human affect. According to the Chinese historian Hao Chang: "The principle of kingship remained an unchanging fixture of Chinese political tradition" with heaven "always upheld as the ultimate source of legitimation, and kingship as the only institutional device to keep the human world in harmony. . . . In the eyes of the Chinese people, the Son of Heaven was not just a ruler of an empire; he was . . . a sort of cosmological linchpin functioning at the center of the world and radiating a universal authority on earth."[11] In the West, the historical lucidity of Athenian and Roman democracy, the rich republican experience of fifteenth-century Italian city-states, and the limitations on kingship under Feudalism, provided constitutional and democratic theorists of the seventeenth and eighteenth centuries with alternative political models to absolutism.[12] But China's history offered few positive guidelines for a radical departure from monarchical authority. Despite strong opposition to the "despot" (*ba*) in the Confucian political thought of Huang Zongxi, Wang Fuzhi, Gu Yanwu, and Tang Zhen, Chinese philosophy did not produce the recurring rejection of traditional patriarchal authority and political paternalism prominent in Western thought from the Reformation onward.[13] Since the Song Dynasty (960–1279 AD) in China, Neo-Confucianism had instead cultivated a widespread political "quiescence" (*jingji*) and "meekness" (*rou*) fundamentally at odds with the Faustian-Promethean ethos of the West. More recently, nineteenth century "practical statesmanship" had linked China's quest for "wealth and power" with "the kingly way" (*wangdao*), while even rebels against the existing order, such as the Taiping leader Hong Xiuquan, had accepted kingship as his model for a new political regime.[14]

The weakness of an antimonarchical impulse in China also reflected the absence of the critical social foundations for an assault on kingship. The path to democracy in the West, especially in sixteenth- and seventeenth-century England, followed profound changes in the religious, political, and economic order. The rise of separatist Puritanism emphasizing the moral worth of the individual and the church congregation as a voluntary "fellowship of equals"; the radical egalitarianism of Cromwell's New Model Army; the growth of a legal profession willing to use common law tradition to oppose royal prerogatives; the assertion of the nationality of the English people in conjunction with the insistence on the people's right to political participation in parliament; the weakening of family control over inheritance, plus the massive shift in land ownership from monastic to private hands and the beginnings of an industrial economy: all these constituted a social prelude to the transfer of authority from king to parliament and people.[15] But in China an archaic social structure and underdeveloped economy apparently robbed the country of the broad social forces that support a shift away from monarchy.[16]

The responses of Chinese political reformers and intellectuals beginning in the late nineteenth century to this historical context were diametrically opposed. The more conservative among them believed that the country's political and economic "backwardness" necessitated a strategy of political change that emphasized continuities with the monarchical tradition. But others, especially those attracted to Western-style democracy, believed that the very depth of influence by the monarchy in Chinese society demanded a wholesale, iconoclastic assault on the institutional structure and social-cultural bases of imperial autocracy.

"Enlightened Despotism" versus Democracy: 1895–1912

"We are still only a patriarchal people."

Yan Fu

The traditional Chinese view that monarchy and civilization were inseparable was first challenged by Kang Youwei in the 1890s.[17] Kang argued that over the course of two thousand years the long line of despots in China had created an excessive reverence for hierarchical status and servility that had become firmly embedded in the country's social and political norms.[18] But Kang also realized that corrupt imperial advisers and an unwieldy bureaucracy were equally to blame for China's inability to meet the challenge of the dynamic West and an emergent Japan.[19] A key supporter of the 1898 Hundred Days of Reform, Kang feared the impact of Sun Yatsen's emerging revolutionary program and thus he opted for a "reforming monarch" to create a strong government with the authority to inaugurate fundamental social and economic changes. By relying on the people's "supreme regard for monarchical power" and by exploiting popular belief in Confucianism that Kang advocated converting into a religion, the modernizing monarch would instill the Chinese people with a collective spirit and energy that Kang (and Yan Fu) believed was the key to Western and Japanese strength.[20]

Kang Youwei's views closely paralleled eighteenth-century Western theories of "enlightened despotism." Where the social order posed major obstacles to modernity and democracy, political thinkers, especially on the European continent, supported the king's use of political fiat as a temporary, though necessary, measure for enforcing fundamental reforms. The imperial despot commanded the authority necessary to cut through the maze of intermediate corporate groups—guilds, estates, and the "feudal" family—to establish the foundations of a modern society. Although personally committed to reason and enlightenment, the monarch elicited blind obedience from the common man and thereby provided the common bond among "the competing rights in a diversified society" that had previously obstructed progressive change.[21] In 1765 Voltaire proclaimed that "the cause of the king of France was the cause of the philosophes"; and in 1805, Hegel believed that only a modern "Theseus" could combat the particular interests that mired Germany in feudalism.[22] Hegel believed that a modern German state should ultimately be based on "self-determination" with political power devolving into a meritorious, "universal" bureaucracy and a constitutional monarch. But in the absence of a common will emanating from German civil society, the "world historical individual" must, Hegel argued, first exploit his absolutist authority as the "God" of the general population in order to forge a common political consciousness and national sentiment. Without a leader such as Napoleon I—admired by Hegel—to guarantee the rights of property and security that were prerequisites for the social contract, Germany could not create a political order based on constitutional democracy.[23] Together both enlightenment and despotism were necessary to produce a modern polity.

Kang Youwei also looked to Napoleon I, as well as Peter the Great and the Meiji monarch, as political models for leadership in a modernizing China. Contrary to the passive, unobtrusive emperor of orthodox Confucianism, Kang favored an activist, monarchical hero—a "Chinese Caesar"—to carry out institutional reform and alter the old customs that Kang believed perpetuated Chinese parochialism and fostered national weakness.[24] In Kang Youwei's view, the emperor should build his personal authority throughout society by establishing a "joint rule of monarch and people," relying on such measures as distributing his picture to the general population and publishing copies of his reform decrees so as to foster popular trust. Such a strategy would not only allow the monarch to circumvent the opposition of the conservative bureaucratic elite, but also close the yawning gap between ruler and ruled that Kang believed had traditionally robbed China of the collective unity so necessary to inaugurate modernization.[25] Popular reverence for the imperial mystique would spur Chinese society to begin the difficult process of political and economic modernization. At the same time, maintaining the monarch's authority would prevent the social chaos that a precipitous leap from autocracy to republican government could bring to China's immature polity. In the opinion of Kang Youwei, China needed to concentrate power, not divide it.[26]

"Enlightened autocracy" (*kaiming zhuanzhi*) was also advocated by Liang Qichao.[27] In the 1890s, Liang had initially expressed his support for Jean Jacques Rousseau's doctrine of popular participation and the general will as a "spiritual medicine" for breaking China's " 'three thousand year tradition of despotism' " that, Liang believed, had ravaged its people and stifled progress. At that time, Liang argued that political reform "has never been accomplished in a country which relied on one or two men to do it" but instead must rely on " 'the whole people.' "[28] Following a trip to Chinatowns in America in 1903, however, Liang took a dimmer view of democracy in general and entertained serious doubts about the Chinese people's ability to participate in popular government. Chinese "slavishness" (*nulide*) was not just the creation of the monarchy, as he had previously believed, but seemed inherent to Chinese culture. "Chinese people simply hope for humane government from their lord. Thus, when they run into humaneness, they are treated as infants; when they meet inhumanity, they are treated as meat on a chopping block."[29] The incessant factionalism and corresponding absence of a "national consciousness" made liberty and political order incompatible in China. Contrary to the positive image of the people underlying Western—especially Rousseauian—social contract doctrine, Liang now believed that the Chinese were fundamentally incapable of resolving political conflict through self-government. In a society in which social relations were "atomized" by the traditional family, Chinese people were parochial, closed-minded, and lacking in the basic "collective" (*qun*) identity and "public morality" (*gong de*) necessary for democracy. "[T]hey have no regard for the common good," Liang averred in criticizing his countrymen. "They can neither organize an association of more than three people nor maintain a [political] party for over a year."[30] Similar to Hegel's view of early nineteenth-century Germany, Liang believed that China was constituted by an aggregate of particular interests such that any expression of the "general will" by the population would produce chaos instead of order. Incapable of representing itself, Chinese society lacked the common bond and communitarian ethic that was necessary to create "a people" out of "a multitude" to establish the foundations of a modern, democratic state.

Based on this profoundly cynical view of his countrymen, Liang Qichao argued that the only escape from this enveloping culture in China was a temporary, "enlightened" ruler, modeled on Germany's Frederick the Great or Bismarck. With China confronting an increasingly fierce international environment, despotic authority was absolutely necessary to foster national unity and create the centralized political structures and rational values central to a modern society.[31] Although democracy remained Liang's long-term goal for China, the general absence of a unified population and "universal" state bureaucracy created a temporary need for a single law-giver—a political demiurge—to lead the country's political transition to modernity, while such single-minded leadership would also avoid a chaotic social revolution. The heroic spirit and personal genius of the great leader would transform the Chinese people, imparting to the "lethargic" population the aggressiveness and unifying will that they desperately lacked, especially in comparison to Westerners and the Japanese.[32] In Liang's view, the historically familiar Legalistic tradition of China that legitimized the strong leader was a more appropriate authority in China's political transition than the unfamiliar Western doctrine of democracy. Enlightened despotism would serve as the catalyst for creating a "new people" who would be politically active, energetic, and, most importantly, nationalistic.[33] Such a regime would also construct the permanent state apparatus that, consistent with the doctrines of the Swiss-German thinker Johann Bluntschli and the German legal jurists Conrad Bornhak and Rudolph von Jhering that Liang now embraced, were the key ingredients to achieve "wealth and power." Liang's Carlylian hero would set into motion a process of fundamental institutional reform culminating in the creation of a corporate and ultimately democratic state that would be based on a rational authority and would be free from the parochial and narrow concerns of "village China" that thoroughly infused the traditional political order.[34]

The model of an enlightened monarchy advocated by Kang Youwei and Liang Qichao never became a political reality in the Qing Dynasty, except perhaps during the short period of the 1898 Hundred Days of Reform. But similar concepts of authority informed the views of many early anti-Qing revolutionaries, though generally in a nonmonarchical framework. Espousing vaguely democratic goals and intensely opposed to imperial tyranny, student opponents of the Qing in the early 1900s still yearned for a strong heroic leader. Lacking an indigenous model of opposition politics and organization, these young rebels often worked through existing secret societies and relied on a vision of political leadership that was fundamentally conservative in content. In a society in which, they believed, the overwhelming superstition, apathy, and ignorance of the population prevented a democratic alternative, revolutionary change could only be effected by a movement energized by a single, powerful leader. Although most anti-Qing radicals were strongly committed to the immediate formation of a democratic government after the

impending collapse of the dynasty, their intense individualism, romanti-
cism, and disdain for building permanent organization often drove them
to embrace strong heroic leaders as a temporary expedient.[35]

"Enlightened despotism" was also espoused by Sun Yatsen in reaction to the political disunity that accompanied the collapse of the Qing
Dynasty in 1911.[36] Despite his earlier outrage over Liang Qichao's retreat
from constitutional monarchy to absolutism, Sun espoused a paternalis-
tic leadership doctrine as the second "stage" in his long-term plan for
China's political evolution. For Sun the personal authority of "geniuses"
and "men of determination" would reshape the consciousness of what
he characterized as China's "unthinking majority" who were "disposed
toward war and killing" and generally incapable of creating organization
because of excessive "individual freedom" and a general lack of "a [sense
of] collectivity."[37] Citing the crushing effects of the "slave system in China
that has been in existence for thousands of years," Sun argued that "the
common people do not yet know that they should assume the role of
ruler. Therefore, we have no other method than coercion to force them
to become the ruler and teach them to practice it. This is what I mean
by political tutelage."[38]

These principles were reflected in Sun's practical approaches to
political leadership. Following the failure of the Second Revolution in
1913, Sun personally organized the Chinese Revolutionary Party on
whose members he attempted to impose an all-encompassing leader
principle.[39] Responding to intense factionalism, disloyalty to the leader,
and absence of centralized control that Sun believed had destroyed the
earlier prorepublican *Tongmenghui*, he argued that the only way to
"achieve revolutionary social change without abandoning national unity"
was to enforce absolute obedience to "his"—the leader's—personal
authority. In a society where Sun's ally Dai Jitao stated that "partisan
struggle is destroying the nation," Sun considered an abstract, institutional form of democratic authority inappropriate for a people who were
just emerging from centuries of monarchical rule.[40] Like Kang Youwei,
Sun believed that the Chinese people would most readily respond to a
highly personalized political authority that exhibited strong continuities
with the past. The personal "will" of the single leader would generate the
unified action that proliferate factions, regional loyalties, and excessively
divisive opinions of the parliamentary parties formed after the fall of the
Qing, had failed to achieve.[41] In a paraphrase of the French political sci-
entist Robert Michels, Sun stated that "political parties most dedicated
to popular rule have to be obedient to the will of one man." Since "there
are many things that you [the members] do not understand," Sun insisted

that the rank-and-file of the party must "blindly follow me."[42] Never again would the Chinese revolution falter as it had in the past because of "the unwillingness to follow the commands of one leader."[43] Led by a single, all-powerful leader and composed of self-sacrificing, heroic activists, the authoritarian party in Sun Yatsen's vision would be the temporary expedient to forge a new, more unified political order.

The Democratic Critique of Chinese Monarchy

This combination of enlightenment with the strong, despotic leader was rejected as inherently contradictory by advocates of democracy for China from the late Qing Dynasty onward. Although in theory the enlightened ruler would be the architect of his own destruction by voluntarily giving way to representative institutions once the social and economic foundations of democracy were achieved, Europe's experience with self-appointed enlightened monarchs suggested a different political outcome. If China replicated regimes similar to that of Frederick the Great or Catherine II, the results would fall far short of a liberal polity. The assaults by monarchs in Germany and Russia on the economic, religious, and ideological pillars of feudalism, and reform of the administrative and legal machinery, had not led to democracy, but rather to highly centralized states.[44] In the view of aspiring Chinese democrats, "enlightened despotism" would not lead to democracy, but was simply a way to achieve a more efficient, and oppressive, state structure.

Some political reformers and revolutionaries in China, therefore, argued that democracy had to be the starting point rather than the final indeterminate outcome of modernization. Influenced by antidespotic themes in New Text and Han Learning philosophy and by the failure of "enlightened despotism" during the 1898 Reform movement, these activists believed that China's historical problem was not an entrenched feudalism of powerful estates and corporate privileges that obstructed political centralization. Contrary to "feudal" Germany, where resistance to modernization in the early nineteenth century had provoked Hegel to support the political strong man, China confronted two thousand years of unbroken monarchical absolutism that even the reform-minded Guangxu emperor had failed to break. Maintaining the despotic political structure with the support of broadly based social values of "loyalty" (*zhong*) and "filial piety" (*xiao*) would not transform the country, but only perpetuate its political weaknesses and block the cultural renovation of the Chinese people. Democracy in China could not wait on a "necessary" period of political transition, but should, instead, be realized immediately. If imperial despotism was the primary cause of China's ills, then destruction of all despotic authority and its underlying social-cultural values was the first order of political business.

The most ardent advocates of such a view in the early 1900s were Chinese anarchists and radical nationalists. Fired by the collectivist and egalitarian doctrines of the Russian thinkers Bakunin and Kropotkin (as well as by Rousseau), Chinese anarchists, such as Liu Shipei and Wu Zhihui, were among the strongest critics of enlightened autocracy, constitutional monarchy, and other such "compromises" with hierarchical principles of political authority. Foreshadowing the May Fourth iconoclasm, these proponents of radical change believed that the depth of despotic traditions embedded in China's social fabric—particularly the family—demanded a frontal assault on the autocratic structure of traditional authority relations throughout the entire polity and society. "In any dispute between emperor and subjects," Wu Zhihui argued, "help the subjects; in any dispute between father and sons, help the sons."[45] The anarchist prescription for China was that revolution should not only "exterminate kings and emperors," but also radically alter familial relationships by elevating the role of women and creating social collectives organized along egalitarian lines. Autocratic authority so distorted the people's personality that the transition to voluntary organization and mutual aid required the total destruction of Chinese despotism in all its social and political manifestations.[46]

The same contradiction between maintaining China's despotic traditions and achieving political modernity was emphasized by radical nationalists, though without a total assault on all authority. Wang Jingwei—whose intense nationalism in the early 1900s belied his later World War II collaboration with the Japanese—argued that nationalism and the modern state structure incorporated a concept of political authority that was fundamentally at odds with Chinese monarchical traditions. In Wang's view, authority in the modern state was impersonal, collectivist, and abstract with loyalty to the corporate order superseding and transcending personal attachment to the ruler.[47] Despite the tradition in China of equating the state with the "personal property" of the dynasty, Wang Jingwei did not argue for a total break with the country's past. Since Wang believed the Chinese people already possessed the common identity underlying modern nationhood and even a democratic "spirit," he argued that once the monarch was destroyed and a "new morality" replaced Confucianism, the institutions of the modern state would easily take hold in China.[48]

Democracy and nationalism as an alternative to monarchy was promoted most vehemently by the fiery, young radical Zou Rong. Inspired by Rousseau's democratic doctrine and by the French and American revolutions, Zou Rong demanded the immediate abolition of the Manchu monarchy in favor of an American-style democracy. Mass participation, he believed, would generate popular loyalty to the nation and replace the submissive obedience to individual monarchs that had characterized Chinese political life for centuries.[49] In his 1903 messianic tract *The Revolutionary Army*, Zou argued that as long as Chinese "live peaceably under a despotic government they are bound to be slaves." "Under the Yellow Dragon flag of China there exists a people," he bellowed, "who might be a nation, but it is not one." Instead, Zou continued: "We Han are particularly good at being slaves. Fathers teach it to their children, elder brothers encourage their younger brothers, wives urge it on their husbands . . . they (all) practice every day the art of being a slave. . . . They have no thoughts apart from dependence, no character apart from obedience . . . and no spirit apart from servility." In the democratic West by contrast, Zou believed that "citizens have a capacity for self-rule, they are independent by nature and have the right to participate in government." Thus in order for China to "uproot slavishness," its people must cultivate a "spirit of dignity and independence" by expelling the Manchus, killing the emperor, and setting up a government with "all the powers . . . to defend popular rights."[50] Anything less than such radical change—even constitutional monarchy—would, Zou believed, leave the Chinese people excessively "loyal to the prince" and incapable of forging national unity or practicing self-government.

Hu Hanmin and Song Jiaoren expressed equally radical views, though with considerably less emotion than Zou Rong. In a rebuttal to the arguments by Liang Qichao for "enlightened autocracy," Hu Hanmin wrote in *People's Gazette (Minbao)* in 1906 that the "first concern of those who wish to establish a new political order must be the destruction of autocracy root and branch."[51] Since China had already experienced an "enlightened autocracy . . . long ago, at the height of the Han and Tang dynasties," Hu claimed that Liang's proposals for authoritarian government were outmoded and obsolete. China, like America, lacked an aristocracy, which in Europe had been the major obstacle to modernity and the primary target of the enlightened despots. Thus Hu concluded that since the Chinese people already possessed a democratic "spirit," the "establishment of a constitutional regime [in China] would be a simple and easy matter."[52]

Song Jiaoren voiced similar views on fundamental issues of institutional power in the vigorous debate over the structure of republican government and political parties that took place between anti-Qing proponents in the early 1900s. The parliamentary system of collective responsibility between prime minister and cabinet was preferable for China, Song argued, because it avoided the excessive concentration of power in a single leader, the president.[53] Democratic principles should also be instituted in China's new political parties. Although Song Jiaoren believed that politicians should aggressively pursue official position—thereby rejecting the traditional value of seeing "virtue in declining an official appointment" (*tuirang*)—he did not believe that this justified Sun Yatsen's highly authoritarian and personal leadership of the Chinese Revolutionary Party. Instead, Song Jiaoren envisioned a mass-based party led by a collegial leadership and organized around common commitments to a political program and ideological principles rather than a blind loyalty to the single heroic leader.[54] A clean break with autocracy not only required a redistribution of power, but a purge of the intense personalism in Chinese politics that Song believed was deeply rooted in Confucian tradition.[55] Political authority and decision-making power in a democratic China, Song concluded, should inhere in the impersonal, institutional order itself.

Even the most avid supporters of democracy found some appeal, however, in the concept of political tutelage underlying the theory of enlightened autocracy. Although they portrayed Chinese society in more positive terms than their conservative counterparts, radical democrats, such as Chen Tianhua, still recognized a need to "prepare [the Chinese people] for popular rights and democracy by means of enlightened autocracy."[56] When Sun Yatsen demanded in 1911 that " 'we cannot adopt a political system which restricts the power of the man we trust,' " Song Jiaoren reluctantly agreed to a strong presidency.[57] Despite the theoretical appeal of an antidespotic, institutional democracy, the most influential model of political authority in early republican thought was still the strong, single leader who, invested with nearly absolute authority, would lead China through the rigors of revolution and modernization.

The Cultural Basis of Despotism: 1915–1922

"The prejudices of the magistrate have arisen from national
prejudice."

Montesquieu

The failure of the revolutions in 1911 and 1913 to establish a functional democratic order in China had a profound impact on emerging Chinese views of political authority, especially among New Culture and May Fourth intellectuals. Despite the overthrow of the Qing Dynasty, they believed that China had not undergone a basic institutional or cultural transformation of political authority away from the country's long monarchical traditions. As one writer in the progressive magazine *New Youth* (*Xin Qingnian*) lamented in 1918: "Our contemporary politics . . . is not republican but is instead a despotic politics."[58] After the exceptionally low voter turnout in the 1913 election and following the near fatal blows delivered to democracy by the attempted restorations of the militarists Yuan Shikai in 1915 and Zhang Xun in 1917, New Culture-May Fourth intellectuals, such as Chen Duxiu, believed that despotism infected China's entire political structure and popular culture. Contrary to the views of Hu Hanmin and Wang Jingwei, the May Fourth generation did not ascribe a democratic "spirit" to the Chinese people. Nor did May Fourth intellectuals think that China's transition to institutional democracy would be "easy." Although they generally opposed such conservative political reforms as constitutional monarchy, the May Fourth group assumed that blind obedience and submission were at the core of Chinese culture, interwoven in all its ethical, religious, philosophical, and linguistic dimensions.[59] In the absence of a functional civil society that could marshal popular support for democratic institutions in China, political and intellectual leaders had, therefore, to effect a fundamental change in popular "habits and customs" (*fengsu xiguan*)—but without a resort to a new despotism.

May Fourth era opposition to monarchical authority was first expressed by Chen Duxiu in 1916 in a rebuttal to Kang Youwei's endorsement of constitutional monarchy.[60] Even a limited monarchical authority, Chen argued, would hamper China's transition to democracy. Echoing the views of Zou Rong, Chen revealed a strong cultural iconoclasm in his political thought by arguing that democracy and monarchy were diametrically opposed: "One is based on a spirit of equality and the other on an adulation and subservience to the [upper] classes."[61] By supporting the establishment of a constitutional monarchy, Kang Youwei had deprecated the political character of the Chinese people, which Chen Duxiu believed only encouraged aspiring despots, such as Yuan Shikai, to assert that the country was more "fit" for military dictatorship and imperial restoration than for republican government.[62] For a social basis of democracy to emerge in China, Chen asserted that the people had "to struggle [on their own] for survival . . . and bring it about [themselves] that there is a public [authority and not rule by one individual]." "Otherwise," he concluded, "monarchy will persist."[63]

Despite this pronounced antiauthoritarianism, Chen Duxiu still questioned the capacity of the Chinese people to support democracy. The experience with fragile republican government that from its inception in 1912 was under constant threat of extinction by attempted restorations had left untouched the deeper values and beliefs that, Chen believed, led the general population to consider monarchy part of the "natural" political order. Basic democratic principles espoused by John Locke and Rousseau—that government was held in trust instead of by ordained right and that the monarch was a mere agent of society with "no will, no power but that of law"—were alien in a society that was still suffused with hierarchical relationships and patriarchal values, and where authority was traditionally vested in the state not the people.[64] In the absence of a "patriotic consciousness," which Chen described as a "love for the collectivity," despotism remained firmly entrenched in Chinese thought, particularly Confucianism, and in everyday life, where Chen Duxiu believed it robbed the newly established Republic of critical popular support.[65] Until this formidable tradition was broken among the general population, the prospects for democracy in China were exceedingly dim.

On the surface, Chen blamed the new, post-1911 political leadership of the country for the persistence of prodespotic sentiments among the people. Instead of educating the populace in basic democratic principles, these new politicians in China had actively reinforced Confucian traditions antithetical to republican institutions. Thus Chen protested in 1917 that "members of parliament proclaim a republic on the one hand but on the other, they rely on such old fashion concepts of rule as the Mencian principle that 'the duty of all kings (from [the ancient dynasties of] Xia, Yin, and Zhou) is to illustrate proper human relationships so that benevolent feelings will prevail among the inferiors below.'"[66] Instead of trying to cultivate an assertive citizenry and to encourage popular participation in the new republican government, political leaders in China "call for obedience to the Confucian school and loyalty to the monarch, filial piety to the father, and servility [of a wife] to the husband." In a similar complaint, Chen's ally Li Dazhao proclaimed that although the 1912 constitution guaranteed political freedom, the document "takes Confucianism as the basis of personal cultivation. The authors of the constitution force people to respect Confucianism," Li protested, "so how can you believe in freedom?"[67] China's elite seemed intent on freezing the polity in a structure of archaic authority relationships by, in Chen Duxiu's words, "exploiting the people's weak points and fitting into the psychology of the old society."[68]

The tenacity of China's despotic tradition was even more apparent in the prevailing style of executive leadership under the new Republic. Since 1912, the May Fourth group charged, China's presidents had attempted to exercise a totalistic authority that in their reliance on individual "commands" (*mingling*) rather than laws was no different from the country's imperial predecessors. Unlike the West, where the king's role was limited to "securing law and order," China's newly installed presidents had gone far beyond the mandate of a democratic political leader and assumed the role of "teacher" (*shi*) in order to "rectify the mind" (*zheng xin*) and "control people's souls" with a stifling political and intellectual orthodoxy, just as all despotic emperors in China had done since the Song Dynasty.[69] The republican revolution had failed to alter the overlap of politics and "morality" (*de*) in China, thus leading political leaders to act like a "mother and father" to the people, using "edicts" to intervene in virtually every aspect of Chinese life, including education, commerce, religion, and even individual personal hygiene.[70] China's new presidents thus refused to delegate authority as they projected an aura of "sacredness" (*shenshengde*), "imperiousness" (*yuanhoude*), "patriarchy" (*jiazhangde*), and even considered themselves "great teachers" (*shifu*) modeled on the ancient sage kings. Until executives in China assumed the role of a "public servant" (*gongpu*)—with, as in the West, concomitant restrictions on state interference in moral and spiritual matters and backed by an impersonal rule of law impervious to arbitrary whim—republican government could not take hold in Chinese society.[71] "With imperious presidents still in control, the people will do nothing but follow."

The heart and soul of Chinese despotism was not, however, the political elite. In the eyes of many New Culture-May Fourth intellectuals, it was instead the cultural "backwardness" of the general population. "Although the agent of our peril is the powerful foe and the merciless autocrat," Chen Duxiu still believed that "the cause of our doom lies in the behavior and character of our people" particularly the "decline in our own national and public morality."[72] Influenced by two millennia of Confucian influence that excessively subservient scholars had interpreted in a prodespotic cast, especially after the Song Dynasty, the Chinese population had fully absorbed monarchical and patriarchal values. This, in turn, had created what Chen Duxiu described as an "unchallenged adulation for the emperor" and a widespread "susceptibility to the benevolent lord."[73] Whereas Westerners "viewed the nation as the organization that guarantees popular tranquility," Chen believed the Chinese willingly "furnish themselves as sacrificial lambs for the great builder." "The majority of Chinese have their heads full of thoughts for the era of the monarchy," Chen complained, and generally they "disagree with the words 'political democracy.'"[74]

Underlying this political quiescence of the general population was the total "indifference" to national affairs among the general population. Although Chen Duxiu acknowledged that "people's rule" had been practiced in traditional popular organizations, such as "spirit groups" and local "militia" (*tuanlian*), centuries of despotic rule uninhibited in Montesquieuian terms by any mediating groups or institutions had turned the Chinese people into what Chen, echoing Sun Yat-sen, described as a "loose sheet of sand" (*yipan sansha*) and a "bunch of fools" (*yidui chunwu*).[75] Devoid of any public morality or national "consciousness, the general population," Chen argued, "takes patriotism as synonymous with loyalty to the sovereign" and treats the nation as "an enterprise to be passed on by the ruler's clan to his sons and grandsons." Chinese people were, indeed, perfectly willing to "let the emperor take full responsibility for all affairs." Lack of patriotism and blind obedience to the emperor were mutually reinforcing as the average Chinese was all too willing to "greedily sell out" to despotic governments and even to foreign interests.[76]

The Problem of China's "National Character"

The critique of prodespotic sentiments among the population was especially apparent in May Fourth discussions of the Chinese "national character" (*guomin xing*). In the view of *New Youth* contributor Guang Sheng, the long history of monarchy in China had "deformed" the people, leaving them unprepared for democratic government.[77] Although Guang argued that the long-standing racial, national, and religious unity of China had provided the country with certain advantages over the West, he also believed that the Chinese lacked the central elements of a democratic system: "freedom of thought, the rule of law, and popular sovereignty." Guang thus lamented that "since ancient times . . . the emphasis has been on one man controlling the state . . . so for several thousand years we have worked solely to protect despotism." Philosophical orthodoxy and the long experience with absolutist notions of "statism" (*guojiazhuyi*) had led the people willingly to accept despotism. This was clearly demonstrated among the population by their common belief in prodespotic adages such as "without a master chaos results" (*wuzhu nailuan*) and "the lord's duty is to create unity." Confucianism, Legalism, and even Taoism had all produced a "moral and coercive control" that so robbed the people of their "human dignity" (*ren ge*) that they consistently "blindly follow" the sovereign. While Legalists used harsh rule to terrorize the Chinese people into abject submission, Confucianism and Taoism had been equally harmful by lulling the people into centuries of helpless dependence on the "benevolent lord." Thus Guang concluded: "If our countrymen do not alter their expectations for the sage king and wise chancellor we will have great difficulty competing with other nations."[78]

Guang Sheng also believed that Chinese despotism had been fostered by China's underdeveloped legal traditions. In the West, since Roman times the legal relationship between state and society had established institutional limitations on political authority and protected the individual through the inviolate concept of a "legal personality." But in China, Guang argued that the people were left politically and legally defenseless by the Confucian emphasis on "benevolence" (renai) and the Taoist idea of "silent meditation."

> The Confucians advocate that the people obey the ruler (jun) and . . . the ruler love the people. . . . However, when people are loved by someone they must only rely on trust and will not have the power to make demands. As [Immanuel] Kant says, politicians who run the state with benevolence become dictators and by treating the people as immature children, they deprive them of their individual freedom.[79]

Since "morality . . . provides no order" and "no [objective] standards" for checking political leaders, Guang asserted that Chinese despots ever since the Qin Dynasty (221–204 BC) have felt free to "massacre the people." Under "virtuous rule" (de zhi), Chinese society has been perennially "dependent on personalities instead of law," which is why the country's politics "often degenerates into autocracy." Thus Guang concluded: "Moral rule easily becomes despotism, while rule by law produces equality."

In sum, New Culture-May Fourth intellectuals generally believed that the Chinese people were organizationally and culturally unprepared to participate in a democratic system. "China has hitherto had no organization" and thus when the people "hear the words 'democracy' and 'federalism'" they "immediately fear the dissolution of the nation."[80] Although one *New Youth* contributor believed that the establishment of the Republic in 1912 had produced "sprouts of self-awareness" in the populace, the "great majority" on which democracy depends was, he agreed, still largely untouched by democratic sentiments. After centuries of oppression, most Chinese still willingly adhered to such promonarchical sentiments as "heaven is sympathetic and generous."[81] Since the vast majority of the people viewed the Republic with traditional indifference as if "nothing but another change in the dynastic cycle" had occurred, naturally they did not support democratic principles or institutions. Instead, they secretly yearned for the day when they too could all become, according to Lu Xun, "cruel, heartless, and tyrannical, just like despots."[82]

Proof of popular complicity in sustaining despotic authority was readily evident in the several restoration attempts executed by Yuan Shikai and Zhang Xun in the early republican era. Contemporary Western historians have generally treated these political maneuvers as futile charades in a society where, Joseph Levenson argued, "the monarchical mystique was dead," particularly after the death of the Guangxu emperor in 1908.[83] Yuan's 1915 "restoration" lasted only eighty-three days and Zhang Xun's 1917 attempt to restore the Manchu emperor Pu Yi was even less successful, ending in less than two weeks. But at the time, Chen Duxiu did not treat the defeat of restoration forces as the death blow to monarchy, nor did he interpret the restorations as desperate moves by an isolated few. In a society where, Chen believed, sympathy for the monarch outweighed support for democracy, Yuan Shikai and Zhang Xun were considered basically in tune with a popular mood soured on parliamentary rule and political parties that were perennially hampered by institutional gridlock and incessant factionalism. "Yuan Shikai's desire to become emperor," Chen noted, "was no idle thought, since he could see that the majority believe in a monarchy and not a republic."[84] Ultimately, Yuan's restoration failed, but unfortunately this did not result from a popular defense of democracy. The "majority" had only objected to Yuan personally, Chen asserted, as "deep down they do not really oppose monarchy in general."[85] As long as the population remained wedded to monarchical authority, Chen Duxiu predicted that even after Yuan's death in June 1916 "[n]umerous Yuans will certainly appear and reappear to abolish the Republic and restore the imperial system."[86] Just as Napoleon III had "repeated the same mistake" of his uncle and "destroyed the French Republic," Chen suggested that so too would a "'Yuan Shikai II' (*Yuan Shikai ershi*)" arise to subvert Chinese democracy by "attempting to pay homage to heaven and respect for Confucianism in order to fool the people." This constant reappearance of aspiring despots in China, moreover, was "a consequence, not a cause" of deeper flaws in Chinese political culture. The sycophantic desire of Chinese politicians to "stay where power is and ingratiate the despicable" fed the megalomania of leaders. The same was true among the general populace, where the long-term effects of "the sovereign duping the population" with Confucian claptrap still provided fertile soil for the despot.[87] Without fundamental change among both elites and people, China's new Republic would continually be threatened and ultimately undermined by "the resurrection of the old system—the sovereign as master and the people as slaves."[88]

In short, the driving force behind monarchical restoration was popular compliance to despotic authority sanctified by Confucianism. According to Tao Lihong, after "four thousand years of despotism" the vast majority of Chinese supported a continuation of monarchy. "Their ideal politicians are Napoleon and Yuan Shikai," he insisted, "and their most prized morality is loyalty and filial piety."[89] China's short-lived experiment with Western-style democracy had failed, not just because the country lacked democratic leaders, but, more importantly, because no substantive changes in popular consciousness had coincided with the introduction of democratic institutions. As Gao Yihan noted:

> It is a mistake to believe that once the monarchical institution is overthrown, then democratic politics is assured. A real revolution requires a corresponding change in ideas. The label on a government can be changed into "Republic," but its techniques can still be monarchical . . . Even though the monarch may have been deposed, he still exists in the minds of the people.[90]

China's greatest need, therefore, was for an all-out assault on Confucianism as the "evil root" of the "autocratic imperial system." To "strengthen the republic," Chen Duxiu declared, "we must take the people's brains and wash out all those old ideas opposed to the republic."[91] Restoration attempts and popular admiration for the strong leader were merely a "symptom" of a much deeper cultural malaise that had been brought on by an antiquated and outworn tradition that continued to defy a creative transformation into modernity. "If we don't implement thoroughgoing change," Chen Duxiu concluded, "then we will remain powerless, as if in a coma. . . ."[92]

Enlightenment and Despotism in May Fourth Thought

"We believe true reason should be the standard in everything."

Chen Duxiu, 1919

If prodespotic sentiments were rooted in popular culture, as May Fourth intellectuals believed, then the question arose as to where the impulse would arise for the basic political transformation from monarchical to democratic authority. Without broader and more profound changes in the economy and society, how could China break out of a despotic culture that was so deeply embedded in the popular psyche?

Until the establishment of the Chinese Communist Party in 1921, most New Culture-May Fourth intellectuals looked to education and "enlightenment" as the answer to this dilemma. Temporarily avoiding direct political involvement, Chen Duxiu, Hu Shi, and Fu Sinian (publisher of the Peking University student magazine, *New Tides* [*Xin Chao*]), mimicked the French *philosophes* by looking to reason to shatter the mental framework that they believed perpetuated despotic authority. Like their European counterparts, Chinese intellectuals argued that propagating fundamental scientific and analytical principles would erode the "superstitious" traditions and cultural parochialism that supported despotism. Although the direct target for such a transformation were other, especially younger, intellectuals, these changes would, it was believed, gradually seep into the general population and alter the broad social and cultural foundations of despotic authority. In distinct contrast to the intuitive and epigrammatic epistemology of Confucianism, modern theories of "cause-effect," "relativity," and rational "skepticism" would lead to an "objective" understanding of oppression in China and of the basic causes of society's ills, thereby paving the way for democratic social and political possibilities.[93] As long as "subjective, arbitrary thought" and an orthodox belief in "one truth" that had been imposed since the Song Dynasty dominated China's intellectual life, Chen Duxiu believed that the philosophical basis of despotism would remain unshaken, even among the young, Westernized students.[94] The propagation among what was described as the "muddleheaded" population, of scientific thought and reason, and political values of freedom and "self-interest" would, however, gradually produce a new antidespotic culture and politics.[95]

Leadership of this broad and bold campaign of intellectual and cultural transformation would be assumed by "independent" scholars, socially conscious journalists, and literary men whom Lu Xun exhorted to "fight for the light."[96] According to Fu Sinian, editor of *New Tides*, China needed "learned men" modeled on Western scholars of the Renaissance and Reformation who would pursue the truth free from contemporary social conventions or partisan political interests.[97] Employing unemotional, objective analysis comparable to the amoral empiricism of the French Enlightenment, this new generation of scholars would demystify tradition and thus reveal to elites and common people alike the cultural props of Chinese despotism. Novelists too would mobilize popular hatred for despotic authority by translating Russian and Japanese fictional works with a strong antidespot message into the Chinese "vernacular language" (*baihua*) that would make literature accessible to the common man. A new breed of journalists would likewise foster democracy in their writing by "facing up to the evils of society . . . and changing popular attitudes rather than by just responding to the people's backwardness."[98] Contrary to the Confucian practice of strictly limiting education to the elite, May Fourth intellectuals believed that the people could gradually be made to "understand things," but not without the guidance of intellectuals to "enlighten them" in what Hu Shi argued would be a very long, painstaking educational process.[99]

Both *New Youth* and *New Tides* were thus devoted to creating a popular "critical consciousness" and propagandizing modern culture by publishing political tracts and "scientific articles." Translations and commentaries on Western democratic theories of John Locke and Jean Jacques Rousseau were staples in both magazines, perhaps because these doctrines had originated in a similar struggle against monarchical absolutism and social dependency in the West. Chen Duxiu thus used social contract theory to attack fundamental Chinese assumptions on the organic nature of rulership and the mystical aura surrounding imperial authority.[100] "The sovereign is . . . a kind of idol," Chen argued in 1918. "He is totally reliant upon people's blind faith . . . and their idolization of him, and only thus can he take command of the whole land and be proclaimed supreme chief."[101] If the Chinese people would only take a more conventional view of the ruler and the state as institutions that should serve their interests, Chen believed that the populace would break out of the "self-deception" that had traditionally sustained Chinese despotism. "A state is merely something that one or several races of people form together," Chen argued in classical social contract terminology that challenged traditional myths in China linking political authority to the sacred soil and the distant past of Chinese culture.[102] "Remove the people from a territory and the state will cease to exist." The Chinese people should adopt the utilitarian principles of social contract theory by separating the authority of state and ruler from the eternal, immutable values of Chinese "civilization." In this way, a "rational" politics based on nonpatriarchal values of economic interests would finally emerge among the Chinese populace, just as in America where, according to Gao Yihan, basic democratic principles had penetrated the broad masses well before the American revolution.[103]

Gao Yihan also argued that Western social contract theory should become the theoretical "foundation of the nation." Like Chen Duxiu, Gao wanted to replace popular Chinese belief in monarchical principles of authority with utilitarian and even anarchist views that rejected the state as mankind's ultimate "salvation."[104] In a review of Western social contract theories, Gao thus criticized Thomas Hobbes's concept of the absolute sovereign (Leviathan) while, at the same time, he lauded Rousseau's defense of popular sovereignty and the right to rebellion.[105]

As a contrast to Chinese traditional political theory that had "usurped" popular rights, Gao argued that Rousseau's doctrine granted "the highest sovereignty to the people" and "clearly delineated the scope of government action." Gao also admired John Stuart Mill for having "destroyed the dictatorship of customs" and for defending intellectual diversity and minority opinion against absolutist (or majority) tyranny.[106] In Gao's view, Mill had wanted to insure the happiness of all the people by protecting their "freedom to feel, think, talk, and congregate," quite unlike Jeremy Bentham whom Gao criticized for ignoring the legitimate interests of the few against the tyrannical majority. Defense of individual rights to express opinion against the interference of popular orthodoxies was the heart of Mill's theory, which is why Gao saw Mill's principles as particularly appropriate to China. "The ancient tradition of venerating one doctrine," Gao lamented, "has not changed even after the [1911] revolution." Whereas Western governments allow freedom and diversity of opinion, China had so thoroughly "crushed" diversity of views that the masses still yearn, Gao exclaimed, "for one mode of thought just as in emperor Han Wudi's time."[107] "If Mill had lived in China how much more would he have condemned the tyranny of custom and opinion!"

In addition to propagating normative Western theories, *New Youth* and *New Tides* also published local "social investigations" (*shehui diaocha*) that purportedly exposed the deeper roots of social and political despotism in everyday Chinese life. The Chinese enlightenment, like its Western counterpart, stimulated interest in social issues and social reality in China, where popular "habits and customs" ostensibly revealed widespread prodespotic sentiments.[108] Visits by university students to villages in Henan and Hebei reportedly uncovered widespread "superstitions" (*mixin*) that maintained popular support of imperial rule.[109] One *New Youth* "investigator" reported that "absolute obedience" to the "fortune teller" (*suanming xiansheng*) caused the peasantry to willingly do anything they are told, "just like the Germans who in the past blindly followed (*fuzong*) their emperor." With their profound nostalgia for the imperial past, rural people in these two provinces were actually repelled by recent social and political changes brought on during the Republic, especially the entry of military men into politics. " 'Since the Republic's president is not a real dragon emperor,' " one local elder was quoted as saying, " 'he cannot be trusted.' "[110]

Other social and cultural characteristics in Chinese society were similarly interpreted as a reflection of the awesome effects of China's despotic traditions that penetrated virtually every corner of Chinese life. The subservient role of Chinese women, for instance, was seen as a social spin-off of imperial demands for absolute loyalty from ministers and subjects.[111] "Slavish" obedience to the husband and reverence for female chastity were not cultural "constants" in Chinese history. Instead these social practices were the reflection of a patriarchal political structure that had peaked in the late Qing Dynasty and continued to shape the entire social order along despotic lines.[112]

The Chinese Family and Despotism

The most important subject of social and cultural criticism in May Fourth journals was the authority structure of the Chinese family. Like Kang Youwei's previous iconoclastic assaults on filial piety, articles in *New Tides* and *New Youth* attacked the Confucian family system as the basic "evil" in Chinese society.[113] Without the sharp differentiation between familial and political authority traceable in Western political and social thought as early as Aristotle, "the family clan system" in China had developed into the "root of [state] despotism." "The scope of filial piety is all inclusive," argued Wu Yu (who was perhaps the most culturally iconoclastic contributor to *New Youth*), as "the ruler served as none other than the father and mother of the people . . . and the laws governing the realm were no different from family mores."[114] Blind obedience to the family head and to despotic government was virtually indistinguishable, since throughout Chinese history filial piety had formed the basis of "loyalty" to the emperor and the Chinese state. "In the beginning, the Chinese nation was like a big family," Gu Chengyu similarly stated, "with the monarch acting like a 'pater familias.'"[115] As the underlying principle of state organization, the "patriarchal system" (*jiazhang zhidu*) not only reinforced the notion of "divine rule" (*tianli*) by the imperial state, but also inhibited the people from "speaking up" and organizing "rebellion from the lower ranks." In a culture where "filial piety and brotherly love" defined every person's most basic social identity, Yu Pingbo asserted that political authority in China was rooted in a family model that historically was completely unassailable: "Those who sin against superiors are few, and those who like sinning against superiors and stirring up disorder, have never existed."[116]

Responsibility for this intertwining of familial and political authority lay directly with the "two thousand year reign of Confucian tradition." Although the emperor Qin Shihuang had institutionalized autocracy, it was Confucius and his followers who were were primarily responsible for establishing the ideological foundations of a family-based autocracy. "Confucius turned the two characters 'filial piety' (*xiao*) and 'younger brother' (*di*) into the foundation of unity between two thousand years of despotic government and the family system."[117] In writing the *Spring and Autumn Annals*, Confucius had wanted to strike fear into the people so as to stop "disorderly vassals" from "murdering their rulers" and "criminal sons" from "killing their fathers." Mencius too had contributed to the interweaving of family and polity by, Wu Yu suggested, attacking anti-Confucian "heresies," particularly the "egotism" of Yang Zhu and the philanthropy of Mozi.[118] According to Mencius, quoted by Wu Yu: " '[The problem with] the idea suggested by Yang of "acting on my own behalf" is that it denigrates the ruler; [the problem with] the universal love of Mozi is that it denigrates the father. To lack a ruler and father is comparable to being an animal.' "

Wu Yu's toughest criticism, however, was aimed at Xunzi, whom Wu accused of being "largely to blame for the harm wrecked on later generations by the teachings of Confucius."[119] In his commentaries on the *Rites* (*Li*), Xunzi had promoted a reverence for the ruler, Wu Yu argued, that in drawing on filial values fortified Confucian support for autocratic government. Xunzi had, moreover, legitimized powers for the ruler that in exceeding parental authority created a greater personal dependency on the state than had ever existed in the family. " 'The father can produce [the child] but cannot rear him,' " Wu quoted Xunzi as saying, and " 'the mother can feed the child but cannot instruct him. The ruler can both feed and instruct him.' " In Wu Yu's view, this doctrine of Xunzi was the reason that " 'of the five terms enshrined by the Chinese (heaven, earth, ruler, relatives, and teacher) the ruler is the most important with the right to take control of both political power and of teaching. . . .' "[120]

Xunzi was also accused of strengthening Confucian prescripts that modeled the service of government ministers to the ruler on the filial obedience of the son to the father. " 'Ministers remain in office for their entire lives by maintaining the ruler's favor through never displeasing him.' "[121] " 'People were enthralled with this one man (the ruler), who obediently carried out virtuous acts (following those of his ancestors).' " Under Xunzi's tutelage, government ministers had become "willing slaves" who feared issuing the slightest challenge to imperial supremacy, the effect of which froze China in a "clan system (*zongfa*)" that had made the country incapable of replicating European modernization. "Familism" had, in fact, destroyed any concept of the "individual's independence and dignity" that Wu and other May Fourth intellectuals considered so vital for a democratic culture and politics to emerge in China.[122] Until political reform combined with "reform of the family system" broke this seamless web of familial and political authority in China, the vast majority of the people would not support the establishment of a democratic republic or any other nonmonarchical authority.

Conclusion: May Fourth and the Dilemmas of Transforming Political Authority in Modern China

This analysis by Wu Yu of the deep foundations of despotism in the Chinese family demonstrated a basic dilemma in all of May Fourth thinking. Although Chinese intellectuals embraced democratic goals and individualism, their view that despotism was at the core of Chinese culture and traditional thought led to a basically pessimistic judgment on the political capacity of the general population for whom, they believed, political and social dependency on despotism had not yet become a problem. Whereas the French Enlightenment thinker Voltaire believed that a "feeling for freedom [is] alive and immediately present in each of us," May Fourth intellectuals argued that the Chinese people were overwhelmed by the moral and cultural control of despotic traditions in virtually every aspect of their social and political lives.[123] According to Gu Chengyu, the Chinese people "feel the family system is completely appropriate," which led Guang Sheng to complain that "the people's spirit and their political-educational habits are cast in one mode and cannot be moved."[124] The same was true in politics, where Chen Duxiu argued that the broad "decline in our own national public and private morality" was even more important than the machinations of "foreign enemies" in bringing about "China's crisis."[125]

This perception of an overwhelming authoritarian culture in China thus led May Fourth intellectuals ultimately to reject a full Lockian or Rousseauian rationalization for democracy. Instead of embracing the notion of a self-regulating civil society in China or an independent consenting majority of freedom-loving individuals, Chen Duxiu et al. adopted an overriding vision of Chinese society as fundamentally prodespotic. Although based on preciously little empirical verification, a consensus emerged among many intellectuals that the Chinese people were not yet willing to challenge arbitrary or absolute power. On the contrary, the people had been willing collaborators with despotism from the ancient times of Confucius right up to the recent restoration attempts by Yuan Shikai and Zhang Xun. China was inherently conservative, Chen Duxiu believed, exuding a "stale and putrid" air that made even young students appear "mentally old."[126] The destruction of China's experiment with parliamentary rule by warlord power and the reversion of the nascent political parties in the country to archaic politics in the elections of 1913 and 1918, seemed to verify the overpowering influence of the traditional culture and practices on China's supposedly "modern" institutions.

What had begun in the mid-1910s as a truly radical assault on monarchical authority with democratic principles quickly dissipated from the intellectual and political scene in early twentieth-century China. Convinced that Chinese society lacked the requisite cultural foundations, especially individualism, for liberal democracy, May Fourth intellectuals showed little concern for constructing functional democratic and legal institutions. Until a fundamental transformation occurred in the basic thought and values of the amorphous "masses," there was little need to focus on the legal and procedural attributes of democratic government.[127] The key problematique of the May Fourth era was to inculcate the populace through education with the "spirit" of democracy, rather than to build democratic institutions on a preexisting democratic culture.

But whereas such May Fourth luminaries as Hu Shi would remain committed throughout his life to propagating the liberal creed, Chen Duxiu, Li Dazhao, and others grew increasingly impatient with relying solely on education and "enlightenment" to transform the people. Since they generally considered democracy less an end in itself than a means to achieve national power, a democratic solution to China's political problems was quickly abandoned. Influenced by newly emergent Soviet Russia and increasingly alienated from the West, May Fourth intellectuals would, like Liang Qichao and Sun Yatsen before them, rapidly embrace a political theory that they considered more appropriate than Western democracy for transforming "backward" China into a powerful, modern society. By ultimately converting to Marxism-Leninism in the late 1910s and early 1920s, many May Fourth intellectuals would, indeed, legitimate a profoundly cynical approach to politics and an even more derisive view of the Chinese people. Instead of producing a "new culture," the cultural iconoclasm of the May Fourth era would, instead, ultimately lead to the degeneration into a future despotism.

Notes

1. Hao Chang, *Liang Ch'i-ch'ao and Intellectual Transition in China: 1890–1907*, (Cambridge, MA.: Harvard University Press, 1971), 17 & 33 and Hao Chang, *Chinese Intellectuals in Crisis: Search for Order and Meaning, 1890–1911* (Berkeley: University of California Press, 1987), 5–20. "Practical statesmanship" involved setting moral examples by a moral elite immersed in Confucian doctrine.

2. Yves R. M. Simon, *A General Theory of Authority* (Notre Dame, IN: University of Notre Dame Press, 1962), 48 & 57. Simon continues: "The power in charge of unifying common action through rules binding for all is what everyone calls authority." 11.

3. Carl J. Friedrich, ed., *Authority* (Cambridge, MA.: Harvard University Press, 1958), 30.

4. Barrington Moore Jr., *Injustice: The Social Basis of Obedience and Revolt* (White Plains, NY: M. E. Sharpe Inc., 1978), 17. Also, Clarke E. Cochran, "Authority and Community: The Contributions of Carl Friedrich, Yves R. Simon, and Michael Polanyi," *American Political Science Review*, vol. 71, no. 2, (June 1977): 551 and Daniel Bell, *Power, Influence, and Authority: An Essay in Political Linguistics* (New York: Oxford University Press, 1975), 39.

5. Simon, *A General Theory of Authority*, 11, 39, 42, 93. Simon further argues that the "need for authority as a factor of united action [increases] in cases where plurality of the genuine means renders unanimity fortuitous." (45) On the other hand, spontaneous unanimity does not require the exercise of authority.

6. Hannah Arendt, *Between Past and Future: Eight Exercises in Political Thought* (New York: The Viking Press, 1961), 93. Arendt continues: "[A]uthority precludes the use of external means of coercion; where force is used authority itself has failed. [But] authority is [also] incompatible with persuasion, which presupposes equality and works through a process of argumentation." Simon also notes that the "[u]nity of judgment cannot be procured by rational communication . . . and demonstration. . . ," as there is a constant tension between objective truth and authority. Simon, *A General Theory of Authority*, 32. Bell also argues that "authority is obligatory because it is capable of reasoned elaboration. But to demand that such reasoned elaboration be made explicit is to challenge authority." Bell, *Power, Influence, and Authority*, 59.

7. Max Horkheimer, *Critical Theory: Selected Essays*, trans. by Matthew J. O'Connell et al. (New York: The Seabury Press, 1972), 69–72.

8. Max Weber characterized authority as a "system of legitimate domination" and also argued that "no system of authority voluntarily limits itself to the appeal to material or affectual or ideal motives as a basis for guaranteeing its continuance." Talcott Parsons, ed., *Max Weber: The Theory of Social and Economic Organization* (New York: The Free Press, 1947), 325; also, Liah Greenfeld, *Nationalism: Five Roads to Modernity* (Cambridge, MA: Harvard University Press, 1992), 104. Yet another commentator suggests that power is not the basis for its own justified exercise, for the "political system and that which could confer authority on it are, necessarily, separated conceptually." Rex Martin, "On the Justification of Political Authority," in *Authority: A Philosophical Analysis*, ed., R. Baines Harris (Tuscaloosa, AL: University of Alabama Press, 1976), 64.

9. Cochran, "Authority and Community," *American Political Science Review* (June 1977): 556. Cochran further notes: "Authority is possible only on the basis of community and tradition. Outside such a community, the communications of the one in authority are unintelligible." And, "when directly confronted with truth, the mind wavers from lack of confidence. Authority supplies that confidence in the absence of an unattainable objectivity." 554–556.

10. Simon, *A General Theory of Authority*, 57.

11. First quote in Chang, *Liang Ch'i-ch'ao*, 27; second quote in Chang, *Chinese Intellectuals in Crisis*, 5. Beginning in the Song Dynasty (960–1279 AD), increasingly the emphasis was on personal loyalty of Confucian scholars to the emperor. That the Chinese emperor's authority was believed to extend to all nations—"Heaven has divided up territories but not peoples"—strengthened the sense of the monarch's immutability.

12. Quentin Skinner, *The Foundations of Modern Political Thought; Volume One The Renaissance* (Cambridge: Cambridge University Press, 1978); and Reinhard Bendix, *Kings or People: Power and the Mandate to Rule* (Berkeley: University of California Press, 1978), 9 & 249.

13. W. T. De Bary, "Chinese Despotism and the Confucian Ideal, A Seventeenth-Century View," in *Chinese Thought and Institutions*, ed. John King Fairbank (Chicago: University of Chicago Press, 1957) 163–203; and Jerome Grieder, *Intellectuals and the State in Modern China* (New York: The Free Press, 1981) 39–40.

14. Vincent Y. C. Shih, *The Taiping Ideology: Its Sources, Interpretations, and Influences* (Seattle: University of Washington Press, 1967), 129.

15. Bendix, *Kings or People*, 250, 281, & 292; Greenfeld, *Nationalism*, Chapter One; Robert Nisbet, *Twilight of Authority* (New York: Oxford University Press, 1975), 163; Michael Walzer, *The Revolution of the Saints: A Study in the Origins of Radical Politics* (New York: Atheneum, 1973), 234; and Harold J. Berman, *Law and Revolution: The Formation of the Western Legal Tradition* (Cambridge, MA: Harvard University Press, 1983), 4–5. Bendix (264) also emphasizes the impact on the decline of monarchical authority of the growth in a reading public and their involvement in a secular culture. In a similar vein, Gordon J. Schochet argues that John Locke's rejection of the patriarchal authority claimed by kings (and supported by Robert Filmer) reflected broader social changes in the family. Finally, scientific breakthroughs, such as Newtonian physics—which replaced the Cartesian model of a chaotic universe in constant "need" of a supreme ordering authority, with a model of the cosmos as structured by immutable laws—were also employed in political arguments against despotism, especially by Montesquieu. Arguments drawn from Western science would also have similar effects on Chinese politics, as discussed below. Gordon J. Schochet, *Patriarchicalism in Political Thought* (New York: Basic Books, 1975), 72; and Robert Anchor, *The Englightenment Tradition* (Berkeley: University of California Press, 1967), 49.

16. A "conglomeration of village communities . . . where the political authority never relinquished its residual ownership of land" produced an archaic social and political structure that Ray Huang portrays as "like a submarine sandwich. The long piece of bread on the top resembles the literal bureaucracy, large but undifferentiated. The bottom piece simulates the peasantry also lacking firm

organization." This structure that Huang described as "mathematically unmanageable" made a quick transition to capitalism and democratic institutional forms in China highly problematical. Ray Huang, *Broadening the Horizons of Chinese History* (Armonk, NY: M. E. Sharpe, 1999), 3–18. Other historians, such as William Rowe, paint a somewhat different picture, particularly of vibrant urban economies and more complex social structures, such as in the city of Hankow from the late eighteenth to nineteenth centuries. William T. Rowe, *Hankow: Commerce and Society in a Chinese City, 1796–1889* (Stanford, CA: Stanford University Press, 1984). Nevertheless, few Chinese politicians and intellectuals in the late nineteenth and early twentieth centuries believed that Chinese society was advancing to democratic politics from a social order comparable to the West.

17. Chang, *Liang Ch'i-ch'ao*, 101; and Chang, *Chinese Intellectuals in Crisis*, 6. Frederic Wakeman notes the role of the theory of relativity and historical evolution in shaping the radical belief of Kang Youwei that all authority, including the emperor's, was circumstantial. This view by Kang challenged the post-Han Confucian belief that the ideal state of nature could not exist without enlightened kingship. Frederic Wakeman, *History and Will: Philosophical Perspectives of Mao Tse-tung's Thought* (Berkeley: University of California, 1973), 101 & 123.

18. Kung-ch'uan Hsiao, *A Modern China and a New World: K'ang Yu-wei: Reformer and Utopian, 1858–1927* (Seattle: University of Washington Press, 1975), 208. Kang's close associate, Tan Sitong, expressed an equally radical critique of China's monarchical traditions, and even advocated democratizing the monarchy through elections. Chang, *Chinese Intellectuals in Crisis*, 100.

19. Don C. Price, *Russia and the Roots of the Chinese Revolution: 1896–1911* (Cambridge, MA: Harvard University Press, 1974), 43; and Jung-pang Lo, ed., *K'ang Yu-wei: A Biography and A Symposium* (Tucson: University of Arizona, 1967), 4.

20. Quoted in Price, *Russia and the Roots of the Chinese Revolution*, 33, 80 & 198. Also, Benjamin Schwartz, *In Search of Wealth and Power: Yen Fu and the West* (Cambridge, MA: Harvard University Press, 1964), xi; and James Reeve Pusey, *China and Charles Darwin* (Cambridge, MA: Harvard East Asian Monographs, 1983), 337.

21. Leonard Krieger, *Kings and Philosophers, 1689–1789* (New York: W. W. Norton, 1970), 242–47; and Leo Gershoy, *From Despotism to Revolution: 1763–1789* (New York: Harper & Brothers, 1944), 48–9. Puritans believed that the enlightened despot could assault "collectivist" feudal structures and thus clear the way for a democratic politics based on individual interests. Walzer, *Revolution of the Saints*, 151.

22. John G. Gaglioro, *Enlightened Despotism* (New York: Thomas Y. Crowell Co., 1967) 17–18, & 60. Whether the *philosophes* and Voltaire in particular actually supported enlightened despotism is, however, subject to debate. Peter Gay,

The Party of Humanity: Essays in the French Enlightenment (New York: W.W. Norton & Co., 1959), 275. Hegel further argued: " 'The common people in Germany . . . to whom a national union is something totally alien, would have to be collected together into one mass by the power of a conqueror; they would have to be compelled to treat themselves as belonging to Germany.' " Quoted in Shlomo Avineri, *Hegel's Theory of the Modern State* (Cambridge: Cambridge University Press, 1972), 60 & 73.

23. "This leader and founder of a state is the educator of his people; he teaches them how to practice discipline, obedience and a societal action, he forces them to obey the common weal. Out of a multitude he creates a people." Avineri, *Hegel's Theory of the Modern State*, 111 & 230. Napoleon's role as "lawgiver" is described in Robert B. Holtman, *The Napoleonic Revolution* (Baton Rouge: Louisiana State University Press, 1967).

24. Michael Gasster, *Chinese Intellectuals and the Revolution of 1911: The Birth of Modern Chinese Radicalism* (Seattle: University of Washington Press, 1969), 7; Price, *Russia and the Roots of the Chinese Revolution*, 29–62; and Chang, *Chinese Intellectuals in Crisis*, 27. The emperor in the Confucian ideal "radiat[ed] virtue, analogically reflecting harmony to society, not logically interfering with it to move it." Joseph R. Levenson, "The Vestige of Suggestiveness: Confucianism and Monarchy at the Last," in Joseph R. Levenson, *Confucian China and Its Modern Fate: A Trilogy*, vol. II, (Berkeley: University of California Press, 1968), 92. Although ultimately favoring a constitutional monarchy, before 1902 Kang Youwei advocated investing extraordinary power in the hands of the emperor in the transition to a more limited monarchical authority. He also reacted against "the orthodox Neo-Confucian view [that] the prime goal of the Confucian state was the maintenance of Confucian moral teachings rather than collective achievement. . . ." Hsiao, *K'ang Yu-wei*, 215–217; and Chang, *Liang Ch'i-ch'ao*, 28. Yan Fu also considered the possibility that "the Manchu leadership would be able to convert themselves into 'enlightened despots.' " Schwartz, *In Search of Wealth and Power*, 147.

25. Hsiao, *K'ang Yu-wei*, 198, 209, & 214. The appeal of Meiji Japan to Kang lay in what he believed was the apparent intimate tie there between the Japanese emperor and his people. Kang presented Confucius as a "sage king" with the authority granted by the Mandate of Heaven to create institutions. He also viewed Peter the Great as a "king" (*wang*) rather than a "tyrant" (*ba*), and Kang admired Russia over England because of the Russian emperor's relatively greater political supremacy as compared to his English counterpart. Wakeman, *History and Will*, 142; Tse-tsung Chow, "The Anti-Confucian Movement in Early Republican China," in *The Confucian Persuasion*, ed. Arthur F. Wright (Stanford, CA: Stanford University Press, 1960), 289; and Price, *Russia and the Roots of the Chinese Revolution*, 49–50.

26. In this vein, Kang expressed reservations about the constraints on political leaders imposed by democratic constitutions and political parties that he believed caused unnecessary " 'delay' " and inefficiency toward achieving moder-

nity. Edward Friedman, *Backward Toward Revolution: The Chinese Revolutionary Party* (Berkeley: University of California Press, 1974), 33; and, Grieder, *Intellectuals and the State*, 129. Kang also opposed elections that he described as a " 'world of darkness' " that inevitably involved plots, assassinations, and bribery. Jonathan D. Spence, *The Gate of Heavenly Peace: The Chinese and their Revolution* (New York: Penguin Books, 1981), 32 & 37.

27. Liang Qichao, *"Kaiming zhuanzhi lun"* ("On Enlightened Despotism"), *Yinping shiwen jice*, quoted in Andrew J. Nathan, *Chinese Democracy* (New York: Alfred A. Knopf, 1985), 61–62. Also, Chang, *Liang Ch'i-ch'ao*, 106; and Price, *Russia and the Roots of the Chinese Revolution*, 139. Price also notes Liang Qichao's admiration for Peter the Great.

28. Quoted in Pusey, *China and Charles Darwin*, 186. Also, Chang, *Liang Ch'i-ch'ao*, 87 & 195; and Price, *Russia and the Roots of the Chinese Revolution*, 113. Liang stated further: "[A]utocracy wears away the character of the people like the steady drip of water." Quoted in Grieder, *Intellectuals and the State*, 163. Also, Joseph Levenson, *Liang Ch'i-ch'ao and the Mind of Modern China* (Cambridge, MA: Harvard University Press, 1953), 44.

29. Liang Qichao, "On Rights' (*quanli*) Consciousness," (1902) trans. in *Contemporary Chinese Thought* (Fall 1999): 18.

30. First quote from Grieder, *Intellectuals and the State*, 163; second from Andrew J. Nathan, "The Idea of Political Participation: Liang Ch'i-ch'ao and Mao Tse-tung," unpublished paper, 30. Also, Chang, *Liang Ch'i-ch'ao*, 152–54 & 242. This widespread image of the Chinese people as "slavish" was shared by Yan Fu. Price, *Russia and the Roots of the Chinese Revolution*, 106.

31. Price, *Russia and the Roots of the Chinese Revolution*, 139.

32. Liang's condescending view of the Chinese people reflected Yan Fu's notion that Chinese lacked an aggressive attitude and had been lulled into living a life of peace and harmony. This sad state of affairs would be reversed, Liang believed, by the dynamic personality and will power of the despot and his adherence to the ideology of Social Darwinism that Liang found so attractive. Levenson, *Liang Ch'i-ch'ao*, 106; Schwartz, *In Search of Wealth and Power*, 48; Spence, *The Gate of Heavenly Peace*, 44; and Pusey, *China and Charles Darwin*, 287. Pusey also notes Liang's support for the restoration of the Guangxu emperor as a possible modernizing monarch.

33. In 1902 Liang lamented the absence of nationalism in China: "Among our countrymen there is not one who regards national affairs as his own affairs." "On the Public Capacity," in *Yinpingshi heqi* (1941), *Quanji (Collections)* vol. III, no. 10, trans. by Prof. Philip A. Kuhn, Harvard University. Also, Spence, *The Gate of Heavenly Peace*, 43; and Nathan, "The Idea of Political Participation," 24.

34. Liang's admiration of Thomas Carlyle and of Bluntschli—who linked political instability in France to what he believed were pronounced weaknesses

in the French national character—is discussed in Levenson, *Liang Ch'i-ch'ao*, 105–107; and Nathan, "The Idea of Political Participation," 24.

35. Mary Backus Rankin, *Early Chinese Revolutionaries: Radical Intellectuals in Shanghai and Chekiang, 1902–1911* (Cambridge, MA: Harvard University Press, 1971), 14, 39, & 124; and Harold Z. Schiffrin, *Sun Yat-sen* (Boston: Little Brown & Co., 1980), 90. Also, Spence, *The Gate of Heavenly Peace*, 47.

36. Lyon Sharman, *Sun Yat-sen: His Life and Meaning* (Stanford, CA: Stanford University Press, 1934), 297; and Hsiao, *K'ang Yu-wei*, 230. Sun believed, however, that China had democratic roots in its tradition of local government, and so in 1905 he supported the establishment of a Republic "without delay." As late as 1916, Sun also commented that "democracy is suitable for China." Schiffrin, *Sun Yat-sen*, 116; and Sun Yat-sen, "Manifesto on the Restoration of the Provisional Constitution," June 9, 1916, *The Kuomintang: Selected Historical Documents, 1894–1969* ed., Milton J. T. Shieh (New York: St. John's University Press, 1970), 60.

37. Hsiao, *K'ang Yuwei*, 228–30; and Sun Yat-sen, "Manifesto on the Restoration of the Provisional Constitution," *The Kuomintang*, 59. Also, Grieder, *Intellectuals and the State*, 340; Robert E. Bedeski, "The Tutelary State and National Revolution in Kuomintang Ideology, 1928–31," *The China Quarterly*, no. 46 (April–June, 1981): 326; Schiffrin, *Sun Yat-sen*, 36; Sharman, *Sun Yat-sen: His Life and Meaning*, 236; and Charlotte Furth, "May Fourth in History," in *Reflections on the May Fourth Movement: A Symposium*, ed., Benjamin I. Schwartz (Cambridge, MA: East Asian Monograph Series, 1972), 67. Sun Yatsen's opposition to the cultural iconoclasm of the subsequent May Fourth movement is discussed in Tse-tsung Chow, *The May Fourth Movement: Intellectual Revolution in Modern China* (Stanford, CA: Stanford University Press, 1960), 344.

38. Sun Yatsen, "An Explanation of Political Tutelage, Speech to the Nationalist Party Gathering in Shanghai, November 9, 1920," in (*Guofu quanji*) *Complete Works of the Founding Father*, vol. II, 399.

39. Sun Yatsen, "Manifesto of the Chinese Revolutionary Party," September 1, 1914, *The Kuomintang*, 53–55. Before the formation of the Chinese Revolutionary Party, Sun had supported the delegation of full authority to the president of the *Xingzhonghui* that had been established in 1895. From 1900 onward, Sun was determined to impose *his* personal authority over revolutionary organization. George T. Yu, *Party Politics in Republican China* (Berkeley: University of California Press, 1966), 17; and C. Martin Wilbur, *Sun Yat-sen: Frustrated Patriot* (New York: Columbia University Press, 1976), 15.

40. Quoted in Friedman, *Backward Toward Revolution*, 12, 18, 32, & 64. Loyalty to Sun in the Chinese Revolutionary Party was solidified with an oath of personal allegiance to his leadership as the party's "chief" (*zongli*).

41. Friedman, *Backward Toward Revolution*, 61. With provincial branches in the *Tongmenghui* stronger than the central authority, intraparty factionalism

had increased dramatically after the 1911 Revolution, undermining the political force of this revolutionary body. Gasster, *Chinese Intellectuals*, 55 & 95, and Chün-tu Hsüeh, *Huang Hsing and the Chinese Revolution* (Stanford, CA: Stanford University Press, 1961), 148.

42. First quote from Friedman, *Backward Toward Revolution*, 57; second from Schiffrin, *Sun Yat-sen*, 177. Sun still considered political figures other than himself (e.g., Huang Xing) to be capable of serving as the supreme leader. Huang, however, in arguing for allegiance to principles rather than an individual leader, led an effort in the Chinese Revolutionary Party to change the focus of the membership's oath from personal loyalty to Sun to an unnamed " 'leader' " who would be elected. Yet despite such resistance, Sun retained supreme authority by writing the rules of the party, appointing all party bureau heads and officers, and opposing any decentralization of power to party branches. This apparently engendered considerable internal resistance and hampered the growth of party membership, all of which ultimately caused the Chinese Revolutionary Party to degenerate into a small group of Sun's personal followers with little real organizational cohesion. Friedman, *Backward Toward Revolution*, 62, 99, & 212; and Yu, *Party Politics in Republican China*, 120 & 149.

43. Friedman, *Backward Toward Revolution*, 60.

44. The primary goal of Frederick and Catherine was to mobilize society's resources for war. Yet in promoting a freer economy, creating an educated and more religiously tolerant people, and establishing the rule of law (which even Frederick seemed obliged to accept), most enlightened monarchs ultimately contributed to the foundations of constitutional power. Krieger, *Kings and Philosophers*, 245; Gaglioro, *Enlightened Despotism*, 65; and Andrzej Walicki, *A History of Russian Thought: From the Enlightenment to Marxism* (Stanford, CA: Stanford University Press, 1979), 3–4.

45. Gasster, *Chinese Intellectuals*, 158, 169, & 184; Peter Zarrow, *Anarchism and Chinese Political Culture* (New York: Columbia University Press, 1990), 118, 136, 141–43, 161, & 200; Robert A. Scalapino and George T. Yu, *The Chinese Anarchist Movement* (Berkeley, CA: Institute of International Studies, 1961) 10, 30, & 41; and Arif Dirlik, *The Origins of Chinese Communism* (Oxford: Oxford University Press, 1989), 77 & 181. Although profoundly iconoclastic, Liu Shipei looked to Confucianism and Taoism for anarchist precedents and considered Chinese monarchical despotism a post-Han phenomenon. Other anarchists attacked Sun Yatsen for assuming the title of party "chief" (*zongli*), though some defended Sun personally, if not his august title. Cultural iconoclasm as a basis for antidespotism had also been expressed in the mid-1890s, most forcibly by Tan Sitong who believed that the "three bonds and five relationships" of Confucianism had created an excessively meek population on which despotism ultimately thrived. Chang, *Chinese Intellectuals in Crisis*, 93, 100.

46. Liu Shipei acknowledged antidespotic traditions in Chinese political thought, including the late Ming writer Wang Fuzhi. But like most Chinese

iconoclasts, Liu believed that traditional antidespotic thought had merely called for greater communication between the emperor and people, without ever really challenging the rigid hierarchical organization of the state and society. Chang, *Chinese Intellectuals in Crisis*, 167; Liu Shipei, "Textbook on Ethics" (*lunli jiaokeshu*) and Zhang Shizhao, "Self-Awareness" (*zijue*), trans. in *Contemporary Chinese Thought*, (Fall 1999): 42 & 50, respectively.

47. Gasster, *Chinese Intellectuals*, 103 & 111. Wang's study of Western law and constitutional systems of the West during his student days in Japan undoubtedly helped shape these views. Yan Fu had also previously contrasted the loyalty of Westerners to the impersonal state with the Chinese people's personal devotion to individual monarchs. Pusey, *China and Charles Darwin*, 70.

48. Howard L. Boorman, "Wang Ching-wei: A Political Profile," *Revolutionary Leaders of Modern China*, ed., Chun-tu Hsueh (London: Oxford University Press, 1971), 301. Wang so distrusted monarchy that he supported the establishment of a political structure of separation of powers for China's national government. Gasster, *Chinese Intellectuals*, 119.

49. Tsou Jung (Zou Rong), *The Revolutionary Army: A Chinese Nationalist Tract of 1903*, Introduction and Translation with notes by John Lust (Paris: Mouton & Co., 1968). Following quotes from 113, 114, 116, & 123, respectively. Also, see Hsueh, *Huang Hsing and the Chinese Revolution*, 14.

50. Zou thus argued that killing the emperor was important as "a warning to the myriad generations that despotic government is not to be revived." *The Revolutionary Army*, p. 123. Also, Hsueh Chun-tu, and Geraldine R. Schiff, "The Life and Writings of Tsou Jung," Hsueh, *Revolutionary Leaders*, 194. Zou had been strongly influenced by Tan Sitong's equally biting criticisms of imperial authority. Grieder, *Intellectuals and the State*, 171. For a similar argument emphasizing the "collective strength" of citizens in opposing tyrants, see, Anonymous, "On Citizens" (*Shuo guomin*), *National Tribune* (*Guomin bao*), trans. in *Contemporary Chinese Thought* (Fall 1999): 11–13.

51. Quoted in Grieder, *Intellectuals and the State*, 184. Like most supporters of democracy in China, however, Hu Hanmin still favored a short period of political transition by an autocratic state. He also warned of constant threats of restoration even after the establishment of the constitutional order. Noriko Tamada, "Sung Chiao-jen [Song Jiaoren] and the 1911 Revolution," *Papers on China*, East Asian Research Center, Harvard University, vol. 21 (February 1968): 217.

52. Grieder, *Intellectuals and the State*, 186. Chen Tianhua also reportedly argued that "ordinary Chinese would perform well as citizens." In their total opposition to autocracy, Chinese anarchists believed that throughout its history China lacked an aristocracy. Ernest P. Young, "Problems of a Late Ch'ing Revolutionary: Ch'en T'ien-hua," Hsueh, *Revolutionary Leaders*, 237; and Zarrow, *Chinese Anarchism*, 109.

53. Yu, *Party Politics in Republican China*, 70–73; Schiffrin, *Sun Yat-sen*, 173; Tamada, "Sung Chiao-jen," 214; and Chün-tu Hsüeh, "A Chinese Democrat: The Life of Sung Chiao-jen," Hsüeh, *Revolutionary Leaders*, 256–61.

54. Tamada, "Sung Chiao-jen," 216. Song held out the possibility of supporting a single national leader as a "symbol of nationalistic fervor," but he opposed autocratic decision-making authority. The Central China branch of the *Tongmenghui* organized by Song and Tan Renfeng thus opposed a single leader " 'in order to preserve it from autocracy.' " Quoted in Tamada, "Sung Chiao-jen," 204 & 212. Also, K. S. Liew, *Struggle for Democracy: Sung Chiao-jen and the 1911 Chinese Revolution* (Berkeley: University of California Press, 1971), 48 & 177. Song Jiaoren also supported "using a party to create a government" and, contrary to many revolutionaries at that time, he advocated the formation of two parties based on opposing political principles. Zhang Xingyan proposed a similar idea in reaction to the increasingly personal dissensions and conflicts among political leaders following the establishment of the Republic. Finally, Jiang Kanghu's Socialist party actually rejected Sun Yatsen as leader on the grounds that "an egalitarian party like the Socialist party does not have a leader." Friedman, *Backward Toward Revolution*, 25, 36, & 38; and Yu, *Party Politics in Republican China*, 77 & 91.

55. Song evidently drew on the antiheroic and impersonal model of political parties articulated previously by Qin Lishan. Price, *Russia and the Roots of the Chinese Revolution*, 104–10. A discussion of Confucian personalism and its impact on Chinese politics and society is in Levenson, "The Vestige of Suggestiveness," *Confucian China and Its Modern Fate*, vol. II, 33 & 62.

56. Quoted in Grieder, *Intellectuals and the State*, 187. Also, Young, "Ch'en T'ien-hua," *Revolutionary Leaders*, 241.

57. Tamada, "Sung Chiao-jen," 214. Sun Yatsen's admiration for strong leadership initially led him to "give Yuan [Shikai] a free hand in governing the infant Republic," a position Song Jiaoren also supported until 1913. Yu, *Party Politics in Republican China*, 105.

58. Tao Lihong, "Women zhengzhi de shengming" (Our Political Fate), *Xin Qingnian* (hereafter, XQN) vol. V, no. 6 (December 15, 1918): 558 (592).

59. Chen Duxiu thus lamented: "[L]oyalty to the ruler, filial piety, chastity and traditional righteousness are the morality of the slave." Chen Duxiu, "Jinggao qingnian" (An Appeal to Youth), *Qingnian zazhi* (Youth Magazine/hereafter QNZZ) vol. I, no. 1 (September 1, 1915), trans. in *Chinese Law and Government* (hereafter *CL&G*) vol. XII, no. 3 (Fall 1979): 31.

60. "Bo Kang Youwei gonghe pingyi" (A Rebuttal to Kang Youwei's Proposals for the Republic), *XQN*, vol. IV, no. 3 (October 16, 1916): 190–211 (211–32). Chen showed little admiration for constitutional monarchy in Germany under the Kaiser, which was endorsed as a political model for China by Kang.

61. "Jiu sixiang yu guoti wenti" (Old Thought and the National Question), *XQN*, vol. III, no. 3 (May 1, 1917): 1–3 (207–209); and Chen Duxiu, "Jinri Zhongguo zhi zhengzhi wenti" (Political Problems in Today's China) *XQN*, vol. V, no. 1 (July 15, 1918): 3 (7). In the latter article, Chen stressed the incompatibility between the concepts of "law and equality" and the idea of "sacred kings."

62. Yuan Shikai's political adventure was also encouraged by his American political adviser, Frank J. Goodnow, who composed a treatise on the unsuitability of republican government for China that evidently reinforced Yuan's ill-fated inclinations to monarchical status. Schwartz, *In Search of Wealth and Power*, 224–226.

63. Chen Duxiu, "Bo Kang Youwei gonghe pingyi," *XQN* (October 16, 1916): 192 (213). Chen also argued: "If a virtuous, intelligent, and valiant emperor were to use his absolute power to save the day, this would be like giving a torch to a blind man." "Aiguoxiu yu zijuexin" (Patriotism and Consciousness), *Jiayin zazhi (Tiger Magazine)*, vol. I, no. 4, (October 11, 1914), trans. in *CL &G*, vol. XII, no. 3 (Fall 1979): 26. Hu Shi also believed that the only way to achieve democracy was through the actual practice of self-government. Min-chih Chou, *Hu Shih and Intellectual Choice in Modern China* (Ann Arbor: The University of Michigan Press, 1984), 111.

64. Sheldon S. Wolin, *Politics and Vision: Continuity and Innovation in Western Political Thought* (Boston: Little, Brown and Co., 1960), 309.

65. "Aiguoxiu yu zijuexin," *CL&G* (Fall 1979): 19; and Chen Duxiu, "Fubi yu zun Gong" ([Monarchical] Restoration and Obedience to Confucius), *XQN*, vol., no. 6 (August 1, 1917): 1–4 (505–08). Yi Baisha, a frequent *New Youth* contributor, voiced similar sentiments. Chow, *May Fourth Movement*, 301.

66. "Jiu sixiang yu guoti wenti," *XQN* (May 1917): 2 (208).

67. Li Dazhao, "Xinde, jiude!" (The new, the old!), *XQN*, vol. IV, no. 5, (May 15, 1918): 446; and, Li Dazhao, "Kongzi yu xianfa" (Confucius and the Constitution), *XQN*, vol. II, no. 1 (September 1, 1916). Li continued: "A constitution is drawn up [to affirm] the citizens' liberty, not the emperor's or the sages' authority; a constitution is drawn up for the happiness of human beings, not for the dignity of idols."

68. "Yuan Shikai fuhuo" (The resurrection of Yuan Shikai), *XQN*, vol. II, no. 4 (December 1, 1916): 2 (312). In this sense, Chen believed that the post-1911 political elite were like China's ancient sages who as Yan Fu had also argued, failed to develop the capacities and vital energy of the people. Schwartz, *In Search of Wealth and Power*, 65. Chen also believed, however, that Chinese politicians were driven by enormous greed—influenced by the lure of Western wealth—rather than "a sincere desire to save the people...." Chen Duxiu, "Aiguoxiu yu zijuexin," *CL&G* (Fall 1979): 25. For an analysis of the financial corruption in the republican government, see Andrew J. Nathan, *Peking Politics*

1918–1923: Factionalism and the Failure of Constitutionalism (Berkeley: University of California Press, 1976).

69. Gao Yihan, "Fei 'junshizhuyi'" (Anti-"Monarchism"), *XQN*, vol. V, no. 6, (December 15, 1918): 549–54 (583–88). The latter point on post-Song despotism is made by Chen Duxiu in a pre-May Fourth article, "A Discussion of the Concept of Orthodoxy," *Guomin ribao* (*China National Gazette*), October 5 & 6, 1903, *CL&G* (Fall 1979): 8.

70. Influenced by the ideas of Montesquieu, Gao Yihan, like Liang Qichao, believed that the close intertwining of morality and politics in China formed a major foundation of despotism. Gao traced the origins of this tradition in China as far back as to the Zhou Dynasty (1122 BC–256 BC). Gao acknowledged that state interference in moral decisions had also occurred in Western history, but he argued that this was done according to "definite rules" that ultimately restrained the executive.

71. Here Gao Yihan repeated Yan Fu's view that Western rulers were public servants and that in the West the rule of law presided over rule by men. Gao also reflected Montesquieu's comment that the despot does not know law. Similar concepts were also previously espoused by Chinese anarchists. Schwartz, *In Search of Wealth and Power*, 66 & 173; Baron De Montesquieu, *The Spirit of the Laws*, trans. by Thomas Nugent (New York: Hafner Press, 1949), 71; and Zarrow, *Chinese Anarchism*, 122–25.

72. "Wode aiguozhuyi" (My Patriotism), *XQN*, vol. II, no. 2 (October 1, 1916), in *CL&G* (Fall 1979): 40–41. Chen's notion of a linear process of social and spiritual decay in China had also been previously expressed by intellectuals, such as the Buddhist revivalist Yang Wenhui who believed that the country's only hope lay with the reinvigoration of Mahayana Buddhism. Chang, *Chinese Intellectuals in Crisis*, 13. In contrast to Chen's tendency to criticize the promonarchical sentiments of the population, Lu Xun blamed the emperors for the country's susceptibility to despotism: "If [the Chinese] are sand, it is because their rulers have made them so." Quoted in Harriet C. Mills, *Lu Hsun: 1927–1936, The Years on the Left* (Ph.D. thesis, Columbia University, 1963), 241.

73. Chen Duxiu, "Jiu sixiang yu guoti wenti," *XQN* (May 1917): 2 (208); and "Aiguoxiu yu zijuexin," in *CL&G*, (Fall, 1979): 17. Chen believed that ever since the Song Dynasty China's traditional scholars, especially the Neo-Confucians, had provided the ideological props of despotism: "The goal [of education] has been to create deference for the sovereign and disrespect for the common people." Chen also cited as key factors in fostering popular receptivity to despotism the general "ignorance of science" among classical scholars and the hagiographic glorification of "heroic" personalities in Chinese historical writings. Chen Duxiu, "A Discussion of the Concept of Orthodoxy," *CL&G* (Fall 1979): 8–9.

74. First quote in Chen Duxiu, "Aiguoxiu yu zijuexin," *CL&G*, 17; second quote in "Jiu sixiang yu guoti wenti," *XQN* (May 1917): 2 (208); third quote in

"Shixing minzhi de jichu" (Establishing the Foundations of Democracy), *XQN*, vol. VII, no. 1 (December 1, 1919): 14 (18). In the last article, Chen foreshadowed his conversion to Marxism by attributing the backward attitudes of the people to the country's material underdevelopment, although at this time he did not believe that major "class divisions" existed in China.

75. Chen Duxiu, "Bei zhi wu shen gaolun" (Lowly Discourse), "Sui ganlu" (Random Thoughts), *XQN*, vol. IX, no. 3 (July 1, 1921): 3 (419). Although written after his conversion to Marxism, Chen did not diverge in this article from his persistent belief that the absence among the people of a "patriotic consciousness," a participatory ethic, and a "resistant public opinion" facilitated Chinese despotism. Also, "Aiguoxiu yu zijuexin," *CL&G* (Fall 1979):16; Chen Duxiu "Fankang yulun de yongqi" (The Courage of an Oppositional Opinion), "Sui ganlu," *XQN*, vol. IX, no. 2 (June 1, 1921): 3 (277); and Chen Duxiu, "Dikangli" (Resistance), *QNZZ*, vol. I, no. 3 (January 15, 1915): 2 (200). Like Chen, Lu Xun also acknowledged the periodic capacity of the common people to "band together," although Lu too condemned their inattention to national affairs. Quoted in Mills, *Lu Hsun*, 243. For a recent Western analysis of "native democratic tradition" in Chinese guilds in the city of Hankow, See Rowe, *Hankow* 324.

76. Here Chen attacked what he believed was the Chinese penchant for collaboration with foreign enemies that purportedly derived from the tradition of "'waiting for a king to come and bring new life.'" With their excessively diffused and unfocused loyalty, which Chen believed the Chinese people easily transferred to a foreign army, China was constantly ripe for easy takeover. "Aiguouxiu yu zijuexin," *CL&G* (Fall 1979): 17 & 27.

77. Guang Sheng, "Zhongguo guomin xing jiqi ruodian" (Several Defects in the Chinese National Character), *XQN*, vol. II, no. 6 (February 1, 1917): 1–11 (495–505).

78. Guang Sheng, "Zhongguo guomin xing jiqi ruodian," *XQN* (February 1, 1917): 11 (505). Like Yan Fu, Guang considered the Chinese yearning for security and tranquility as the basic cause of the people's political quiescence, although Yan saw evidence of democratic thought in the writings of the ancient sage Laozi. Kang Youwei saw a similar authoritarian spirit rooted in the classical concept of "righteousness" (*yi*) that he believed had legitimized political domination and social differentiation. Schwartz, *In Search of Wealth and Power*, 166 & 199; and Chang, *Chinese Intellectuals in Crisis*, 30.

79. Guang Sheng, "Zhongguo guomin xing jiqi ruodian," *XQN* (February 1, 1917): 11 (505).

80. First quote, Zhang Dongsun, "Xianzai yu jianglai" (The Present and the Future), 1920, cited in Dirlik, *Origins of Chinese Communism*, 141; second quote, Li Dazhao, "Lianzhizhuyi yu shijie zuzhi" (Unification and World Organization) *Xin Chao* (*New Tides*), vol. I, no. 2 (February 1, 1919): 151–52.

81. Chen Daqi "Gonghe xinxi" (New Year's Congratulations), *XQN*, vol. VI, no. 1 (January 15, 1919): 2 (6).

82. First quote, Guang Sheng, "Zhongguo guomin xing jiqi ruodian," *XQN* (February 1, 1917): 1 (505); second quote Spence, *The Gate of Heavenly Peace*, 180. Lu Xun "was in the forefront of those who raised the issue of *guomin xing*," but in accounting for the purportedly "backward" political and social sentiments of the populace, he ultimately blamed the elite and not the common people. Yet, by the time of the May Fourth era, Lu Xun was led by his inherent pessimism to see little hope for the grandiose plans for cultural transformation by students and intellectuals. Vera Schwarcz, *The Chinese Enlightenment: Intellectuals and the Legacy of the May Fourth Movement of 1919* (Berkeley: The University of California Press, 1986), 121; and *Lu Xun: Diary of a Madman and Other Stories*, trans. by William A. Lyell (Honolulu: University of Hawaii Press, 1990), xiii. Tao Lihong lamented that: "When [Chinese] people organize an association, everyone wants to be the head . . . and with power in their hands to give orders in a haughty manner . . . acting as a tyrant. [This] is the core of despotism." Tao Lihong, "Women zhengzhi de shengming," *XQN* (December 1918): 560 (594).

83. Levenson, "The Vestige of Suggestiveness," *Modern China and Its Confucian Fate*, vol. II, 138; and Spence, *The Gate of Heavenly Peace*, 77.

84. Chen Duxiu, "Jiu sixiang yu guoti wenti," *XQN* (May 1917): 1 (207). The preservation of the monarchy in all its pomp and ceremony by the "Articles Providing for Favorable Treatment of the Great Qing Emperor after his Abdication" provided an institutional basis for restoration efforts and apparently reinforced popular promonarchical sentiments, at least in Beijing.

85. Luo Jialun concurred: "[W]e must realize that the crimes of Yuan Shikai and Zhang Xun are not individual crimes but harmful phenomena emanating out of the very nature of the Chinese mentality." Luo Jialun, "Da Zhang Puqun lai xin," (Reply to a Letter from Zhang Puqun), *XQN*, vol. II, no. 2 (December 1919): 367, trans. in Schwarcz, *The Chinese Enlightenment*, 95.

86. "Yuan Shikai fuhuo," *XQN* (December 1916): 2 (312); and Chen Duxiu, "Fubi yu zun Gong," *XQN* (August 1917): 1 (505). In the latter article Chen noted that "restorations require Confucianism and Confucianism requires restorations."

87. Chen thus lamented that "Yuan Shikai committed high treason, and [yet] everywhere men scurried about and worked to the point of exhaustion for him." "Wode aiguozhuyi," *CL&G* (Fall 1979): 43 & 47.

88. Chen Duxiu, "Aiguoxiu yu zijuexin," *CL&G* (Fall 1979): 20.

89. Tao Lihong, "Woman zhengzhi de shengming," *XQN* (December 25, 1918): 559 (593). In fact, Yuan's close aid, Cai E, had advocated dictatorship by a "Chinese Napoleon." Friedman, *Backward Toward Revolution*, 168.

90. Gao Yihan, "Fei 'junshizhuyi,' " *XQN* (December 1918): 551 (585). In an obvious slight against Sun Yatsen's anti-Manchu appeals, Gao attributed this failure to bring about a revolution in popular consciousness on, in part, the fact that the "Chinese revolutionary struggle had used racial thought instead of Republican principles."

91. "Jiu sixiang yu guoti wenti," *XQN* (May 1917): 3 (209).

92. Chen Duxiu, "Jinggao qingnian," *CL&G* (Fall 1979): 36. Also, Yu-sheng Lin, "Radical Iconoclasm in the May Fourth Period and the Future of Chinese Liberalism," in *Reflections*, ed., Schwartz, 56.

93. Chen Duxiu, "Xinwenhua yundong shi shenma" ("What is the New Culture Movement?"), *XQN*, vol. VII, no. 5 (April 1, 1920): 3–5 (699–701); Fu Sinian, "*Xin Chao* fakan zhiqu shu" ("The Basic Aim in Publishing *New Tides*"), *XC*, vol. I, no. 1 (January 1, 1919): 2; Gao Xian, " 'Shi shenma' he 'weishenma' " "('What' and 'Why')", *XQN*, vol. IX, no. 5 (September 1, 1921): 1–9 (589–91); and Gu Chengyu [Gu Jiegang], "Duiyu jiu jiating de ganxiang" ("Reflections on the Archaic Structure of the Family"), *XQN*, vol. I, no. 2 (February 1, 1919): 160. Also, Jerome Grieder, *Hu Shih and the Chinese Renaissance: Liberalism in the Chinese Revolution, 1917–1937* (Cambridge, MA: Harvard University Press, 1970), 106, 140, & 156; Arif Dirlik, *Revolution and History: Origins of Marxist Historiography in China, 1919–1937* (Berkeley: University of California Press, 1978), 263; Charlotte Furth, *Ting Wen-chiang: Science and China's New Culture* (Cambridge, MA: Harvard University Press, 1970); and Schwarcz, *The Chinese Enlightenment*, 100. Despite his commitment to "enlightenment," Chen Duxiu noted that people who abided by "scientific ideas" still believe in "ghosts," so much so that instilling the population with modern thought would not be easy. Chen Duxiu, "You gui lun zhuyi" ("Doubts Concerning the Theory of the Existence of Ghosts"), *XQN*, vol. IV, no. 5 (May 1918): 408 (443).

94. "A Discussion of the Concept of Orthodoxy," *CL&G* (Fall 1979): 9.

95. Chuan Sinian, "Qu bing" ("On Eliminating War"), *XC*, vol. I, no. 1: 26–27; and Luo Jialun, "Jinrizhi shijie xinchao" ("The New Tide in the Contemporary World"), *XC*, vol. I, no. 1 (January 1, 1919): 22. Luo especially emphasized the importance of educating the common man. Also, Mao Ziyong, "Guogu he kexue de jingshen" ("The Ancient Learning and the Scientific Spirit"), *XC*, vol. I, no. 5 (May 1, 1919): 738–39; Wang Xinggong, "Shenma shi kexue fangfa" ("What is the Scientific Method"), *XQN*, vol. VII, no. 5 (April 1, 1920): 1–4 (713–16); and Schwarcz, *The Chinese Enlightenment*, 99. Yan Fu also drew a close linkage between propagating the scientific method and reordering society to make up for previous failures to educate the masses. Schwartz, *In Search of Wealth and Power*, 35 & 39.

96. Mills, *Lu Hsun*, 230. Contrast this view on the political role of scholars with that of Gu Jiegang (also known as Gu Chengyu) who "refused to see a fundamental social obligation for the scholar, and a social function for learning." Laurence A. Schneider, *Ku Chieh-kang and China's New History: Nationalism*

and the Quest for Alternative Traditions (Berkeley: University of California Press, 1971), 75.

97. Fu Sinian, *"Xin Chao* fakan zhiqu shu," *XC* (January 1919): 2. Fu noted that at the end of the Song Dynasty and during the Ming, Chinese scholars had failed to halt political and moral decline, this in contrast to their Western counterparts of the Renaissance. At this time, recent foreign visitors to China, such as Betrand Russell, were hailed by their Chinese hosts for "throwing light on society's basic modern ills and then advocating change," while Chinese scholars, in contrast, were roundly condemned for failing to engage in "an independent search for truth." This occurred despite the fact that Liang Qichao had previously called on Chinese scholars to learn from Western history in his book *New History.* Schneider, *Ku Chieh-kang*, 245; and Chang Sunnian, "Luosu" ([Betrand] Russell), *XQN*, vol. VIII, no. 2 (October 1, 1920): 3 (183).

98. Harriet C. Mills, "Lu Xun: Literature and Revolution," *Modern Chinese Literature in the May Fourth Era*, ed. Merle Goldman (Cambridge, MA: Harvard University Press, 1977), 199; and Zhi Xi, "Chuban jie ping" (A Commentary on the World of Journalism), *XC*, vol. I, no. 1: 121–22.

99. Chou, *Hu Shih*, p. 113; Luo Jialun, "Jinri zhi shijie xinchao," *XC* (January 1919): 22; and Fu Sinian, *"Xin Chao* fakan zhiqu shu," *XC* (January 1919): 2. In the latter article, Fu Sinian also recognized the difficulties of this educational effort by lamenting the Chinese people's general "dislike for science and technology."

100. Chen Duxiu, "Shixing minzhi de jichu," *XQN*, vol. VII, no. 1 (December 1, 1919): 13–21 (17–25); and Richard Kagan, *The Chinese Trotskyist Movement and Ch'en Tu-hsiu: Culture, Revolution, and Polity*, unpublished Ph.D. thesis (The University of Pennsylvania), 81. Einstein's theory of relativity was also translated in *New Tides* as a challenge to what was considered the Chinese tendency to see everything in absolute terms. Schwarcz, *The Chinese Enlightenment*, 120.

101. Chen Duxiu, "Ouxiang pohuai lun" (On Iconoclasm), *XQN*, vol. V, no. 2 (August 15, 1918), trans. in *CL&G* (Fall 1979): 51. Here Chen seemed aware that, as in the West, the single leader's authority was bolstered by an organic theory of the state. Walzer, *The Revolution of the Saints*, 172; and Schwarcz, *The Chinese Enlightenment*, 126.

102. This argument was part of Chen's general assault on the notion of "national essence" (*guocui*), a concept that he believed not only obstructed the development of democracy, but also inhibited China's competitive position in the international arena.

103. Gao Yihan, "Fei 'junshizhuyi,'" *XQN* (December 1918): 551 (585).

104. Gao Yihan, "Guojia fei rensheng zhi guisu lun" (Rejecting the State as the Ultimate End for Humankind), *QNZZ*, vol. I, no. 4 (December 15, 1915): 1–8 (287–94).

105. Gao Yihan, "Minyue yu bangben" ("Social Contract and the Foundation of the Nation"), *QNZZ*, vol. I, no. 3 (November 5, 1915): 2 (206).

106. Gao Yihan, "Du Mier de *Ziyou lun*" ("Reading [John Stuart] Mill's *On Liberty*"), *XQN*, vol. IV, no. 3: 212–16. John Stuart Mill's theory also strongly appealed to Lu Xun. Leo Ou-fan Lee, "Genesis of a Writer: Notes on Lu Xun's Educational Experience, 1881–1909," *Modern Chinese Literature*, 170.

107. In a similar vein, Luo Jialun complained that "a critical spirit has been squelched in China in two ways: by autocratic politics and autocratic thought." Luo Jialun, "Piping de yanjiu: san W zhuyi" ("The Study of Criticism—Three W-ism"), *XC*, vol. II, no. 3 (April 1920): 601–03.

108. Li Dazhao thus urged Chinese youth to go "to enlighten, benighted villages so that the despotic village could be converted into a constitutional one." Cited in Dirlik, *Revolution and History*, 37 & 140; also, Grieder, *Hu Shih and the Chinese Renaissance*, 121.

109. Ma Boyuan, "Hubei, Henan jian de fengsu" ("Customs and Habits in Hubei and Henan"), in "Shehui diaocha" ("Social Investigations"), *XQN*, vol. VIII, no. 1 (September 1, 1920): 1 (109). Just how objective these "investigations" were is unknown. For another account of such "investigations," see Schwarcz, *The Chinese Enlightenment*, 129.

110. Ma Boyuan, "Hubei, Henan jian de fengsu," *XQN* (September 1, 1920): 1.

111. Ye Shaotiao, "Nü renge wenti" ("On the Women's Issue"), *XC*, vol. I, no. 2: 252; and Tang Si, "Wo zhi jielie guan" ("My Views on [Female] Chastity"), *XQN*, vol. V, no. 2 (August 15, 1918): 96–100 (107–11). Also, Schwarcz, *The Chinese Enlightenment*, 115.

112. Identifying female chastity with tradition thus led many women writers and students to flaunt these socially "despotic" conventions by cohabitating outside marriage with male friends. Leo Ou-fan Lee, *The Romantic Generation of Chinese Writers* (Cambridge, MA: Harvard University Press, 1973).

113. Meng Zhen, "Wan e zhi yuan" ("The Origins of All Evil"), *XC*, vol. I, no. 1: 124. Opposition to the patriarchal family in May Fourth thought was traceable to Kang Youwei and Liang Qichao and created an appeal among Chinese intellectuals for the irreverent and socially critical plays of Henrik Ibsen and Oscar Wilde. Hu Shi, "[Yibusheng]zhuyi" ([Ibsen]ism), *XQN*, vol. IV, no. 6 (June 1918): 489 (531); Spence, *The Gate of Heavenly Peace*, 39; and Schwarcz, *The Chinese Enlightenment*, 113. Meng Zhen believed that the oppressive family explained the absence of great figures in Chinese history—comparable to George Washington and Charles Darwin—just as Lu Xun argued that the powerful social and political influence of filial piety had caused China to become "stuck" in history incapable of making progress. Pusey, *China and Charles Darwin*, 205.

114. Wu Yu, "Jiazu zhidu wei zhuanzhizhuyi zhi genzhu lun" ("The Family System as the Root of Despotism"), *XQN*, vol. II, no. 6 (February 1, 1917): 1–4 (491–94). (The order of the quotations is reversed from the original). Aristotle distinguished authority in the patriarchal family from political authority on the basis that the latter involved rule over free men. Schochet, *Patriarchicalism in Political Thought*, 34.

115. Gu Chengyu, "Duiyu jiu jiating de ganxiang" ("Reflections on the Archaic Structure of the Family"), *XC* (February 1919): 161.

116. Yu Pingbo, "Wode daode tan" ("Discussing Morality"), *XC*, vol. I, no. 5 (May 1, 1919): 890. Mao Zedong's philosophy teacher, Yang Changqi, argued that the individual in China would be liberated by breaking the excessive reliance on the indulgent Chinese family, thereby creating the invigorated citizenry necessary for democracy. Wakeman, *History and Will*, 159–62.

117. Wu Yu, "Jiazu zhidu wei zhuanzhizhuyi zhi genzhu lun," *XQN* (February 1917): 2 (492). Gu Chengyu argued further: "The desire of the father to have a peaceful house with nary a word of opposition to his authority is what leads to this [political] notion of 'no opposition.'" Gu Chengyu, "Duiyu jiu jiating de ganxiang," *XC* (February 1919): 163.

118. Yang Chu was a "shadowy figure" in the fourth Century BC who preached individual survival and longevity as the greatest good. Benjamin I. Schwartz, *The World of Thought in Ancient China* (Cambridge, MA: Harvard University Press, 1985), 175, 188, & 215.

119. Wu Yu, "Du Xunzi shu hou" ("After Reading Xunzi"), *XQN*, vol. III, no. 1 (March 1917): 1–3 (9–11).

120. Here Wu is quoting a commentary by a certain Yang Jing. For a description of Xunzi's doctrine of the "hegemonic" ruler (*ba*), see Schwartz, *The World of Thought*, 292–305. This linkage of political authority with doctrinal monopoly was considered by the May Fourth generation as the intellectual core of the patriarchal political structure in China.

121. Wu Yu, "Du Xunzi shu hou," *XQN* (March 1917): 3 (11). Wu's opposition to the subservience of ministers to the monarch also reflected the views of the seventeenth-century thinker Huang Zongxi. De Bary, "Chinese Despotism," *Chinese Thought and Institutions*, 174. May Fourth intellectual Yu Pingbo also traced China's lack of progress to the tradition of "'treating the ruler and father as one,'" though Yu believed this was not the original intention of the sages. Yu Pingbo, "Wode daode tan," *XC* (May 1919): 890.

122. Li Dazhao, quoted in, "Origins of Chinese Communism," *Modern China*, 41.

123. Voltaire as cited in Ernst Cassirer, *The Philosophy of the Enlightenment*, trans. by Fritz C. A. Koelln and James P. Pettegrove (Princeton, NJ: Princeton University Press, 1951), 250.

124. First quote Gu Chengyu, "Duiyu jiu jiating de ganxiang," *XC* (February 1919):157; second quote, Guang Sheng, "Zhongguo guomin xing jiqi ruodian," *XQN* (February 1917): 1 (495).

125. Chen Duxiu, "Wode aiguozhuyi," *CL&G* (Fall 1979): 39.

126. Chen Duxiu, "Jinggao qingnian," *CL&G* (Fall 1979): 30. That Chinese society resembled a physically old and infirm person would be repeated during the 1980s among reformist intellectuals and by democracy movement supporters in 1989.

127. *New Youth* and *New Tides* thus carried few articles on the institutional and legal structures and practices of parliamentary democracy.

Ought We Throw the Confucian Baby Out with the Authoritarian Bathwater?: A Critical Inquiry into Lu Xun's Anti-Confucian Identity

Virginia Suddath

Introduction

The concerns of this paper emerge out of a number of interrelated interests and ongoing intellectual problems; primary among them are those arising from contact between Western and non-Western cultures and values, specifically between post-Enlightenment European culture and that of post-Qing Confucian China. One culture was in the full thrust of its intellectual and expansionist glory, and the other at a moral and political ebb. What took place during this earlier phase of contact and the resultant anxieties and sociopolitical realities necessitated by interchange are still being played out today. The questions are still being debated in China as to how best to respond to the challenges that this encounter and these new options pose to the Chinese worldview. Witness the debate over human rights in China and the process of democratization that is ongoing. What *kind* of a democracy will emerge as a result of the intersection with traditional Confucian socialization? How do assumptions of a rights-based view of autonomous individual achievement intersect with a culture that has an equally powerful, but radically different, understanding of human flourishing? In which domains is free speech, especially speech critical of the central government, to be sanctioned? These are several of a host of areas of ongoing intercultural discussions and discontinuities arising out of initial contact.

More narrowly, this is an inquiry into the practice of remonstrance (*jian*) within the Confucian tradition. *Jian* can properly be seen as an indigenous means of protest, one that has been a documented part of the Confucian state bureaucracy from at least the Han Dynasty, with some elements dating back to the Zhou Dynasty. This topic is one especially worth pursuing at this time given that China is at present experiencing difficulty in negotiating a place for protest within contemporary society. Questions arise as to whom in the government or which policies can be properly or safely criticized and to what degree or level of command this criticism can extend. For instance, the central authorities' tolerance toward localized strikes and tax demonstrations and their overt encouragement of such protests as those against the 1999 bombing of the Chinese embassy in Belgrade contrast sharply with the persistent campaign of repression that has been directed against Falun Gong members and the silencing of those who publicly question the policies of the Central Committee. Exploring such a homegrown means of protest not only demonstrates that this technique has historically had a place within the Chinese tradition, but also is useful in countering those who might claim that protest or freedom of speech need be discussed in rights language and its practice imported. My aim here is not to address directly the applicability of such a conception of protest in contemporary China; rather, in examining *jian* as both a philosophical and an historical phenomenon, I aim to contribute to the project of rearticulating Confucianism, making it more relevant and giving it greater cultural currency.

Recent discussions within social science circles on "Rethinking Confucianism in Asia" have a tendency to depict contemporary neo-Confucianism as some kind of moral "software" informing the "hardware" of East Asian authoritarianism or authoritarian capitalism. The arguments are often between those making positive claims about neo-Confucianism as the moral and cultural software in China's modernization—the glue that holds the culture together and enables stability in the course of rapid change—and negative claims about its role in legitimating patriarchal social relations and authoritarian political habits. "Neo-Confucianism is responsible for the subjugation of Asian women" is a common theme, although studies of elite women in late imperial China increasingly challenge this stereotype.[1] Another is: "Neo-Confucianism provides a liberal vision of human agency and mitigates against autocratic government," even though most Confucians since antiquity have willingly served authoritarian rulers and many late-twentieth-century politicians who call themselves Confucians favor neoauthoritarian governments. Moreover, we know that Confucianism in East Asia has been rife with dissension among elites in the face of state orthodoxy, especially in China during the late Qing and Republican periods. And certainly it can be argued that during the Mao era, the persistence of Confucianism is evidenced by the virulence and violence of the various campaigns to eradicate any of its dogged cultural manifestations.

It is a cliché, but true nonetheless, that one cannot fully understand what is going on in China today if one does not understand what happened there in the past. Thus, while current debates as to the place of Confucianism in contemporary Asian cultures are strongly reminiscent of ones carried on during the early part of the twentieth century, more often than not these contemporary discussions fail to take into account earlier generations of Korean, Vietnamese, Japanese, and Chinese intellectuals who had engaged in just these debates. Many of these earlier thinkers had condemned Confucianism as the primary obstacle to modernity and were advocates of a "turn to the West" in order to get on the fast track to much-needed political change and economic development. Some of these thinkers, most notably Hu Shi in China, had even gone to the West for university degrees and returned home with plans for reform informed by specifically Western ideals. In some analyses Hu and other progressive reformers failed in their elitist conflation of their own understanding of "freedom" (that of individual thought) with the desires of the majority of the people for freedom from hunger and oppression. While this may be the case, Hu's agenda still ought to be seen in the context of those of others during this same era, for instance those associated with the National Essence movement, who advocated less, not greater, freedom as the solution to China's social ills; theirs was a call for a reinstatement of pre-Manchu dynastic and feudal power structures under a neotraditionalist aegis in order to provide the necessary stability to move into an uncertain future. During the years following the end of the Qing dynasty and before the consolidation of Mao's power, there were spirited and wide-ranging debates over the course that China ought to follow and the political framework within which this course ought to be charted, debates that took place on both political and philosophical planes and questioned the suitability of that framework remaining a Confucian one.

This study focuses on the May Fourth period, a time of intellectual and political turmoil in China during the early twentieth century, a time when Confucianism had arguably hit its moral nadir. When morality becomes doctrinaire, it fails; and during this period Confucianism and the political bureaucracy it had sustained had degenerated into a coercive template that had become hopelessly unproductive in effecting social change. This state of affairs was reflected in the poverty, stagnation, and corruption rampant throughout China. Everything that could possibly go wrong, did; cures were worse than the diseases they were intended to treat. In classical Chinese terms, the celestial mandate (*tianming*) had apparently been revoked.

This is also a time when China began seriously to engage with questions and problems arising from extensive contact with the West and military defeats by Japan. Given especially China's powerful past and self-conception as the world center (or centering), there was widespread agreement that, to reverse the tide, considerable political and social change was mandatory. Most agreed that China was mired in a degenerate and authoritarian past, and many began looking to Western concepts as a source of reform. To what degree ought they be appropriated? How was it apt to respond to these new, "modern" ideas and to the unfamiliar, and humiliating, occupations by foreign powers? Indeed, how might the process of change being mandated by the times force changes in how change is itself conceived? In a world conceived as and constituted by the active process of "worlding" (*ziran*), a process of spontaneous arising free of any grounding first principle, what meaning could or should attach to "radical change" called for by the May Fourth reformers? In fact, ought a radical reordering even be sought to emerge out of a particularly degenerate world or situation? Given the Chinese analogy of the chicken and the egg, the question can then be put: what ought to be done with a remarkably rotten egg?

Lu Xun's Confucian Anti-Confucianism

My point of departure in the analysis of *jian* is with the works of Lu Xun, the cultural critic and fiction writer, one of the key figures of the May Fourth or New Culture Movement (approximately 1917–1923), and a potent moral voice in China today. "Rotten egg" is mild in contrast to many of his depictions of China and the Chinese. In 1906, when asked by a friend why he was giving up medicine to become a writer, he replied, "You don't think China's idiots, her wretched idiots, can be cured by medical science?" The May Fourth *literati* saw themselves as the rejuvenators of Chinese culture—the key to China's future, in their view—and much of what was taking place in the May Fourth period replicates contemporary aspects of China's process of modernization. I choose to focus on Lu Xun because he is a paradigmatic example of one who remonstrates, as the strategy of *jian* is employed within the Confucian construct; his criticism of the culture was at the same time a defense of the culture. He is widely considered one of the predominant anti-Confucian intellectuals of the May Fourth period, and yet, I will argue that almost uniquely Lu Xun's vociferous critique of Confucianism can be seen to remain within the Confucian tradition and to avoid the dichotomous thinking—to either turn to the West or back to the Han—of many of his contemporaries. Finally, the voice of Lu Xun, more than any others from that period, still resonates.

It could be argued that the history of Lu Xun is the history of twentieth-century China; it is the history of a man whose life and whose values, both during his lifetime and after his death, represent and typify China's struggle to transform itself in the face of its own internal degeneration and stagnation, while simultaneously confronting the increasing presence and influence of foreign cultures and powers. Lu Xun was born into a family of tenuous nobility, whose station was further threatened by his father's profligacy, opium use, and ill health. As the eldest son, Lu Xun was educated and began to sit for the series of state exams when a combination of factors diverted him from this path: the state bureaucracy that the exam system was designed to support was in turmoil; an uncle was found guilty of corruption (within a corrupt system) and dismissed from government service, bringing shame upon the family and limiting Lu Xun's chances for official success; and, after a long illness, his father died a preventable death. Lu Xun then studied both marine science and medicine in Japan, read widely and was influenced by Western thinkers, became profoundly disturbed by the apathy of his fellow Chinese to their country's downhill course, and returned to China, determined to participate in reform. He then began a life of teaching, writing, and protest, all to great acclaim. After his death, Mao took advantage of Lu Xun's fame and moral stature, distorted his positions to advance his own political agenda, and by the 1970s the Communist Party was producing posters depicting Lu Xun's image and carrying such slogans as "Take over the brush of polemics, struggle to the end," "Carry forward the revolutionary spirit of Lu Xun," and "Study the revolutionary spirit of Lu Xun; become a pathbreaker in the criticism of Lin Biao and Confucius." Finally, in 1989, his words were inspiration for the protesters at Tiananmen Square and could be found on placards and banners during the demonstrations, demanding accountability from those in power.

Lu Xun had the good fortune to die in 1936 before he could be denounced by Mao, as he surely would have been had he lived to witness the development of Mao's policies; instead Mao was at liberty to later use him for his own devices. Lu Xun's avowed intellectual and literary preferences tended toward the "counter-traditions" in Chinese culture—strains of thought and sensibility in opposition to, or removed from, the orthodox Confucian tradition. These heterodox interests emerged from his research into the traditional literature of Daoism—especially of Zhuang Zi—and folk literatures, and helped to shape both his iconoclastic thinking and his writing style. In "A Madman's Diary," one of his best-known works of fiction, he depicts China as mired in a feudalistic and "cannibalistic" past, writing in the voice of a man who is self-avowedly mad. And yet in even such an extreme example, in terms of both style and polemic, we are able here, and throughout his oeuvre, to trace important remnants of a formative and, indeed, an inescapable Confucian worldview and methodology. As opposed to those of his contemporaries who proposed specific cures—in the form of systematic political change—Lu Xun's role remained that of the indignant critic, one at times verging on despair.

In the literature, beginning in 1918 and extending to the present day, Lu Xun has invariably been labeled as anti-Confucian. Indeed, there is in most representations of his life and intellectual development an assumption about a teleology that moves from a young man grounded in tradition, to evolutionist, to May Fourth iconoclast, to leftist revolutionary. Only recently has scholarship begun to move beyond this teleology. For example, Wang Xiaoming's biography *Wufa zhimian de rensheng: Lu Xun zhuan* (*A life that cannot be faced directly: a biography of Lu Xun*, 1992) seems to be working to counter the Lu Xun myth; in English, Leo Ou-fan Lee's scholarship (1987) and the new biography by David Pollard (2002) have contributed to debunking the Marxist canonical representation of Lu Xun's development, even as they succumb to different ideologically motivated representations. Why, we must ask ourselves, is it not possible for him to be both critical of Confucianism—what most would label "anti-Confucian"—and, at once, Confucian? Answering this question leads to an investigation of the strategy of *jian* and a consideration of some distinctions between the relationship between criticism and change in the Western and Chinese philosophic traditions.

Criticism and Change

While the earlier claim and project of comparative philosophy—the attempt to determine overarching commonalities between the Western and non-Western traditions—has been debunked, most would agree that an essential part of what we call philosophy in any cultural tradition involves thinking critically about serious issues. In the Western tradition this pursuit has involved questioning assumptions, revealing and interrogating underlying values, clarifying the meaning of key terms, determining relationships between cause and effect, and making important distinctions about important things. The pursuit of Truth "at all costs" has been paramount. This may seem antithetical to the aims of Confucius, who understood social harmony as instrumental in bringing about the cultural unity that is the most distinctive characteristic of Chinese culture. Harmony is valued above most other types of values as it goes hand in hand with social stability, whose alternative is perceived as chaos and a general burden on social structure. Thus, although values typically associated with Confucianism such as social harmony and deference to authority might be taken to show that critical thinking and Confucian thought are divergent, in the Confucian tradition, too, the very activity of doing philosophy has involved thinking critically, by way of developing a critical attunement and making distinctions on a wide variety of subjects.

However, what can be seen to distinguish the two traditions is their response to impasse and the resultant recognition that change or transformation of some sort is necessary. In the Western philosophic tradition, with the realization that a problem seems to be unsolvable, the tendency is to go back to the essential basis of our assumptions and to question them. The paradigm in which we are working is one in which change is thought of as a from/to process—from A to B. Criticism leads to an understanding of a problem that leads to a return to question basic assumptions that leads to a system changed in its fundamental components and structure. The Chinese tradition, by contrast, is one in which change is not *from* one thing *to* another; rather it is change *by way of*— that is, it is a change from A to A'. Within the Confucian framework the strategic employment of *jian* leads to an appreciation of a divergence from *dao*, which leads, in turn, to critical reevaluation and rearticulation of the tradition.

"Apparent contradictions always demand attention," writes John Dewey in *The Ethics of Democracy*. By most accounts, Lu Xun is represented as anti-Confucian, but to what degree is this representation borne out? While taking into consideration his own anti-Confucian claims, along with Mao's strategic cooptation of him, I understand Lu Xun to be working within a Confucian methodology—change from (or becoming) A to A'—and in support of a Confucian tradition open to rearticulation through internal critique. He was madly critical, that cannot be argued. However, early in his journalistic career he claimed, "If we want to preserve our national characteristics, we must first make sure that they can preserve us." And this critical attitude—this protest as protestation—can be seen to underlie his anti-Confucian stance and is key to understanding his method of critique. The way in which he approached the process of critique and change was one that involved a process of becoming, as distinct from a change from being (one way or thing) to being (another).

In the following sections I will explore some possibilities for opening up the concept of *jian* (official remonstrance) within the Confucian tradition. Given the institutional tendency toward stability that characterizes Confucianism through the millennia, one might think that such an effort would indicate a lack of appreciation of the concomitant resistance to critique that has also been a defining mark of the tradition throughout its history. While it is true that by the beginning of the twentieth century there was growing dissatisfaction and pockets of anger at the strongly negative socioeconomic effects of a corrupt and decaying, but still powerful, Confucian bureaucracy that ruled China, and yet the cultural landscape of premodern China could still be fairly described (as it has been by Tu Weiming) as one dominated by "despotic, gerontocratic, and male-oriented practices," a description that held through the twentieth century, one could add. If we compare this history to our own European past, it can be argued that these practices remained entrenched to an even greater degree in a dynastic culture that reveres tradition in such ritualized ways on both institutional and individual levels and had yet to experience a widespread period of antiroyal protest such as took place during the Enlightenment. And yet, I will claim that there exists within Chinese Confucian discourse a fertile ground for extending the possible meaning of the practice of *jian* and that a deeper exploration of its history will work to destabilize the fixed meaning and power it has acquired.

In what follows I discuss the history of remonstrance within the Confucian tradition and some distinctly Confucian aspects to the act of remonstrance in order to demonstrate how *jian* integrates with other Confucian values and practices. I will then illustrate the manner in which Lu Xun employed his critique of Confucianism by looking closely at one of his short *zawen* (essays) from 1918. Here we will see an example of Lu Xun as cultural critic, wielding the sword of *jian*. Cultures need to change, not merely to survive, but to prosper and to permit better lives for their members. The Chinese cultural archetype—that of the critical official, the one in the position to remonstrate the emperor and to advocate change—has traditionally been as powerful a focus of loyalty as the figure of the oppressive emperor. After all, it is criticism that makes much philosophizing a social endeavor, and usefully so.

Remonstrance within the Confucian Tradition

A discussion of the history and role of remonstrance in China runs the risk of becoming an excessively complex one, complicated in part by its very success as an institution in the evolving bureaucracy of the dynasties. Unlike in Japan, where those in the Imperial court bureaucracy held positions that were little more than status markers, the Chinese bureaucracy actually functioned as a government. As a result, throughout its long history it continued to evolve and respond to political circumstance. Posts were created, and occasionally eliminated, as deemed necessary; as well, bureaus and posts were renamed and responsibilities shifted among them. This leads to difficulties when trying to chart a simple history.[2] Yet, as we shall see, throughout the history of Imperial China, the positions of official critic (remonstrator) and censor were ones that endured without rupture in the Confucian bureaucracy until the end of the Qing Dynasty in 1911. And not only did this office and these roles persist, but from Qin times on (second century BCE) the organization of the central government, although it grew and changed, fell into an established pattern that emphasized and depended upon the censorial functions. In fact, the top stratum of government, directly under the Emperor, was always tripartite: a supreme military establishment, a supreme general-administration establishment, and what has been translated into English as the Censorate (*yushitai*), officials whose numbers varied but who for the most part had unmediated access to the emperor.[3]

The theoretically absolute power of the emperor has thus in practice been subject to highly effective constraints. Although for over twenty-two centuries the Chinese emperor was reverently considered the Son of Heaven, he was compelled not only to uphold the institutions established by the founder of the dynasty, but also, ideally, to observe the customs, felt as commands, of his long list of ancestors. These practices are what would evolve into the Confucian *li*, established in the Confucian tradition by the sages of antiquity, those wise enough and virtuous enough to comprehend the requirements of heaven. The emperor would have been instructed in this tradition from earliest childhood by teachers specially appointed to educate future rulers. As well, he would have internalized the understanding as to how his actions would be noted and evaluated by historians, as the writing of history was a long-established state institution. And in addition to these powerful, but relatively amorphous controls, there were explicit institutions that were established to meet the same ends. There was the system of remonstrance (*taijian*), by which officials were charged with the solemn duty of closely observing the Emperor's behavior and decisions and advising him of his faults. As well, there was the Censorate (*yushitai*) that performed similar duties with regard to officials.[4]

As it developed, especially in its neo-Confucian evolutions, there is a strong emphasis in the tradition on the importance of the cultivation

of the self and the role that self-cultivation plays in maintaining relationships. But it is important to keep in mind the conceptual continuity
between the individual self with its intimate relations, and the social and
political realm. The relationships to be maintained are not ones that
remain solely in the personal sphere, but are ones that extend outward
from the family to the community and to the state. In addition, these
relationships are marked not just by their continuity, but by their inherent reciprocity and their "differentiated manifestation" as well.[5]

The continuity between self and the political realm was conceptualized early on in the tradition. We see a clear path depicted in the *Great
Learning*: "Their persons (the self) being cultivated, their families were
regulated. Their families being regulated, their states were rightly governed. Their states being rightly governed, the whole kingdom was made
tranquil and happy."[6] What originates with the self, in other words, is
made manifest in a well-functioning society. A standard neo-Confucian
reading of this passage emphasizes the cultivation of one's personal life
for the sake of society, indeed the world at large, and seems to declare
that when the state is not functioning well, this is a time for a necessary
reemphasis on individual self-cultivation.

> Implicit in the statement that 'when the personal life is culti-
> vated, the family will be regulated' is an assertion that, as long
> as the family is not yet regulated, the cultivation of the personal
> life must be continued. By analogy, if the body politic is not yet
> in order or if peace has not yet pervaded all under Heaven, the
> effort of self-cultivation should not be interrupted. Learning
> (*hsüeh*), in the Neo-Confucian sense, requires an ultimate and
> continuous commitment.[7]

However, it is important to note that the *Great Learning* continues:
"From the Son of Heaven (the emperor) down to the mass of the people,
all must consider the cultivation of the person (the self) the root of
everything besides (the most essential thing)."[8] While self cultivation as
the "root" is clearly both the conceptual starting point and the site of
ultimate return, it is a mistake to conceive of this root as located within
the family of the populace exclusively. That is, it is clear in the passage
above that the emperor himself is not exempt from the admonition to
develop a high level of *de*, of virtue, in order to preserve his power to
rule. In fact, as we will see, he has a special duty, for the sake of the
kingdom, to maintain a level that transcends what is required of the
ordinary person.

It is not surprising, then, that one distinguishing feature of
Confucianism is the emphasis that it places on *jian* as a duty. In English,

the term "remonstrance" has come to mean "a formal statement of griev-
ances or similar matters of public importance." To remonstrate is "to
protest against (a wrong); to point out, state, or represent (a grievance,
etc.) to some authority." It has the sense of voicing a reproach, but in an
official capacity, in the public realm, and in matters of importance. It is
not something that one would undertake casually; as well, it is an objection that is made in some formal manner to a person in a position of
authority. In Western democratic culture, this kind of official protest most
commonly takes place when we vote. As David Hall and Roger Ames
note in their work on the history of democracy in China: "[In the West]
remonstrance has been associated ideally with the power of the bour-
geoisie and intellectual classes to influence government through the
exercise of the ballot, and through participation in the actions of educational and voluntary associations."[9] Given the very real political and
economic powers at work to counteract this influence, it is arguable to
what degree this impact is felt; nonetheless, the framework is there in
Western democracies for official protest to be voiced. However, in traditional China, this would have been impossible. The institutional structure was not one that permitted the general populace from having a voice
that could be heard, or even expressed, in such a way to the emperor.
In the orthodox Confucian tradition, it was the ruler's ministers who
were given this role. Indeed, the role of minister was defined such that
there was an expectation that he would not only serve to carry out the
policies of the emperor, but would also be expected to advise and, if
necessary, to criticize.

One important distinction that needs to be made at this point is the
different meaning that the verb "to protest" has in English and in Chinese.
A Western understanding of the term is "to object to," "to dissent or
dispute." The position that one takes is one of an adversary. One is in
opposition to the original stance and is voicing disagreement and mounting a challenge, at least implicitly. The Chinese interpretation, however,
is more along the lines of the alternate English meaning: "to affirm with
solemnity", as in "I protest my innocence." Roger Ames has argued that
many features of the Chinese world order work to challenge and limit
the nature of protest, that they circumscribe it within the limits of the
second of the two meanings. And that this latter meaning is ineffectual
in mounting substantive challenge to prevailing modes of authority.
Instead, what takes place is a reaffirmation, a resuscitation of an ideal
template.

It is a recurring feature of the history of Confucianism that
individuals will arise to dispute the claims to orthodoxy of a
current dominant type of Confucianism... Most major

claimants to reinterpretation would offer their own commentaries and draw from other earlier commentaries that supported
their viewpoint. However, the most fundamental claim in each
reinterpretation was not to a novel vision—which would have
been abhorrent!—but to having perceived the original and true
meaning of the Classics.[10]

This "return to the future" becomes the desired end of *jian*.

The termination of each of the historical dynasties was marked by
a period of corruption and a falling away from the central tenets of the
Confucian tradition; the beginning of each succeeding dynasty a restoration in the form of a powerful leader committed to the Confucian Classics.
Historically, China's future has been a series of adaptations on the past,
and protest has had as its overarching goal the realignment of the traditional path; one might, in fact, see the whole history of political authority
in China as, "meet the new boss, same as the old boss." And yet, ideally,
the "boss," the authority, has been freshly interpreted in the light of
current political realities, and this authority is made manifest in the
person of the Emperor, in a sense dressed, not in new, but freshly restored
ceremonial robes.

Given the above limitations of protest in the Confucian tradition,
how then can we interpret the role of the minister, whose duty it was to
advise and protest? What might he have to say beyond affirmations of
the status quo? Indeed, his role did go beyond that of cynical window
dressing that one might assume, given the Confucian understanding of
protest noted above; but in order to conceive of the possibility of his
effectiveness, it is necessary to explore the status of the emperor and the
manner in which, on a conceptual level, his power is accrued.

Looking briefly at early Chinese history, we see that the sense of
ming (to command, to cause to happen) had been closely tied to a notion
of fate, and the ruler was one who happened to be endowed, as if by fate,
with a particular amount of royal virtue. However, by the eleventh
century BCE, with the establishment of the Zhou dynasty, the position
of emperor became invested with a different conception of *tianming* (the
"mandate of heaven"), and the legitimacy of his rule became closely tied
to the degree to which he either augmented or dissipated his *de* (his
virtue). A proper ruler would be one who paid great attention to his
conduct and understood his moral and religious obligation to take proper
care of his virtue. This care came to involve an elaborate set of ritual
duties, of *li*, that were incumbent upon him performing, and performing
well. If he failed, especially by putting his own desires first, then he would
be understood to be dissipating his *de*. Eventually he would lose his

power and, more importantly, his legitimacy to rule, and the position would be transferred to someone who had shown himself to be morally worthy to hold it. Given such an understanding, virtue that is made manifest in an ordered society trumps all else—strength, heredity, wealth—as the necessary condition for power and authority.

If the conditions under which the emperor was to remain in office were so closely connected to his ability, indeed his *suitability*, to represent the power conferred on him by *tian*, then—given the natural tendencies of all human beings, emperors not excluded, to stray from the moral straight and narrow—we begin to see the necessity for the position of remonstrator among the Emperor's ministers. In the Confucian tradition, the issue and the aim is not to be good, but to be *good at* whatever project or interaction one is involved in. In order to live properly, to follow the *dao* (the "proper way"), is for most neither a facile nor an effortless undertaking. In fact, what is easy is to be led astray. In this light, a conceptual space begins to open for *jian*, for correcting the path.

In the Chinese Confucian tradition order in the society and the state is evidence of the personal ordering of the constituents of that society. Yet at the same time, it emphasizes the degree to which personal order is possible only within the context provided by social and political life. In other words, individuals and the state are never viewed as an instrumental means to serve the realization of the other. Instead, they serve as mutually implicating ends. Repeatedly throughout the *Analects* Confucius emphasizes this interdependence and thus marks an understanding of political relationships that is distinctly unfamiliar to categories of Western philosophical theory. Even in contemporary China the concept of inalienable rights remains foreign to the culture. What underlies the distinction between ruler and ruled, in the West, is a clear distinction between rules as procedures for promoting and maintaining social order, and those elements of a society that require ordering. We rely on theory to justify and order our practice; the two are seen as necessarily different realms altogether, with the latter flourishing when it is most in conformity with the former. A Confucian order, or flourishing social structure, emerges rather from a valuing of the conditions in which all the particular constituents of the order can best manifest their particularities, especially in the performance of the ritual duties (*li*).

Jian: Alteration as Preservation

Remonstrance involves a number of important philosophical terms central to the Confucian tradition. Those discussed here are ones especially relevant to and intimately concerned with an understanding of the crucial role that remonstrance plays in upholding that tradition: specifically, *dao*, *yi*, *de*, *li*, and *xiao*. None of these "organic" or correlative concepts, as we shall see, can easily be spoken of without reference to the others. What are we doing when we engage in remonstrance? When we use this term (if we ever do), what we mean is a kind of admonition. We might be reminding someone of her duties or obligations or, with more of a caveat in mind, expressing a warning or disapproval. In a more stern tone, to remonstrate would carry the weight of a reproof or a censure, even. Oftentimes, too, remonstrance has a formal quality to it; one thinks of a letter addressed to an official, to someone in government. Most often, the word implies a formal protest (a letter to a sovereign from a subject, for example) or a serious investigation at play.

When we put the term in a Confucian context the best way in which to think about *jian* is as a correction, as when one adjusts the tiller after checking the compass. The goal is to get back on the path, the *dao*.

> A sustained image that the Chinese text presents is Confucius finding his way. That is, in reading the *Analects* in the original language, a term such as *guo* that is often nominalized as "faults," or if its verbal aspect is acknowledged, translated as "to err," has the specific sense of "going astray" or "going too far": not just erring, but straying from the path.[11]

When erring in this way, what we most require, if our internal compass is not fully functioning, is someone who understands that it is her responsibility to guide us back. Yet it is important to note that, as in other contexts, *dao* here is not meant to convey the sense of a one, single, correct path. It is not the idea of "staying on the straight and narrow." One's energies are not directed at discerning precise footsteps to follow. Rather it ought to be thought of as a process of adjusting to the terrain, and of thereby building up a road, or, more aptly, participating in shaping it. This road will not be THE right road, but it will be the right road, nonetheless.

The goal of correction is to be brought back into balance, into harmony, and one gets here the sense of optimism in the flexibility of a person, an openness to change, that is fundamental to the Confucian project. Now if bringing us back into balance is the goal, how is this harmony to be accomplished? In the Confucian understanding, harmony is brought about by appropriate actions, with special attention paid not just to which specific actions one chooses to perform, but more to what *kind* of actions and to how one performs them. *Yi*, or appropriate actions performed appropriately, carries with it the sense of doing one's duty, but especially in a way that would fit together with other actions and the actions (and needs) of others. It is a kind of social "sixth sense" that transmutes those actions into meaningful ones, given especially an attentiveness to the communal context in which they are performed.

How is harmony made manifest? The measure is those individuals who have most realized their *de*. Examples in history include King Yao and King Shun and, of course, Confucius. These are individuals who more often than not we can say were "broadening the way."[12] They are the ones against whom others gauge themselves, the models within the community whose characters "command" deference. The way they are broadening, *dao*, is the character of the culture accumulated over time that is realized ("made real") in the world by the efforts of such persons of *de* who act as mediums for its manifestation. As Confucius concludes, it is a human being actively engaged in the world who makes the way great; hence, it is the duty of the leader to develop and preserve the way.

Finally, the opportunity through which one might demonstrate harmony and the guide to its expression is *li*. These are the observations of rites, the observance of which allows us all to have meaningful contact with one another; they ought also be seen as providing us the opportunity to develop or to deepen relationships. We shake hands, we acknowledge successes, we go to funerals, we make special dinners, we open doors.

> Master You said: "Achieving harmony (*he*) is the most valuable function of observing ritual propriety (*li*). In the ways of the Former Kings, this achievement of harmony made them elegant, and was a guiding standard in all things large and small. But when things are not going well, to realize harmony just for its own sake without regulating the situation through observing ritual propriety will not work.[13]

We perform these acts not in a rote manner and not with the aim of maintaining order or control over others. Rather, we invest these responsibilities with meaning that is both their due (as ritual acts) and the expression of our investment in the relationship. We act as daughters, friends, teachers, neighbors, citizens; learning to rightfully perform *li* is part of what both develops one as a person and contributes to the flourishing of the community of persons one inhabits.

All of these terms are to be placed within the context, not simply of harmony, but of harmonious relationships; for the harmony that one is aiming toward is not an abstract Pythagorean perfect pitch, not the application of laws of cosmic harmony, but a Whitmanesque mélange, where self and other are in vital dynamic relationship, one to the other, and where human perceptions overlap and form a web of experience: "And these tend inward to me, and I tend outward to them, And such as it is to be of these more or less I am, And of these one and all I weave the song of myself."[14] Whitman here expresses an imagined sense of connection to those in a world extending beyond one he has physically encountered, and yet his harmony, too, differs from the Confucian in this important sense: a Confucian experience would have as its goal the *actualization* of such a harmony, a process beginning close at hand, at home, and extending out into the world, and finally the cosmos. This harmony is actualized through the appropriateness of one's daily interactions. It is not "just for its own sake," but to "regulate the situation," a situation that is at base relational.

It must be stressed, finally, that the primary characteristic of relationships in the Confucian universe is filiality. It is family that is the primary model of order and *xiao*, filial relationships (parent/child, teacher/student, sovereign/subject), are the basis of all order. "That's what it's all about," is what Confucius is saying in the following passage from *The Classic of Familial Deference*:

> The Master said, "Do you understand how the former Kings were able to use their consummate character (*de*) and their visionary way (*dao*) to bring real order to the world, how the people were able to use it to become harmonious (*he*) and to live in accord with each other so that superior and subordinate alike did not resent each other?"
>
> Zengzi arose from his mat to respond, and said, "I am not clever enough to understand such things."
>
> "It is familial deference (*xiao*)," said the Master, "that is the root of character (*de*), and whence education (*jiao*) itself is born."[15]

Xiao is what ties all the other values together, like a river that runs through them, always demanding, always adjusting. It is how the goal of harmonious relationships, from family to cosmos, is achieved and it is what is required of us, implicitly, in all our interactions.

> Someone asked Confucius, "Why are you not employed in governing?" The Master replied, "The Book of Documents says:
>
> It is all in filial conduct (*xiao*)! Just being filial to your parents and befriending your brothers is carrying out the work of government.

In doing this I am employed in governing. Why must I be 'employed in governing'?"[16]

That is, everything that one does, or ought to be doing, is in the context of, with regard to, and under the rubric of familial deference.

However, if *xiao* is the root of *ren* (authoritative conduct),[17] then in what sense or to what degree can we fit *jian* into this equation? It would seem that if duty and obedience were the primary values at work, and if the relationships in question were always hierarchical, then any suggestion of wrongdoing by an inferior to a superior would be acutely inappropriate. Not surprisingly, there is more complexity to this concept, as *xiao* is not simply straightforward obedience or the fulfillment of one's duty, as might be implied from these guidelines. A clear example is that of the Confucian parent-child relationship, which is one not based on a specific age association, but is, rather, a generational one. Parents must care for children; but then, later, children are above all bound to care for elderly parents.

It will be useful here to distinguish three central and interrelated aspects of *xiao*: care, obedience, and moral vigilance.[18] Numerous references to *xiao* in the *Analects* refer to the first of these aspects: respectful care, especially of one's parents. "The Master said, 'When your father and mother are alive, do not journey far, and when you do travel, be sure to have a specific destination'."[19] "The Master said, 'Children must know the age of their father and mother. On one hand, it is a source of joy; on the other, of trepidation'."[20] And, in addition, this care must be carried out with the appropriate attitude.

> Ziyou asked about filial conduct (*xiao*). The Master replied: "Those today who are filial are considered so because they are able to provide for their parents. But even dogs and horses are given that much care. If you do not respect your parents, what is the difference?"[21]

> Zixia asked about filial conduct (*xiao*). The Master replied: "It all lies in showing the proper countenance. As for the young contributing their energies when there is work to be done, and deferring to their elders when there is wine and food to be had—how can merely doing this be considered filial?"[22]

Filial care, in other words, emerges from a feeling of responsibility and appreciation for what one's parents have done for one and is based on a sense of reciprocity that runs through all manifestations of *xiao*.

Xiao also has an aspect of obedience, a habit that can be easily shifted from parent to ruler. Here one is fulfilling one's duty, but the feeling of care is backgrounded and the more dominant focus is, appropriately enough, on stability of rule and effective submissiveness to power.

> The Master said, "It is because exemplary persons (*junzi*) serve their parents with familial deference that this feeling can be extended to their sovereign as loyalty (*zhong*), because they serve their elder brothers with deference (*ti*) that this feeling can be extended to their elders as compliance, and because they maintain an organized homelife that this sense of organization can be extended as proper order to the governmental offices. Thus when one is successful in what one does at home a name is established that will be passed on to posterity."[23]

And Mencius, too, notes this tendency. "Mencius said, 'There is a common expression. "The Empire, the state, the family." The Empire has its basis in the state, the state in the family, and the family in one's own self'."[24] It is on this aspect of *xiao* that many critics of Confucian authoritarianism rightly focus their concerns, and many of the May Fourth reformers will denounce the kinship system as the ideological basis for despotism.

However, the third dimension of *xiao* is meant to work as a corrective to the possibility of such blind obedience. This is the aspect that Heiner Roetz calls "moral vigilance," and it takes the form of remonstrance. While certainly one always must maintain proper respect and show deference to ones "superiors," Confucius is unequivocal as to the additional duty to remonstrate with even one's parents: "The Master said, 'In serving your father and mother, remonstrate with them gently. On seeing that they do not heed your suggestions, remain respectful and do not act contrary. Although concerned, voice no resentment'."[25] And he was even more forceful (agitated, one might say) in *The Classic of Familial Deference*, when questioned as to whether a child should opt for narrow obedience:

> Zengzi said, "Parental love (*ai*), reverence and respect (*jing*), seeing to the well-being of one's parents, and making a name for oneself for posterity—on these topics I have received your instructions. I would presume to ask whether children can be

deemed filial simply by obeying every command of their father."

"What on earth are you saying? What on earth are you saying?" said the Master. "Of old the emperor had seven ministers who would remonstrate with him, and although he had no vision of the proper way (*dao*), he still did not lose the empire. The high nobles had five ministers who would remonstrate with them, and although they had no vision of the proper way (*dao*), they still did not lose their states. The high officials had three ministers who would remonstrate with them, and although they had no vision of the proper way (*dao*), they still did not lose their families. The scholar-officials just had a friend who would remonstrate with them, and they were still able to preserve their good names.

If a father has a child who will remonstrate with him, he will not sink into immorality (*buyi*). Thus, in confronting immorality, a child has no choice but to remonstrate with a father, and a minister has no choice but to remonstrate with a sovereign. Hence, remonstrance is the only response to immorality. How could simply obeying every command of one's father be deemed filial?"[26]

Here we can see that filiality is more than just "honoring thy father and mother," and certainly it goes far beyond mere obedience. From the above example it is clear that even though neither the emperor, nor the high nobles, nor the high officials, nor the scholar-officials were adept at ruling, yet because they had ministers or friends who would correct them, then the kingdom was effectively ruled.

Then again, a more problematic state of affairs would be one in which the Emperor, or someone in position of power in the government, was unresponsive to remonstrance. A skillful person might be able, with the help of some luck, to maneuver his way into a solution that would be the appropriate one for all involved; however, there is very little that a remonstrator can do if those in the position of political power nonetheless refuse to take their counsel. More often than not during the history of the Censorate in China, when the Emperor was unresponsive to criticism, it was the remonstrator who was the loser—often in a very literal sense, indeed losing his life. And yet, it is at such a juncture that the technique of *jian* might manifest itself most forcefully.

A Call to Arms

We may now ask ourselves what might be the outcome if a censor emerged to critique not just the individual emperor, but the *role* of the emperor, as well? What might be the consequences within the tradition when the ultimate goal of the critic becomes not that of preserving the tradition, but seemingly to radically change it, overthrow it even? Is it possible to be an advocate for such radical change without at the same time supporting wholesale revolution?

Lu Xun was an example of such a critic. By the time he had turned to journalism in the second decade of the twentieth century and become a much-published gadfly, the political struggle was engaged most directly against the feudal-minded *literati*, and those aspects of Confucianism that we identified earlier as constituting the authority of *jian* now lacked all effectiveness for political regulation. The state had become one in which tradition was an old man; worse, in Lu Xun's prose that tradition had become cannibalistic, devouring those it was to protect.[27] The *li* had become impoverished, hollowed-out forms,[28] devoid of meaning; simply rules to be followed and external guides to conduct imposed by others.

"The 'village worthy' is excellence (*de*) under false pretenses."[29] What Confucius draws our attention to here is the duplicitous behavior of those in positions of power, such as the Dowager Empress Ci Xi, whose deceptive actions in the last years of the Qing dynasty belie their true intentions or abilities. Such a "village worthy" might have the outward appearance of a superior person, but be lacking the necessary constitutive elements of a true leader. They no longer have the ability to govern, they do not have the good of the common people as their objective, and they have nothing of their own to contribute to governance. Such a person might be mistaken as a model, but through the practice of a desiccated form of *li*, devoid of personalized and creative elements, they have a decidedly detrimental effect on those around them. Ci Xi's attempt to shore up the Qing dynasty was a decades-long hypocrisy, causing much greater harm than good; it had all the pretensions of taking the high road, just to get to the low road more quickly.

Lu Xun saw these rulers for the empty shells that they were. The problem was that many others in China were allowing themselves still to be duped. His appraisal, a "call to arms," is characteristic both of his asperity and the pragmatic, nonideological stance he would maintain for the rest of his life; at the same time, however, it suggests an underlying aspiration to recover certain values. He writes: "If we want to preserve our national characteristics, we must first make sure that they can preserve us."[30] This power to preserve will be the criterion by which to judge what (or rather *how*) to recover those values. It is important to note that we ought to read his use of 'preserve' here not in the sense of pickling, certainly; rather, it is more the sense of sustaining and upholding both the individual and the culture. The challenge will be to discover a method by which the Confucian underpinnings of the state ideology can be *made* to serve again, in other words to revitalize and repersonalize *li*. As we shall see, Lu Xun is not advocating obliterating all remnants of Confucian culture, rather his focus is on making what is worth preserving stronger, while jettisoning those aspects that are consuming its members.[31]

This process will be one not of disjunction, not a break with the past tradition, but of self-transcendence, and thereby self-renewal, a process consistent with the cyclical history of China. Throughout its long history, Confucianism was able to survive and thrive as a system of thought, as well as the basis for an effective political system by constantly engaging in creative philosophical debates with its opponents. In this process it was being repeatedly reformulated, adapting to the times and to the influences of opposing schools of thought, both indigenous and foreign.[32] The May Fourth period provided Lu Xun and those others engaged in the struggle to determine the course for China's future with yet another opportunity for such productive syncretism.[33]

Here we can distinguish the principal distinction that must be drawn between the political impetus behind the views of the majority of the New Culture advocates for change and those of Lu Xun. Cultural innovation is not an easy process to program; and yet there was a belief during that period in China in a strategy of cultural transformation—whether in Hu Shi's liberal democracy or Chen Duxiu's eventual push toward Communism—that was "scientifically" reliable. Implicit in this strategy was the assumption that a society, or a culture, can be disassembled piece by piece, its parts evaluated as to their usefulness, and then put back together altered in social form and intellectual substance. "It is always reason that guides and directs," wrote Hu Shi.[34] This was at the core of the progressive political agenda. Its strategies for social and political change were based on the assumption that desired ends could be achieved through reforms in the political institutions alone. That is, once an understanding of what progress would depend upon (acquisition of technology and democratic political institutions, for instance), then change would be a matter of acquiring the knowledge necessary to achieve this goal.[35] In contrast, Lu Xun's vision of society was as a living entity; it was a Confucian view of moral community as a vital organism that cannot be dismembered—even with the sharp edge of reason—without lethal consequences to the life force that animates it. Radical change, therefore, would be for him not a matter of redefining ends, but of revitalizing the very conditions for the possibility for the production of change.

"My Views on Chastity"

In order to understand why most analyses of Lu Xun's critical stance depict him as straightforwardly anti-Confucian, we can now turn to an example of his essay writing during this period. In 1918 Lu Xun published an essay, "My Views on Chastity," in which he addressed the great attention being paid by writers and public speakers to the "insufficient level of chastity" of contemporary Chinese women. Their purported concern was to prevent women from joining the ranks of those who were "growing more degenerate every day." As is common in a time of crisis, women were being given the moral responsibility to save the nation, or at least to shoulder the burden of preventing further decline. However, Lu Xun was able to perceive this movement as a clear example of the worst of the Chinese tendency to retreat to the past and viewed all related arguments about what "forward direction" to take as being variations on the worthless.

> This is the twentieth century, and dawn has already broken on mankind. If *New Youth* were to carry an article debating whether the earth were square or round, readers would almost certainly sit up. Yet their present arguments are pretty well on a par with contending that the earth is not square.[36]

Lu Xun saw this movement as merely "raising old banners" and the focus on the issue of chastity as especially retrograde. In this regard, women were not only expected to be chaste if unmarried, but also if and when her husband died. "In short, when a woman's husband dies she should remain single or die. If she meets a ravisher she should also die. When such women are praised, it shows that society is morally sound and there is still hope for China. That is the gist of the matter."[37]

In his opposition to this crusade and its ilk Lu Xun is seen by many as advocating a turn in a straightforwardly Western direction as a solution. He begins his argument by asking in what ways unchaste women injure the country. China, he admits, is a country faced with ruin, but it is certainly not the case that the men in power have become dissipated because they have been corrupted by women. It is rather because the leaders have brought the crisis on themselves through their crimes and their mismanagement of the years of wars, famine, flood, and drought. Lu Xun argues that it is not the louche behavior of the women that has led to this state of affairs; rather the moral and political decadence is "owing to the fact that we have no new morality or new science and all our thoughts and actions are out of date."[38]

In demonstrating how such a view had come to hold such sway, he charts the path that the virtue of chastity had followed in the Confucian tradition to the current point where both men and women were unable to do much to change the situation. Many women, after being taught that submission is the cardinal wifely virtue, had a "spirit as distorted as her body"—a reference to foot-binding—and were thus unable even to conceive of objecting to this "distorted morality."[39] And, according to Lu Xun, the ones who did dare to express their desires were chastised—at the very least—for challenging the "eternal truth" that good women were above such aspirations. As to the men, they had been silenced as well by those that he calls the "professional Confucians."

> The fact is that after the Han Dynasty most mediums of public opinion were in the hands of professional Confucians, much more so from the Song and Yuan dynasties onwards. There is hardly a single book not written by these orthodox scholars. They are the only ones to express opinions. With the exception of Buddhists and Taoists who were permitted by imperial decree to voice their opinions, no other "heresies" could take a single step into the open. Moreover, most men were very much influenced by the Confucians' self-vaunted "tractability." To do anything un-orthodox was taboo. So even those who realized the truth were not prepared to give up their lives for it. . . . [S]o they turned "tractable" and held their peace. This is why there has been no change right up till now.[40]

In Lu Xun's analysis Confucianism, as the state ideology, had by this time successfully achieved a high degree of interior colonization; the culture had become one in which a primary characteristic of its people was self-abnegation and the willingness to be led. It is this sense of the word "tractable" that so horrifies and angers Lu Xun. And given such a depiction of Confucianism as a system by which to "manage" its populace, to make them easily controlled, one might easily understand why Lu Xun, like a number of his intellectual contemporaries, might then want to turn to such available Western values as those of self-determination and autonomy and away from a Confucian social framework and sense of self. While indeed this might have been the path he chose to follow, in fact those who see this turn misread not only Lu Xun, but important aspects of Confucianism as well.

One of the most significant of these misreadings is the degree to which many Western encounters with China have historically been based on notions of the Chinese as being "selfless," most especially when viewed in the light of unquestioned understandings of 'Western' individual selves. While the full dimensions of this distinction are too complex to cover here, it needs to be noted that this view of a "selfless self" is a misunderstanding and leads to such elisions as that between "tractability" and "self-abnegation." While, as we saw above, Lu Xun was angered by the degree to which he saw those around him having lost their backbone and having become easily managed—"tractable" in the worst sense of the word—we can by no means assume that he would therefore be advocating, as a "cure," a turn toward an autonomous self, in the Western understanding of this term.

During his student years in Japan, Lu Xun had read and translated some Nietzsche and had been quite taken by the image of the *Übermensch*, as the symbol of the individual daring to take a stand against conformity and smallness. Yet still, we must not think that he is advocating the development of a separate, individual sense in the Western sense of "individual." As Roger Ames and David Hall observe, this would be anathema to the Chinese. They note: "We should not . . . think that because we most often associate self-actualization with individuated existence, there can be no appreciation and personal enjoyment of an alternative understanding of uniqueness among the Chinese."[41]

> The term "individual" can mean either one-of-a-*kind*, like a human being, or *one*-of-a-kind, like Turner's "Seastorm." That is, "individual" can refer to a single, unitary, separate, and indivisible thing that, by virtue of some essential property or properties, qualifies as a member of a class . . . by virtue [of which] it is substitutable. . . . Individual can also mean unique. Under this definition, . . . equality can only mean parity. It is this sense of "unique individuality" that is helpful in understanding the traditional Confucian conception of self. . . . Attributing the ideal of self-abnegation to the Chinese tradition involves importing both the public/private and the individual/society distinctions. To be selfless in the sense presupposed by some commentators on Chinese culture requires that an individual self first exist [as an achievement], and then that it be sacrificed for some higher public interest.[42]

It was the loss of a person's uniqueness, his "*one*-of-a-kindness" that Lu Xun saw as the humiliating inheritance of the Confucian tradition during the early part of the twentieth century. However, it was the tractability, the acquiescence in the face of humiliation, that angered him more and what he considered to be the greatest hindrance to change. We see here one of the characteristics that most distinguishes Lu Xun from his contemporaries in their shared critique of the effects of the Confucian tradition. His criticism was directed not solely at the rotten framework within which the deterioration had occurred, but took aim at those who, through their silence and inaction, had allowed the temple to rot.

Conclusion

One of the dogmas of Confucian culture is that "harmony" and "unity" come necessarily at the expense of individual liberty and are a defining element of "Chineseness." Correct thinking, articulated and enforced by a class of scholar-officials and later by Party officials, has indeed been a defining feature of East Asian societies, where authority has often been enforced by such Confucianist dogma. However, to blame Confucius for this would be to miss the mark; as we have noted, repeatedly Confucius insists that those in the position to do so are required to speak truthfully to ones in the position of power, however unwelcome this truth might be. In *Analects* 13.15, Confucius responds to an inquiry by Duke Ding by declaring that there is no one thing that those in power can say or do that can ruin a state.[43] States, like the human beings and the institutions that constitute them, are complex entities and can withstand occasional abuse and offense to their bodies. However, what Confucius goes on to say is that what will effectively poison them in the long run are silence, and cowardice, and the inability to care enough about the relationships that sustain them to speak out in their defense. Lies corrupt politics; only if the truth can be told—and false names rectified—can good government follow.

Values are real to the degree to which we are willing to risk something to make them prevail. When commitments we express are not followed by action, then these values remain in the realm of the virtual. They remain rhetoric about what we claim to be important. For most of the twentieth century in China, the value of *jian* had been emptied of meaning, possibilities for protest have been grotesquely virtual, and both at the beginning and the end of the century many of those who hoped for reform turned to Western concepts of rights in order to argue for protest in a meaningful voice.

However, by examining more deeply the concept of *jian* from within the framework of the Confucian tradition, my aim here has been to begin to explore the possibility of opening up a space for argument, of loosening the hold that the prevailing modes of interpretation have had on possibilities for change. Within the terrain of this discursive space, there are possibilities that have not yet been articulated. The question becomes: How do you open up a discursive terrain so it is more hospitable to its own inchoate possibilities? Specifically, how might we begin from within the Confucian tradition itself to make room for internal transformation? My hope is that by exploring an earlier period when the very legitimacy of the term "Confucianism" was being contested that we shed some light on this question today.

Notes

1. See especially Francesca Bray, *Technology and Gender: Fabrics of Power in Late Imperial China*, University of California Press, 1997 and Wang Zheng, *Women in the Chinese Enlightenment: Oral and Textual Histories*, University of California Press, 1999.

2. See Hucker (1985) for an extensive and quite detailed dictionary of official titles in Imperial China.

3. Hucker (1966): 11–12.

4. There was also a long tradition of literary criticism in China. Both by necessity and intention more subversive than the state-sanctioned criticism of censors and remonstrators, this literature could have a strong affect on public opinion, something of great concern to the government. See especially François Jullien's *Detour and Access: Strategies of Meaning in China and Greece*, Chapter III, "Under the Cover of the Image: Insinuated Criticism."

5. Tu (1985): 138.

6. Legge: 45.

7. Tu (1985): 135.

8. Legge: 45.

9. Hall and Ames (1999): 154.

10. Mungello: 37.

11. Confucius, trans. Ames and Rosemont (1998): 46.

12. "The Master said, 'It is the person who is able to broaden the way (*dao*), not the way that broadens the person." Confucius, *Analects*, 15.29.

13. *Analects*, 1.12.

14. Whitman: 15.

15. Ames and Rosemont (unpublished manuscript): 1.

16. *Analects*, 2.21.

17. Master You said: "It is a rare thing for someone who has a sense of filial and fraternal responsibility (*xiaodi*) to have a taste for defying authority. And it is unheard of for those who have no taste for defying authority to be keen on initiating rebellion. Exemplary persons (*junzi*) concentrate their efforts on the root, for the root having taken hold, the way (*dao*) will grow therefrom. As for filial and fraternal responsibility, it is, I suspect, the root of authoritative conduct (*ren*)." *Analects*, 1.2.

18. Roetz (1993): 53.

19. *Analects*, 4.19.

20. *Analects*, 4.21.

21. *Analects*, 2.7.

22. *Analects*, 2.8.

23. *The Classic of Familial Deference*: 14.

24. *Mencius*, Book IV, Part A, 5.

25. *Analects*, 4.18.

26. *The Classic of Familial Deference*: 15.

27. See most especially Lu Xun's "Diary of a Madman," first published in *New Youth* magazine in 1918, where the society itself is depicted as "man-eating."

28. "The Master said: 'What has a person who is not authoritative (*ren*) got to do with observing ritual propriety (li)? What has a person who is not authoritative got to do with the playing of music (*yue*)?'" *Analects*, 3.3.

29. *Analects*, 17.13.

30. Lu Xun (1980) Vol II: 30.

31. The Master said: "Learning without due reflection leads to perplexity; reflection without learning leads to perilous circumstances." *Analects*, 2.15.

32. There have been many instances in the China's history of this process of reinvention. For instance, Confucianism adapted to the influence of the Legalist school by evolving into a bureaucratic ideology fit to further the interests

of the empire. More notably, Neo-Confucians in the Song era absorbed the influences of both Buddhism and Daoism, syncretizing them in a way that gave
Confucianism more of a mass appeal.

33. See *Zhongyong* 28 for Confucius's own reflections on mining the past
for a certain sustenance during periods that lack direction. What Confucius aims
to provide are not so much examples of *li*, but reminders of the way in which *li*
were performed and the effect that such performance can have. These are
reminders that the importance and the sustaining power of *li* rest in their original
idea, not in their present form.

34. Hu Shi, "A Reply to Mr. Ch'en Hsü-ching," quoted in Grieder: 268.

35. See Mary Tiles, "Balancing acts: rational agency and efficacious action,"
in *International Studies in the Philosophy of Science*, Vol. 13, No. 3 (1999) for a
comparison between the ancient Greek and traditional Chinese valuations of
those skills necessary for attaining stable political order (or "the good life," more
narrowly conceived). Action that is efficacious is that which tends toward
harmony (*he*), but that action is not attuned to any predetermined end. Rather,
its attunement is to the variety of factors and influences that make up the environment in which it is unfolding.

36. Lu Xun (1980) Vol II: 14.

37. Ibid., 15.

38. Ibid., 15.

39. Ibid., 21.

40. Ibid., 22.

41. Hall and Ames, (1998): 25.

42. Ibid., 25.

43. "Is there any one saying that can ruin a state?" Duke Ding asked. "A
saying itself cannot have such effect," replied Confucius, "but there is the saying,
'I find little pleasure in ruling, save that no one will take exception to what I say.'
If what one has to say is efficacious (*shan*) and no one takes exception, fine
indeed. But if what one has to say is not efficacious and no one takes exception,
is this not close to a saying ruining a state?" *Analects*, 13.15.

References

Ames, Roger T., "*The Confucian World View: Uncommon Assumptions, Common
    Misconceptions*," The ASIANetwork Exchange Newsletter, Vol. V, No. 2,
    Oct. 1997.

————, "Protest in the Chinese Tradition," Occasional Papers No. 2, D.W.Y. Kwok (ed.), Center for Chinese Studies, School of Hawaiian, Asian and Pacific Studies. University of Hawai'i at Manoa. 1989.

————, "New Confucianism: A Native Response to Western Philosophy," *Chinese Political Culture, 1989–2000*, Shiping Hua, ed. Armonk, NY: M. E. Sharpe, 2001.

Ames, Roger T., and David L. Hall, *Focusing the Familiar: A Translation and Philosophical Interpretation of the Zhongyong*. Honolulu: University of Hawai'i Press, 2001.

Ames, Roger T., and Henry Rosemont, Jr., *The Classic of Familial Deference*, unpublished manuscript.

Bell, Daniel, and Hahm Chaibong, *Confucianism for the Modern World*. Cambridge University Press, 2003.

Bray, Francesca, *Technology and Gender: Fabrics of Power in Late Imperial China*. Berkeley: University of California Press, 1997.

Buruma, Ian, *Bad Elements: Chinese Rebels from Los Angeles to Beijing*. New York: Random House, 2001.

Chow, Tse-tsung, *The May Fourth Movement: Intellectual Revolution in Modern China*. Cambridge, MA: Harvard University Press, 1960.

Confucius, *The Analects: A Philosophical Translation*, trans. Roger Ames and Henry Rosemont. New York: Ballantine Publishing Group, 1998.

Creel, Herrlee Glessner, *The Birth of China: A Study of the Formative Period of Chinese Civilization*. New York: F. Unger Publications, 1937.

Gálik, Marián, "Studies in Chinese Intellectual History III. Young Lu Xun (1902–1909)," *Asian and Oriental Studies* 21, 1985.

Goldman, Merle, "The Political Use of Lu Xun in the Cultural Revolution and After," *Lu Xun and His Legacy*, Leo Ou-Fan Lee, ed. Berkeley: University of California Press, 1985.

Grieder, Jerome, *Intellectuals and the State in Modern China: A Narrative History*. New York, NY: The Free Press, 1983.

Hall, David, and Roger Ames, *Thinking Through Confucius*. Albany: State University of New York Press, 1987.

————, *Anticipating China: Thinking Through the Narratives of Chinese and Western Culture*. Albany: State University of New York Press, 1995.

————, *Thinking from the Han: Self, Truth and Transcendence in Chinese and Western Culture*. Albany: State University of New York Press, 1998.

————, *The Democracy of the Dead: Dewey, Confucius, and the Hope for Democracy in China*. Chicago: Open Court Press, 1999.

————, "Confucian Democracy," in *Confucianism for the Modern World*, Daniel Bell and Hahm Chaibong, eds. Cambridge University Press, 2003.

Hucker, Charles O., "The Traditional Chinese Censorate and the New Peking Regime," in *The American Political Review*, XLV, Dec., 1951.

————, "Confucianism and the Chinese Censorial System," in *Confucianism in Action*, David Nivison and Arthur Wright, eds. Stanford, CA: Stanford University Press, 1959.

————, *The Censorial System of Ming China*. Stanford, CA: Stanford University Press, 1966.

————, *A Dictionary of Official Titles in Imperial China*. Stanford, CA: Stanford University Press, 1985.

Jullien, François, *Lu Xun: Écriture et révolution*, Paris, Presses de l'École Normale Supérieure, 1979.

————, *Detour and Access: Strategies of Meaning in China and Greece* (trans. Sophie Hawkes). New York: Zone Books, 2000.

Lee, Leo Ou-fan, *Voices from the Iron House: A Study of Lu Xun*. Bloomingtoon and Indranapolis: Indiana University Press, 1987.

Legge, James (trans.), "The Great Learning (*Da Xue*)," in *The Chinese Classics*, vol. 1, Hong Kong: Hong Kong University Press, 1970.

Lin, Yusheng, *The Crisis of Chinese Consciousness: Radical Antitraditionalism in the May Fourth Era*. Madison: The University of Wisconsin Press, 1979.

————, "Lu Xun, The Intellectual," *Lu Xun and His Legacy*, Leo Ou-Fan Lee, ed. Berkeley: University of California Press, 1985.

Louie, Kam, *Critiques of Confucius in Contemporary China*. Hong Kong: The Chinese University Press, 1980.

————, *Inheriting Tradition: Interpretations of the Classical Philosophers in Communist China, 1949–1966*. New York: Oxford University Press, 1986.

Lu Xun, *Selected Works*, Volumes I–IV, ed. and trans. Yang Xianyi and Gladys Yang. Beijing: Foreign Language Press, 1980.

————, *Diary of a Madman and Other Stories*, trans. William A. Lyell. Honolulu: University of Hawaii Press, 1990.

Mao Zedong, "On Lu Hsun," *July* (*Zhiyue*), March 1938. Source: Maoist Documentation Project, http://www.etext.org/Politics/MIM/.

————, "Talks at the Yenan Forum on Literature and Art," May 2, 1942. Source: Maoist Documentation Project, http://www.etext.org/Politics/MIM/.

Mencius, D. C. Lau, trans. Hong Kong: The Chinese University Press, 2003.

Mungello, David, *Curious Land: Jesuit Accommodations and the Origins of Sinology*. Honolulu: University of Hawai'i Press, 1989.

Murphey, Rhoades, *The Chinese: Adapting the Past, Facing the Future*, Center for Chinese Studies. Ann Arbor: University of Michigan Press, 1991.

Pollard, David E., *The True Story of Lu Xun*. Hong Kong: The Chinese University Press, 2002.

Rankin, Mary, *Early Chinese Revolutionaries: Radical Intellectuals in Shanghai and Chekiang, 1902–1911*, Cambridge: Harvard University Press, 1971.

Roetz, Heiner, *Confucian Ethics of the Axial Age:* Albany, State University of New York Press, 1993.

Schaberg, David, "Remonstrance in Eastern Zhou Historiography," in *Early China* 22, 1997.

Tiles, Mary, "Balancing Acts: Rational Agency and Efficacious Action," *International Studies in the Philosophy of Science*, Vol. 13, No. 3, 1999.

Tu, Wei-ming, *Humanity and Self-Cultivation: Essays in Confucian Thought*. Berkeley, CA: Asian Humanities Press, 1979.

———, *Confucian Thought: Selfhood as Creative Transformation*. Albany: State University of New York Press, 1985.

———, *Centrality and Commonality: An Essay on Confucian Religiousness*. Albany: State University of New York Press, 1989.

———, "Cultural China: The Periphery as the Center," *Daedalus* 120 (2), 1991.

———, "Confucianism: Humanism and the Enlightenment," *Encyclopedia of Chinese Philosophy*, Antonio S. Cua, ed. New York: Routledge Press, 2003.

Walker, Richard L., "The Control System of the Chinese Government," in *The Far Eastern Quarterly*, Vol. VII, November 1947.

Wang Zheng, *Women in the Chinese Enlightenment: Oral and Textual Histories*. Berkeley: University of California Press, 1999.

Whitman, Walt, *Leaves of Grass and Other Writings*, Michael Moon, ed. New York: Norton, 2002.

Yu Ying-shih, "The Radicalization of China in the Twentieth Century," *Daedalus*, Spring 1993.

Contributors

Roberta E. Adams is professor of English at Fitchburg State College, Fitchburg, Massachusetts, where she has been on the faculty since 1988, teaching courses in British and world literatures and writing. Dr. Adams has served as a Fulbright Scholar at Sofia University, Sofia, Bulgaria, and taught for one semester at Hangzhou University, China. She is an active member of the Asian Studies Development Program of the University of Hawai'i/East-West Center and of the Japan Studies Association. Dr. Adams earned her Ph.D. from Indiana University, Bloomington.

Roger T. Ames is professor of Philosophy and editor of *Philosophy East & West*. His recent publications include translations of Chinese classics: *Sun-tzu: The Art of Warfare* (1993); *Sun Pin: The Art of Warfare* (1996) and *Tracing Dao to its Source* (1997) (both with D. C. Lau); the *Confucian Analects* (with H. Rosemont) (1998), *Focusing the Familiar: A Translation and Philosophical Interpretation of the Zhongyong*, and *A Philosophical Translation of the Daodejing: Making This Life Significant* (with D. L. Hall) (2001). He has also authored many interpretative studies of Chinese philosophy and culture: *Thinking Through Confucius* (1987), *Anticipating China: Thinking Through the Narratives of Chinese and Western Culture* (1995), and *Thinking From the Han: Self, Truth, and Transcendence in Chinese and Western Culture* (1997) (all with D. L. Hall). Recently he has undertaken several projects that entail the intersection of contemporary issues and cultural understanding. His *Democracy of the Dead: Dewey, Confucius, and the Hope for Democracy in China* (with D. L. Hall) (1999) is a product of this effort.

Peter D. Hershock is coordinator of the Asian Studies Development Program at the East-West Center in Honolulu, Hawai'i. He has earned degrees from Yale University (B.A., Philosophy) and the University of Hawai'i (Ph.D., Asian and Comparative Philosophy) and has focused his research on the philosophical dimensions of

247

Chan Buddhism and on using the resources of Buddhist thought and practice to address contemporary issues, including technology and development, education, human rights, and the role of normative values in cultural and social change. His books include *Liberating Intimacy: Enlightenment and Social Virtuosity in Ch'an Buddhism* (State University of New York Press, 1996); *Reinventing the Wheel: A Buddhist Response to the Information Age* (State University of New York Press, 1999); an edited volume, *Technology and Cultural Values on the Edge of the Third Millennium* (2004); and *Chan Buddhism* (2004).

Wenshan Jia, Ph. D. in Communication from University of Massachusetts at Amherst, is associate professor in the Department of Communication Studies, Chapman University. He is the holder of the Wang-Fradkin Professorship 2005–2007 and the recipient of Early Career Award from the International Academy for Intercultural Research. Jia is a Fellow of International Academy for Intercultural Research and author of the award-winning book *The Remaking of the Chinese Character and Identity in the 21st Century: The Chinese Face Practices*, a dozen research articles and book chapters as well as coeditor of several books.

Tao Jiang is an assistant professor in the Department of Religion at Rutgers University New Brunswick, NJ, teaching Buddhism and classical Chinese religion and philosophy. He received his Ph.D. from the Department of Religion at Temple University in 2001. His articles appear in *Philosophy East & West, Journal of the American Academy of Religion, Journal of Chinese Philosophy, Journal of Indian Philosophy*, and *Dao*, etc. His book, *Contexts and Dialogue: Yogācāra Buddhism and Modern Psychology on the Subliminal Mind*, is forthcoming from the University of Hawai'i Press. He is currently working on Confucianism and law.

Keith N. Knapp is associate professor of History at The Citadel, The Military College of South Carolina. He is the author of *Selfless Offspring: Filial Children and Social Order in Early Medieval China* (University of Hawai'i Press, 2005). Currently he is translating two Chinese manuscripts on the lives of filial paragons that have been preserved in Kyoto, Japan.

Steven B. Miles received a Ph.D. in history from the University of Washington in 2000 and is currently an assistant professor in the

Department of History at Washington University in Saint Louis. His first book, *The Sea of Learning: Mobility and Identity in Nineteenth-Century Guangzhou*, to be published by the Harvard University Asia Center, is a cultural history of the Xuehaitang academy, urban Guangzhou (Canton), and the Pearl River delta. He is currently working on a book project that will examine Cantonese migration, trade, and travel along the West River basin in Ming-Qing times.

Henry Rosemont Jr., Distinguished Visiting Professor of East Asian Studies at Brown University, is concurrently professor of Philosophy Emeritus at St. Mary's College of Maryland and Senior Consulting Professor at Fudan University in Shanghai. A founding member of the Society for Asian & Comparative Philosophy in 1967, he served as its president (1976–78) and received a Distinguished Achievement award from the society in 1993. From 1972 to 1988 he was book review editor of *Philosophy East & West*. Holder of fellowships and grants from the NEH, Fulbright Program, ACLS, and NSF, he is the author of several books including the forthcoming *Radical Confucianism*. He has also edited and/or translated eight other works, including *Explorations in Early Chinese Cosmology* (1984) and *Leibniz: Writings on China* (with Daniel J. Cook, 1994).

Virginia Suddath received her Ph.D. in philosophy in 2005 from the University of Hawai'i with a dissertation entitled "The *junzi* Doth Protest: Toward a Philosophy of Remonstrance in Confucianism." She has a B.A. in French literature and language from Connecticut College, a B.A. in philosophy from the University of Massachusetts, Boston, and a M.A. in philosophy from the University of Hawai'i. She is currently a Program Associate with the Asian Studies Development Program at the East-West Center in Honolulu.

Lawrence R. Sullivan earned his Ph.D. in Political Science from the University of Michigan, Ann Arbor, and is currently an associate professor of Political Science, Adelphi University, Garden City, New York. His recent work includes the cotranslation and co-edited volume *Tiananmen Follies: Prison Memoirs and Other Writings* (EastBridge Press) by Dai Qing, one of China's most noted investigative reporters, and an article titled "Debating the Dam: Is China's Three Gorges Project Sustainable?" in *The Global Environment: Institutions, Law, and Policy* (Congressional

Quarterly Press), Regina S. Axelrod, David Leonard Downie, and Norman J. Vig, eds.

Robin R. Wang is the director of Asian and Pacific Studies and associate professor of Philosophy at Loyola Marymount University. Her publications include *Chinese Philosophy in an Era of Globalization* (State University of New York Press, 2004), *Images of Women in Chinese Thought and Culture: Writings from the Pre-Qin Period to the Song Dynasty* (Hackett, 2003), and articles in *Philosophy East & West*, *Journal of Chinese Philosophy*, *Journal of the History of Ideas* and *American Academy of Religion*.

Index

251